AFRICAN PHILOSOPHY IN THE GLOBAL VILLAGE

Theistic Panpsychic Rationality, Axiology and Science

AFRICAN PHILOSOPHY IN THE GLOBAL VILLAGE

Theistic Panpsychic Rationality, Axiology and Science

Maduabuchi Dukor

malthouse

Malthouse Press Limited

Lagos, Benin, Ibadan, Jos, Port-Harcourt, Zaria

First Published 2021
ISBN: 978-978-58789-1-2

Malthouse Press Limited
43 Onitana Street, Off Stadium Hotel Road,
Off Western Avenue, Lagos Mainland
E-mail: malthouselagos@gmail.com
Facebook:@malthouselagos
Twitter:@malthouselagos
Istagram:@malthouselagos
Tel: 0802 600 3203

Distributors:

African Books Collective Ltd, Oxford, UK
Email: abc@africanbookscollective.com
Website: http://www.africanbookscollective.com

DEDICATION

FOR

My Father: Cyril Dukor (Uwuabunkonye) 1916-2001 School Teacher, Educationist And Cathechist/Interpreter For The Irish And British Catholic Missionaries In Obiaruku, Midwestern Region Of Nigeria (1951-1967) My Mother: Monica Dukor (Ujuagbalu) (Nee Isaac Ezeobi) And All Africanists Living And Departed

ACKNOWLEDGEMENTS

I acknowledge with innumerable thanks the Journals that published my papers which are relevant to this work and which are hereby reproduced namely: (1) *The Arts and Humanities Quarterly*, Nnamdi Azikiwe University; (2) *Nnamdi Azikiwe University Journal of Arts and Humanities*;(3) *Nnamdi Azikiwe Journal of Philosophy*; (4) *Essence, An Interdisciplinary-international Journal of Philosophy, Essence Library*; (5) *British Journal of Economic, Management and Trade*; (6) *US Open History and Culture*, U.S.A.; (7) *American International Journal of Social Science*, Center for Promoting Ideas, U.S.A; (8) *Philosophy Study*, David Publishing Company, U.S.A.; (9) *Open Journal of Philosophy*, China and U.S.A.

I am also indebted to the Philosopher's Information Centre, Bowling Green State University, Ohio, and U.S.A for indexing most of these articles and their book/journal donations to Essence Library. See footnotes for specific articles for when and where they were first published.

I owe a lot to my late father, Cyril Dukor (1916-2001) and my mother, Monica Dukor, for their responsibilities to me as their son. The same goes to my brothers and sisters. Above all my wife, Anderline Dukor (*nee* Atuliama), Fellow of West African College of Pharmacy and my children Kenechi Frank, Obumneme Stanley and Amarachi Amanda who have been major sources of inspiration to me and whose motivations and supports sustained me through the research for this book.

Finally, I must register my sincere acknowledgments of my colleagues at the Department of Philosophy, Nnamdi Azikiwe University, Mrs. Roseline Nkechi Obiozor, the University Librarian who did the indexing and Emeritus Professor Godwin Sogolo at the University of Ibadan.

TABLE OF CONTENTS

INTRODUCTION

This thesis is essentially matters arising from all philosophical endeavours and works of scholars since the knowledge and awareness of the need and significance of what is called African philosophy but most importantly from my previous works on African Freedom, theistic Humanism and scientific paradigms .It is important to note that the vigorous and strenuous efforts exerted in defence of African philosophy produced arguments in defence of African freedom. Yet African philosophy is not a reclusive philosophy that subsists as a philosophy of primitive or ancient people of Africa or the philosophy of Africans that serves the aesthetics, ethical, political social and technological needs of the Africans alone. It is a philosophy of the post-modern age justified and sanctioned by post-modernism as a doctrine of post-imperialist new world order. In some unique and particular sense African philosophy in the global village highlights special features of what I call theistic humanism in all areas of human life - aesthetics ethics, politics and science- which I think are of global significance and could make the earth a better place for human habitat. African philosophy in the global village is therefore theistic humanism of African philosophy and secondly a cosmopolitan philosophy.

In this post-modern era international community recognizes what individuals, societies; nations could contribute to a united world. Under the current aegis of United Nations, slavery, colonialism and racism are now anathema. The regime of superiority of our races over the rest and the dominations of the 'other' with the ideology of monotheistic reason have all been castrated by superior postmodern reason that every culture has a legitimate place in a free worlds. Above all every culture has something to contribute to values, literature or history, science and technology. African philosophy in the global village as cosmopolitan philosophy therefore, contribute meaningfully to the world ethical, literary and scientific heritage. This is the sense in which we discuss African philosophical contributions in Axiology, literature and science. The Book is a collection of my works already published in International and national Journals but which are related to the common theme of an African literature, values and science in the global.

Axiology and Epistemology

This chapter recognizes the animistic and transcendental epistemological nature of axiological values in African philosophy. Hence "Artistic Symbols and Aesthetic Values in African Philosophy" in Arts and Humanities quarterly, vol.3, 2009 and "Proposition of African Cultural Values" in *Arts and Humanities Quarterly*, vol. 2, January, 2010 and "The concept of Justice in African Philosophy" in *Perspectives of African Communalism* (Canada, Trafford Publishing 2006) are revised and reproduced. Einsteins theory of special relativity is similar to African theistic panpsychic epistemology on the plank that the Relativity theory acknowledges the place of intelligible but powerful powers and forces in the superfluously densed magnetic world. The same transcendental and animistic foundation and paradigm define the complexion and nature of arts and aesthetics in African philosophy. This is accomplished in a pronounced way by the use of symbols and sculptors in an imitating and mimicking nature as the object of arts and aesthetic. The concept of art and aesthetic are also subterranean and God intoxicated understanding of the universe. On the question of axiological values, African mind especially that of the Igbo nationality in Nigeria uphold fundamental human right and consensual democracy, yet amidst occasional dictatorship and abuse of powers. Political leadership which is part and parcel of the natural or monarchical leadership runs justice at animistic level and from communalistic perspective. Hence the concept of justice is hinged on the framework of communalism and kingship system.

Theistic Panpsychic Rationality

The issue here is the philosophy or rationality of literature, communication and poetry in African philosophy. Hence I reproduced here my papers, "Theistic Panpsychic Rationality of African History". Theistic Panpsychic Communicative Rationality" and "Life-Here-after Poetics and Metaphysics" in *Kpim of Death* (Canada, Trafford Pub.} 2007. The idea of theistic panpsychic rationality is meant to be used to justify every facet of study in African philosophy, we call it Theistic panpsychic because the framework for understanding the African mind which is both theistic and panpsychic are irreconcilable factors in Christianity and some philosophies. Literature is the mirror of a people's experience and life using the medium of language propositions and poetry. African literature incidentally is suffused and characterized by Theistic animism and panpsychicism so also is its history. Because of its God intoxicated nature, the African history, literature and means of communication are theistic, pantheistic, communistic and panpsychic. A story-teller tells in an animistic and panpsychic way; a dancer dances in an animistic style; a sculpturer sculptures in a pantheistic undertone and modern African literatures have followed the animistic panpsychic method because they could not start beyond a people's ideas and cultures to recognize their talents, achievement and failures. Also death or life-after-death is rationalized animistically and panpsychically as a reality.

African Philosophy in the Global Village The question here is the significance of African philosophy to the global village and the scientific nature of African myths and symbols in my papers included here: "Globalization and African identity", first published in *Essence, Interdisciplinary International Journal of Philosophy*, no. 5, 2008; "Feminism in Theistic Humanism" in Philosophy Study, Vol 3, No. 11 2018, USA and in Proceedings of World Congress of Philosophy, 28, 2028, 63-75; "Globalization and African Development" in *Essence, Interdisciplinary-International Journal of Philosophy* in No. 4, 2007; "Epistemology of Outer space" *in Essence, Interdisciplinary-International Journal of Philosophy*, vol. 6, No.1, 2009; "Symbol and Symbolism in InfoTech Epistemology" in *Nnamdi Azikiwe Journal of Philosophy*, vol. 2, No.1; *Journal of the Department of Philosophy Nnamdi Azikiwe University*, Awka, Nigeria and "Philosophy and African Salvation", The vision of this work is to locate African philosophy in the context of globalism, cosmopolitanism and science and what it could contribute to the emerging global culture. The practices of retrogressive cultures and traditions have been responsible for the lack of African science and the inability of the Africans to contribute to scientific growth. Many factors like atavism, selfishness, witchcraft and sorcery have contributed a lot to the retardation of African civilization not only to science but also to the epistemology or science of the outer spaces, where the local folks have perfected somewhat artistic and mystical vehicles for journey to and from the outer spaces. Another area of the current global pool where the African is needed urgently to intervene is the area of feminism and women liberation which has truncated the equilibrium and balance of relations between man and woman. African contribution to this class-struggle between man and woman is a neutral one that absorbs the man and the woman to their respective natural places in the nature's womb.

Chapter 1

Epistemology and Axiology

ARTISTIC SYMBOLS AND AESTHETIC VALUES IN AFRICAN PHILOSOPHY*

African arts and aesthetics have the background of Theistic Pansychism, Polymonotheism and Theistic Humanism. Like the Western Art, the African appreciation of beauty expresses certain emotions, attitudes or expressionism as well as geometrical properties or formalisms. In the mimesis or mimetic theory of Aristotle and Plato, art imitates or depicts an object, whether individual, ideal or universal. For Aristotle, tragedy is an imitation of human action in which a good man comes to disaster because of some failing or defect, its purpose is to effect a pleasurable catharsis (purging) of the emotions of pity and fear in the spectator.[1] The African has a conception of tragedy in real and imagined life. Similarly, the African Art is hedonistic in as much as the beauty or aesthetic value lies in the capacity of an object to aesthetic contemplation. For Santayan, beauty is pleasure objectified, that is, our pleasure projected spontaneously as a quality of the object, which then appears to us as beautiful.[2] African cultures and natural artefacts are Santayanic pleasure objectified. For Hegel and Schopenhauer, art embodies in concrete sensuous form a higher reality[3] such as Platonic idea, the absolute idea, the African polymonotheism and African Panpsychism. African music as an aesthetical commodity is transcendental. Art enables human imagination to operate freely through the order it imposes on the playful activity of the imagination. For the African, as against Freud view, art may not be an escape or illusion. It is not a socially relevant expression of repressed wishes and desires neither is it, as Lange would argue, a self-

---

* "Artistic symbols and Aesthetic values in African philosophy" was first published in *Arts and humanities Quarterly,* vol 3 April 2009.

[1] Aristotle, quoted by Hafstadfer A, Principle of Philosophy, A Simplified Summary and Instant Reference - Data - Guide, Quick Chard (New York Data Guide, Inc. 1967).

[2] Ibid.

[3] Ibid.

deception by which one escape into an ideal world. African world is predicated on the transcendental world and as such art expression cannot be an escape into but a utility derived from the ideal world. Art is an expression of impression and spiritual transformation of the raw material of experience into intuitions, lyrical vision, of the concrete and individual. For Collingwood, art is the expressive objectification of feeling, raising feeling to a level of consciousness.[4] Tolstoy views artistic expression as activity in which the artist transmits his emotions by means of consciously constructed external signs to other persons, who may then experience the same feelings.[5] Art is a language of emotion experienced in apprehending a significant form rather than the represented content. In aesthetic experience, that is, empathy, we project our own life-feelings, emotions, attitudes, activities to the object, and thus experience it as beautiful like in African sculptures, paintings and drawings. Arts, according to Dewey, therefore, purifies and heightens the features that make experience satisfying or consummatory, raising them above the threshold of perception so that we may enjoy them for their own sake.[6] Art is therefore an intellectual clarity on every subject of nature and experience. It is an approximation of truth in the abstract and subjective world.

Aesthetics as an Art

African aesthetic value as an art is communicative in nature, its main purpose is to communicate the aesthetic relish through emotive means. There is a relationship between the work of art and the spectator. There is also a common ground on the basis of which there is the transference of feeling. The African believes that human beings have the potentiality to experience as well as understand certain primary emotional states, such as sorrow, happiness and fear. Aesthetic emotions should not be confused with real emotive states experienced by man in real life.

According to Tandra Patnaik, 'Relish' is the keyword in aesthetic universe:

> In real life a man avoids the feelings of sorrows, fear disgust, etc. But when such emotive contents are presented in a work of art, the reader/spectator enjoys them. Otherwise, tragedies would not have

---

[4] Ibid.
[5] Ibid.
[6] Ibid.

> been successful as a form of drama. Therefore, the emotive content present in a work of art is not the writer's or artists utterly private feeling, nor are they projection or readers or audience's own mental states. Though man has the potentiality to experience varied emotional states, everybody is not universally capable of experiencing the relish from a work of art projecting these emotive contents. The subtle aesthetic pleasure can be experienced only by a sensitive mind.[7]

Art represents the realities of life and society. The African conception of society is generally considered to be purposive and ordered according to human nature and habit. Therefore, contrary to Marxian view man's psychic and moral constraints inform the nature and form of society, not vice-versa. Individuals' psychic and emotional pattern is not determined by the society. It is also presumed that basic qualities of human nature are more or less universal."[8] These two presuppositions lead to the belief that the work of art reflects man's social ambitions, goals and values. These goals and values are integral parts of human nature. These values are in no way imposed by society. A work of art aims to reflect man's need for the realization of values through the display of fundamental emotive and psychic qualities. Also specific artistic works, carvings, images and impressions are surrealisms showing nostalgia of the idyllic past, the good nature and moral ideal of man as well as his predicaments. Fundamentally, an artistic and aesthetic value of the African is transcendentally 'theistic Parapsychic'[9] and 'polymonotheism'.[10] Most carvings are representations of different gods, ancestors and spirits (good and bad ones). Contrary to western evaluation,

---

[7] Tandra, Patnaik. "Purusarthas in Aesthetics" in *Indian Philosophical Quarterly* Vol. *XXII, No. 1, Jan. 1955* p. 59

[8] Ibid., p. 60

[9] The Conception of Theistic Panspychism is deduced from the idea that Africans have a panspychic and theistic view of the universe. This is shown by their understanding of the relationships between the Supreme God and the lesser gods or divinities, man and natural objects. African panpsychism is the belief that everything in the universe is spiritual and that spirits, divinities, man plants, animals, physical objects, rivers and water are creatures of God, the Supreme being. Theistic Panpsychism underlines African conceptions of values like arts and music. For more details on this principle, See M. Dukor, "God and Godlings in African Ontology" in *Indian Philosophical Quarterly Vol. XXII, No. 1, Oct. 1990*, Pp. 80-87. Also, M. Dukor, *God and Godlings in African Ontology* in Philosophers Index Bowling Green State University, (Winter, 1990) p. 130.

[10] Polymonotheism is the African belief in God and gods. The Polymonothestic culture of the Africans is not doubtful and is based on good evidence. The gods and spirits in African religion can be criticized when they seem to have failed in their duty to the society. Polymonotheism is the existential pragmatism of African civilization.

these images or carvings are not idolatrous but representations of the gods, ancestors or spirits they symbolize. Therefore symbolism is one important aspect of African art, with a high aesthetic relish. Symbolism in a broader sense spans beyond godish, ancestoral and spiritist expression to glorification and aestheticizing the Mother Nature like the beauties of trees, rocks, waters and inanimate objects.

In African art, the desire for love between man and woman in African context is a symbolism in carvings, tales, stories, folklores, poems and drama. Love is not only isolated to the relation between man and woman, it is also extended to material gain as well as righteousness and morality. The art has their corresponding negative impression and projection in drama and poem of greed, heartlessness, selfishness and cruelty. This may lead the spectator/reader to realize the ill-effects of materialism through cruelty, selfishness, etc. Similarly, the qualities of enthusiasm, righteousness, nobility, tendency for self-sacrifice and so on are projected through dramatic and poetic stories and folklores. More often than not, the hero or a noble person is taken as a symbol of morality and righteousness. The object of a work of art is therefore to make a man aware of goals and values of life. However in Plato's theory of form, art is based upon and contingent with his doctrine of external and timeless forms (or ideas). In Plato's philosophy, for instance in "*Dialogues*" we assume the existence, or rather the being, of the form of absolute Beauty as one among the other forms or ideas, but in our search for this ultimate and supreme Beauty, we are never able to behold it directly; by means of earthly vision."[11] Whatever we see and take to be beautiful in this earth is perfect and beautiful only in the highest degree because it partakes of an absolute Beauty. Similarly, in Theistic pansychism or African philosophy there exists in transcendental realm a pure spiritual beauty of goodness of unity among others, apart from the relative likeness of these things which we possess in perceptive experience. In African thought, therefore, absolute beauty is only a reality in the spiritual realm. Also in Plato's *Pheadrus*, "beauty of this world available through sense perception serves only as a reminder of an absolute true beauty which can only be

---

[11] See M. Dukor,"African Polymonotheism: An Existential Humanistic Culture" in *Philosophy and Social Action: An Interdisciplinary International Quarterly* Vol. 15, 1-2, 1989. Pp. 45-30. Also, M. Dukor, *Theistic Humanism* Lagos, NCN, 1994. Pp. 45-53. Also, M. Dukor, "African Polymonotheism: An Existential Culture" in *Philosophers Index* (Cumulative Edn), 1989, pp. 396.

contemplated but not seen."[12] In Plato's epistemology, metaphysics, logic, etc., are aesthetical and on the other hand, aesthetics is both epistemology, metaphysics, etc.

Aesthetic as a branch of study basically deals with man's psychic and emotional dimension. Unlike the ancient western theories, emotion and intuition as sources of knowledge are never looked with suspicion in African tradition. Along with sense-experience and intellect, emotive experience too finds a place in the scheme of wisdom. "Bliss is a matter of emotive experiences. It is also believed, that when a man transcends the narrow confines of *Ego* and selfishness and identifies himself with the universal and ultimate reality, his experience is the experience of pure happiness."[13] The state of transcendence is a release from the bondage and suffering of the worldly life. But its part is the part of emotive experience. Man has physical, psychic, moral as well as spiritual needs. Therefore, Art, while dealing with the aspect of human emotions cannot do away with the cherished values of human life and the quest for realization of the ultimate truth. Art is viewed as a means of passing from the empirical level of simple sensual pleasure to the experience of a pleasant object through sight and sound aesthetic imagination. This preliminary level of empirical enjoyment stimulates the imagination of man.

> In real aesthetic experience, a man forgets all factors that constitute the limitedness of his 'Ego' or individuality, such as space, time surrounding objects, even the felling of „I' ness. All barriers between the experience and the experienced, „I' and "thou" are resolved. In short such factors which contributed to our idea of individual is pushed back. Any work of art which contributes to our idea of individual is pushed back. Any work of art which fails to raise man to his emotive height is not a true work of art.[14]

In the context of recent development in the area of aesthetics (especially poetics and literary criticism) and philosophy, an African aesthetic theory may seem out of place. It may be argued that the metaphysical explanations like Theistic panpsychism and Theistic humanism[15] may provide support to the Western dogma about the mystical overtone of the African way of

---

[12] Albert, W. J., "Art and Otology" in Indian Philosophical QuarterlyVol. XXII, No. 2, April, 1995 p. 133

[13] Tandra, Patnaik, *op. cit.*, p. 56

[14] Ibid, p. 56

[15] Ibid, p. 62

thinking. The criticism is valid to a certain extent. With the triumph of science and positivism in the West subject dealing with non-empirical or rather supra-empirical is looked with suspicion. But it seems that the modern intellectuals have shut their eyes from the fact that in ultimate level of analysis every branch of wisdom points to the direction of the transcendental' or 'Supra-Empirical'.

> If we come down from the level of abstract theories to the level of practical experience, then we note that the work of art can definitely raise us from the level of mundane to the super-mundane. A piece of good music, poem or drama (also cinema) does enthrall us and often our narrow limits of space, time and Ego are pushed back, and we are lost in the world of pure bliss. This state is definitely obtainable through aesthetic modes of experience.[16]

Art as a form of language artist craves for communication with an audience that can understand his ideas. Music as an art "is a language where the artist tries to convey information in terms of say, ideas or motifs or themes whether melodic, rhythmic, harmonic and so on and their treatment, form, structure order and so on."[17] In music, information content may vary from moods to motivation, from action to motifs to the order of the work itself and so on while ordering forms may vary from classical forms like fugue to aleatoric forms and so on. Art is therefore, a language though, an aesthetic language. Art has both syntax and semantics like natural and formal languages. The syntax of a work is its structure while its semantics is what it attempts to express. "The artist tries to communicate order in his idea. Music is an art and an aesthetic language."[18] A good language obeys forms of aesthetics just like a good music is determined by its aesthetics.

African Music as an Art

Studies of African music fall into two main categories the vocal music of "the Acholi, the Hausa, the Dagomba, the Wolof while the Homophonic parallelism is characteristic of that of the Igbo, the Iawo people."[19] It emphasizes the percussive and aesthetic nature of African music in contrast

---

[16] See Theistic "Humanism African Philosophical Tradition" in Journal ofIndian Council of Philosophical ResearchVol. XVIII, No. 3, July - September 2001 Pp. 47-76.

[17] Ibid., p. 65

[18] Saam Trivedi, "An outline of some problems in the philosophy of Music Composition," in *Indian Philosophical QuarterlyVol. XIX, No. 3, July 1992,* P. 11. The article offers enormous insight into the philosophy of music.

[19] Ibid, p. 1

to the European, Indian, Chinese, Japanese music cultures. It tends to emphasize the features of African music such as the use of polyrhythms, speech-related melodies, percussive techniques, improvised variation and audience participation. Also the act of panegyrizing and eulogizing is an important common feature of music in Africa especially, the Yorubas and the Igbo. Africans love to praise and love being praised:

> Being essentially agrarian societies with high level of craftsmanship, the various communities of West Africa created drums, flutes, horns, trumpets and gongs from various materials such as wood, gourd, clay, stone, rock, iron, hides and skins of animals. The instructions are then used in various modes of communication.[20]

The place of emotion and intellectual appreciation of music art is less emphasized in Western music than in African music which is full of love and praise. As appreciated by the African and pointed out by Schoeberg, "order is needed for music to be understood and comprehended as well as appreciated emotionally and intellectually."[21] It is needed in order to communicate, and is generated primarily through form and structure. In music written in thematic-motive style order is brought about by unity of form thereby making music monistic. Like most African music, music which is written in a thematic-motive style derives its order from a single theme of motif or subject or idea. Such music exhibits the unity of form mentioned above, e.g. the works of Oliver de Coque, Ebenezer Obey, Fela Ransom Kuti etc. Each of these works attempt at generating order and communicating. As Schoenberg points out, "communication is the sole purpose of the composers' efforts, perhaps even that of other creative artists' efforts."[22] In communication and generation of order by the composer, the audience should be able to perceive order. There can be communication in the language of music only when information or idea, the semantics, can be transmitted from the composer to the audience through form or structure, the syntax. The audience may perceive order through the aural/aesthetic level/ear, that is, where order is perceived largely through an aural experience

---

[20] Tunji, Vidal, "Music and Musical instruments as modes of Communications in West Africa" in *African Unity: the Cultural Foundations*. The author offers an array of musical philosophy in African setting. I am indebted a lot to him.

[21] Ibid., p. 44.

[22] Saam, Trivedi, *op. cit.* p. 12.

by listening carefully to a piece of music."[23] This preserves the conception of art, or music as both emotive and cognitive, while the intellectual level corresponds very closely to cognitive. In pre-twentieth century music, order can be perceived easily,[24] the aural or aesthetic level by aurally following motif and their functions. The same cannot be said, perhaps, of modern music.

The pre-twentieth century classical music is very often traced to the African aboriginal music which was aural and aesthetic as well as intellectual and emotional. An average African music is also cognitive. Order and communication are facilitated through natural and traditional voices, drums and crafts. African music, no matter what is being communicated is laden with emotion, intellectualism and cognition. The thoughts being communicated are forms of folklores, stories, proverbs, wise-sayings, eulogies, messages and senses of nostalgia. One of the most important modes of communication is the drum. Yoruba oral traditions ascribe the invention of the *Dundun* talking drum to Alaafin Abipa, *Ogbolu* who reigned in 1650. The Akan of Ghana also have similar drum. It is customary for *dundun* drummers to play epithets and praises of community leaders. "The royal *Gbedu* drums are often sounded to announce the passing away of Yoruba monarchs into the ancestral world. The *Kalagua* is used even in a wide area of the northern parts of Nigeria in the speech mode."[25] There are also semblances of the use of this drum among various ethnic groups in Africa.

Music as means of communication

There is a three-fold classification of contemporary music, that is: Serialism/Atonalism which is exemplified by such British composers as Peter Maxwell, Davies, Alexander Goehr, Harrison Birtwistle, Oliver Knuseen, etc. Minimalism is exemplified by composer like Philip Glass, Steve Reich and Terry Riley. Alestorian/Electro - Acomatism /Non-Romantism is exemplified by such diverse composers as John Cage, Richard Rodney Bennett, etc.[26] In serialism, order is entirely perceived by the mind at the intellectual level. Upon analysis of the score; there is such that the ear, even the most trained ear, can discover, for such music is too complex for the ear. In minimalism,

---

[23] Ibid., p. 12.
[24] Ibid.
[25] Tunji, Vidal, *op. cit.* p. 145.
[26] Saam Trivedi, Ibid., p. 13

order is entirely perceived by the ear at the aural/aesthetic level upon hearing the music; there is not much that the mind can discover, for such music, like popular music, is too simple for the mind. In Alestorism/Electro Acomastism/New Romantism there is not much order to be perceived at either the intellectual or aural/aesthetic levels, which is why these three diverse movements have been grouped together here. However, the concept of minimalism could be discovered in African musical tradition.

The human voice is an important aerophone in the West African music repertory. It is a mode of musical communication between hawkers of trade articles and consumers in many towns. Each article of trade has its own melodic formula by which the trader or hawker announces his or her trade article to consumers. The town-crier is also an important message bearer who uses his voice as the principal mode of delivering messages from the rulers to the ruled. Also many religious cults especially in Yoruba and Igbo announce their appearance in the public through the use of passwords which are hollered to members of the public.[27] The human voice, as used in musical communications in trade, announcement and religious festival are form of popular music and could be classified as minimalism where order and message is perceived by the ear at aural and intellectual level.

When it comes to serial music, it is not the ear but only the mind which matters. Order cannot be perceived through the object-language, that is, the language of modern music via the aural experience, which is what the composer would want, but only through a meta language, that is analysis in ordinary language of modern music via an intellectual experience. Serial music, being the generic specie of classical music is found to be common in Africa, which is why classical music is traced to African aborigines. Music as a means of communication or earophone through the horns, trumpets, flute is a form serialism or classical music. Among the Hausa "the *Kakori* or the long trumpet is used to salute the Emir at daybreak, awaken the community and recently, to announce the close of the month of fasting. The *Ntahera* horn of the Ashanti is used to recite the praises of the *ashantehene*."[28] Besides the signal, the speech and the symbolic modes of communication, a fourth mode which the earphone plays in musical ensemble vis-a-vis other instruments may be called the music mode. This musical mode includes all forms of herald music, welcome music, praise music and processional music

[27] Tunji, Vidal, *op. cit.* p. 146
[28] Ibid.,

when, for example, music ensembles accompany a monarch at public functions.

There are kinds of musical communications known as idiophones. They are talking instruments. Most important among this class of talking instrument is the *Ikolo;* the Igbo wooden slit-gong. The *Ikolo* is used primarily to send messages, summon people into an assembly and recite people's names and title. These kinds of instrument are also found among the *Efik, Ibibio, Igbodo* and *Ekira.* "Metal idiophones such as the iron bell or gong which form the largest number of idiophones musical instruments are used to carry messages, signal danger and warn people of curfew. Metal idiophones have a high carrying power, and this is able to penetrate larger distance."[29] The flutes, trumpets, horns and idiophones, as forms of serial or classical communications are meta-language, analysing ordinary language of the language of modern music. Their mythical historical and religious imports generate a lot of philosophical interests on 'art', 'aesthetic', 'language', 'music', 'order communication', etc.

In Africa, music is an important mode of communication that contributes to the maintenance and persistence of religious, political and social ethos of which it is a part. Through musical expressions, rulers re-affirm their sovereignty, communities preserve their history for posterity while the young are socialised into values of the society. In the courts of certain West African monarchs, certain repertories are played at various times of the day and for special occasions. Musical repertories may be used to communicate different periods of day, approach and commencement of festivals or seasons and progression of ceremonies. Among children, folktale and songs constitute a mode of communication and education. In pre-colonial days, the recital of folktale stories and singing of songs under the moonlight was an important part-time amusement and a source of informal education. In all religious, social and political musical communications, the aural experience and intellectual experience are both necessary and neither is sufficient by itself. The African mind, in enhancing order, comprehensibility and beauty receives the aural/aesthetic and the accompanying feelings, if any, and then comes the organizing, analysing, unifying intellect which classifies catalogues and identifies modes of making order. The science so developed

---

[29] Ibid.,

can enhance the intrinsic joy of creating or comprehending or communicating beautiful expression/perception.

The metaphysical undertones of sound (theistic panpsychism or humanism) make music an important mode of communication of religious rituals. Musical sounds have referential and symbolic roles. Several West African divinities have their corresponding repertoires by which they are identified, summoned and communicated with. The communication may take the form of invocation, propitiation, purification, eulogising or absolution in which the divinity is asked to intercede to prevent catastrophy in a community. The verbal mode of communication is associated with the linguistic functions of West African musical instruments and its verbal arts such as changing and singing. Because of the close relationship between music and language, musical instruments can use the verbal mode of communication while the verbal arts can use the musical mode. The non-verbal mode is symbolic and is perhaps the most significant for multi-lingual and ethnic society. It may be visual, aural or both. In the visual form the appearance of the musical instruments in public signals the message. Each musical instrumental appearance is associated with a specific message. Thus, among the Yoruba, the appearance of *Igbin* drums will be associated with *Obatala* festival, *Apesi* with *Ifa, Agere* with *Ogun*, *Aran* with *Gelede* and *Bata* with *Sango.*[30] The sounds of this kind of drum is theistic pansychic, animistic and humanistic. In the aural form, musical sounds are codified into rhythmic or melodic patterns with corresponding connotation. The connotation may be associational in which the hearing of a characteristic sound is always connected with commencement of a war or curfew. The connotation may also be referential in which case a rhythmic or melodic pattern is ascribed to or identified with a god.

Contemporary African musics although heavily diluted or influenced by contemporary Western musical traditions and cultures have the re-enactments of the old but authentic black artistic and musical cultures and modes. In regenerating the black consciousness most of them, making use of traditional musical instruments, folklore and proverbs and songs, generate both African theistic panpsychic or mysterious consciousness relevantly weaved into the post-colonial Eurocentric contemporary African society. To

---

[30] See Dukor. M., "Theistic Humanism - African, Philosophical Tradition" in *Journal of Indian Council of Philosophical Research* Vol. XVIII, No. 3, July – September 201 pp 47-76.

achieve this objective, most contemporary African music and musicians adopt the serial and minimal semantic and synthetic characterization.

The subject matter of music and nationalism had been an important concept among contemporary theoreticians of Africanism. It is all the more surprising given the fact that the effect it has on the lives of people is second in importance only to religion among a host of other variables like ethinicity, ideology, democracy, etc. Art has many forms like music, painting, sculpture and literature. All these art forms have exerted a mysterious power over the human spirit. Among them, it seems that music has tended to be the most universal and language like. In talking about music and society, mind and spirit are often used interchangeably. It is in the broadest sense, the spirit or the mind that feels, not emotionally, but aesthetically; that is, it perceives, responds to, and is moved by beauty and feeling religiously.

The ideological commitments of contemporary African musicians to today's challenges would contribute immensely to the upliftment of pluralistic, democratic and ethical values and to the overall advancement of the continent. But the contemporary African musical scene is a flood of highlife, juju music, rock, rap, etc., with a preponderance of ethnic backgrounds and with a plethora of negative consequences to individual and national psyche. If some artists can claim to have engaged in changing the society positively, there is no denying the fact that the African musical terrain still subsist with a lot of poison in the youth's minds.

Music, by definition, is a universal idea and language predicated on the social nature of man. It is an idea communicated to the rich, the poor, the high and the low. Man as a social being receives whatever message is anchored in the music except if he is a beast or god. In music, vices and virtues could be communicated. While listening to music, you can float away in day dream on a sea of sound in glorious, thrilling, wishful, sentimental and usually delightful ways; you see yourself in hundreds ennobling situations; situations in which you are a democratic, Nigeria is seen as a world democracy, where there is a high ethical values, where there is no election rigging, no money laundering, no cocaine or drug to sell or smoke and where education and values are emphasized above crass and primitive materialism. However, in experiencing these visions and emotions you are being introduced only to yourself, a glorified version of yourself though sceptics would argue that this glorified version of a music listener would not transform him in the face of the budding corruption and material ism of our time. But from historical point of view, the values in music imparted on individuals can affect the society positively or negatively. At least we know that the music of Bob Marley, Peter Tosh, Lucky Dube, Fela Anikulapo-Kuti among others have ideologically united the blacks all over the world, they articulated the cause and the plight of the black in Africa and the Diaspora. Similarly European artists like Bach, Scarlatti and Handel Beethoven, Schubert, Haydn and Mozart are product of European culture and problems. Each artist could, in his own time contribute in one way or the other to the development of his society.

Music is not meaningless; it must have a message, which could be ideological, political, cultural or ethical. When musicians sing or even act out on stage, what effect does this have on listeners and viewers? In a modern society, rock stars are promoting a life style and band members do influence the kids very much. Music influences the society and vice-versa. In the colonial times and immediately after the achievement of independence, highlife music was in vogue in Africa. The highlife music after Independence was a consequence of the celebration galore that followed the departure of colonial masters. But today, the complexities of musical lyrics and traditions have informed wide diverse forms of life. There are *ipso facto* diverse consequences of modern music. Do you know that music can lure one to attempt suicide believing that the answer to life is death? Researchers have discovered that most fascination with death begins with heavy metal music. It has been revealed that many of those involved in youths and satanic cults are heavy drug users who listen to heavy metal music which glorifies drug use and encourages sexual immorality, certain music makes vulnerable young people in universities today get attracted to satanic and secret cults. Most often when you go to any circles or squares on any campuses in Nigeria, you see young people of these secret cults in round table drinking and smoking *razzmatazz* listening to heavy metal music that often spur them into senseless butchering of their fellow students.

The value orientation of contemporary music in Africa, especially in Igbo society, from the critical point of view, is lopsided. The first question relevant to Igbo society and her musical scene is are there not Mariam Makebas, Lucky Dubes, Peter Toshs and revolutionary singers who could change the today's materialistic trends in Igbo society? Are there no artistes among the Igbo who could see the dangerous dwindling interest in education? When the leader of Igbo societies were crying out against the fall of male enrolment in schools, the musicians are busy stimulating the males into the business world through their music. Today, the values highly cherished in Igbo society are money, chieftaincy titles, kingship, the music of praise and self-adulation. There were quite a good number of great maestros like Osita Osadebe, Oliver de Coque, Muddy Ibe, and so on, who had made names in the musical field and who should honestly not be blamed for assembling a great number of fans and becoming rich therefrom but whose music have lured greater number of people into satanic materialism. In ancient African Igbo society, musical songs centred around praising noble deeds, eulogies, celebration of feasts and success, heralding the appearance of kings and in praise of the gods and goddesses. But, to uphold these musical tenets of the ancient society completely is to march behind changing times and civilization. Culture is not static but dynamic; there have been emergence of values consequent upon the complexity of modern society. Society that fails to meet up the challenges of modern time would degenerate and asphyxiate in the competitive environment of scientific world order. Contemporary Igbo musicians, while being largely influenced by Africanness of Igbo music, have failed to use their vocations to address some of the ills plaguing Igbo society. May be they don't know that in terms of lyrics, songs and stage demonstration, some Igbo music is crudely materialistic and completely devoid in content and form of any message for the need for education.

The old, the young, the lame and the blind nod heads and gesticulate at hearing the Oliver de Coque's lyrics. Oliver became a household maestro in Igbo society. He was a legendary and musical avatar as far as the cream of Igbo society is concerned. Oliver's music is an incentive to business and perhaps hard work put in whatever form. If Oliver were to be a late Greek composer and singer, he would have been an oracle of music. Like Claude Debussy, an outstanding French figure of the impressionist movement in music between nineteenth and twentieth centuries, Oliver was a frontline and heavily outstanding impressionist figure in music in contemporary Igbo society. But unlike Richard Wagner who elevated Germanic Racism to intellectual and international heights, Oliver elevated class materialism to oracular height, perhaps not deliberately. The spheres of influence of Oliver's music are not at all complementing the efforts of some individuals to encourage young boys to go to school. In his music, Oliver conveys melodic, rhythmic and harmonic ideas, motifs or themes which in their treatment, form and structure appeal to the business and money making classes. Take for instance, his record on '*peoples club*' is nothing but a celebration of crass material ism, and the idea of *"Nnukwu-Mmanwu na onye-otimkpu ya"* (big masquerade and his heralder) in one of his records has become not only a way of life but also an incentive to become rich at all cost to the detriment of morality and integrity. Oliver's music had always been a masterpiece composition appealing to the largest audience or greatest number of people in Igbo society. One could, on occasions when the sound of Oliver's music is on, see a lot of teenagers, boys and girls of primary and secondary school age being carried away in thoughts on how to belong to the class of Oliver's audience. Old men and women at hearing the sound of Oliver's music would go into trance and day-dreaming how soon their sons would become rich. The point at issue is that the musical trends in Igbo society had spurred young people out of educational career into money making through means that are more foul than fair. We would want to acknowledge against this foreground, that the musics of Oliver De Coque and some notable artists in Igbo society could be powerful media for fighting the retrogressive trends in the society. Just as the Oliver's medium seems to sell the ideology of commerce and trading, it could have been used to campaign for mass education in contemporary African society in order to have a balanced socio-political awareness and development in the continent.

Fela was amorist, immoralist, immoral crusader; he was 'a sexual pervert, a drug addict, a non-conformist, and a rascal,' people said. But he was the greatest Afro-beat musical jazz in the world. He was a freedom fighter, a vanguard of black redemption. These propositions and judgements are all about one man. But when examined within the context of a finite and mortal world, Fela is meaningful. In existentialist parlance, his-existence precedes his essence and as he entered into the trajectory of his Odyssey, the musical maestro acted out a full-blown essences and quintessence. In Fela Ransome-Kuti is a concept of goodness that is both abstract and real. Both senses are considered in terms of utility that are comprehensible negatively or positively depending on individual. Fela, the maestro is good in abstract and real terms. On the stage, Fela was a partisan actor. He used partisan language and unique style. His language is a combination of pidgin-English and Yoruba and he generated universal pidgin-Yoruba and English language to communicate to his audience the extent, form and nature of decadence in the society. As an Africanist and social reformer, he had the knack of permuting and communicating the syntax and semantic of Yoruba and English language in serial and minimal orders amenable to the appeal of popular audience. The unique language, rhythmic and melodic style is liberative and irredentist. In short in Afro-juju music no musician can imitate him, falsify him or deny him in the annals of musical ontology now and in the future. Therefore, one can say that the value he created in art and music is an enduring Afrocentric, Africanist jazz music comparable in classic and erudition to that of Handel and Mozart. He was ideological in composition and conduct of his music. If he were not a racist, then, he was a freedom fighter in the pursuit of black consciousness and redemption. This is the positive dimension of the goodness of Fela and his musical band – Egypt. His beliefs were such as the world's numerous beliefs like atheism, animism, humanism and Africanism. They are judgements and propositions among numerous ones that define world-views, peoples and individuals. The world has enough beliefs, theories and philosophies that define individual characters and dispositions. In philosophy of existentialism, it is difficult to distinguish badness and goodness. For existentialists, men are active and creative. Men make their essence as they go along and do not live out a predetermined essence or blueprint. The reality and nature of freedom is one of the chief concerns of existentialists. Fela's beliefs, against the background of his mission in life, life-style and thoughts, therefore, could be classified as existential.

In conclusion, the nature and mode of African conception of aesthetic value in music is a natural and utilitarian one. It is pleasure objectified in the sense that it is psychically emotion laden and hedonistic. African art is a symbol of the appreciation of nature which the African holds very dear. Through African sculpture, carvings, surrealisms, folklores, legends, the artistic expression of the African finds an outlet. As African culture is a celebration of life, so is its musical repertory. The celebration is a re-enactment of the purpose of existence, communion with God, gods and ancestors. Accordingly, the transcendental principles of polymonothesistic humanism and theistic panpsychism underline the nature and mode of aesthetics in African culture. Modern African artists have built upon the traditional artistic fabric, and writers exhume African culture for relevance in the world scientific order.

PROPOSITIONS OF AFRICAN CULTURAL VALUES[+]

Any discourse on this subject matter with the intention of translating or canonizing African cultural values, that is, believing that there is a set of

---

[+] Propositions of African Cultural values was first published in *Arts and humanisties* Quarterly, Vol , 2, January 2007.

values common to all African people, in the manner in which we have Western or Islamic values that gave birth to Western and Islamic laws, would require a rigorous and vigorous logical analysis of the values which are largely epistemic and ontic in their transcendental origin. Here, we are concerned with some moral normative values in the cultural values of Igbo (Nigeria) philosophy of culture and by implication the African Theistic Humanistic philosophy. 'Value' is such a broad concept that mistake is often made when seen from only the point of view of ethical values. However, the values of a people go beyond ethic to values of technology, architecture, food habit, poetry, music, sculpture, painting, farming, swimming and a whole of arts. These are values, but different from values concerning ought, obligation, duty, right, wrong, valuable, desirable, otherwise called axiological ethics. The former are called non-moral values while the later belong to what is called moral normative value.

Categories of Values

Every ethnic group in Africa has a set of cultural values, which is in her cultural environment, poetry, architecture, food habit, farming and fetching of water. But the issue of moral normative cultural values of the African is the concern here and which would require logical analysis in terms of propositions, predication and entailment and finally into magisterial, legislative and universal law-like statements or propositions which can be true or false. These values when enacted would be like Thomas Paine right of man, the American declarations of independence and the United Nation Charter on human rights. We have sorted out two main categories of African cultural values, i.e. the moral normative values and the non-moral normative values. The moral normative values consist in what can be called ethical or axiological values while aesthetic and artistic values make up the non-moral normative values in African philosophy. Now the issue of propositions and entailments of African cultural ethical values arise because these values are embedded in African folklores, proverbs and wise-sayings on one hand and on the other hand are propositions within the kinship or communalistic system.

An ethical or moral normative cultural value can be extracted propositionally from a set of proverbs or folklores or from the African communication philosophy. In Igbo speaking group of Nigeria, the entire structure of value system can be configured with this diagram illustrating their origin and evolution.

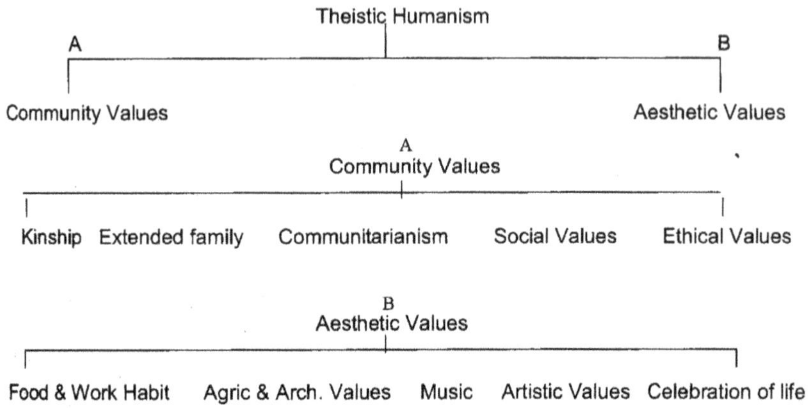

This structural diagram shows that Theistic Humanism is the defining principle of African cultural values and from it spring community values A (like kinship, extended family, communitarianism and social values, ethical values, etc.) and B (the aesthetic value like food and work habit, agricultural and architectural values, music, artistic values and celebration of life).

As shown in the above diagram, categories A - community consciousness and B - Aesthetic Consciousness, both have their roots in the religious, scientific and existential value, which I called Theistic Humanism. The subcategories in A and B that is, Kinship, extended family, communalism, social values, ethical or normative values and celebration of life, artistic values, music, Agricultural/Architectural values, food and work habit and other scientific concepts supplement one another in creating an objective and spiritually immanent universe for the progress, peace and good of the community. In other words communal consciousness informs and supplements the aesthetic/artistic or scientific consciousness and vice-versa.

African cultural values as legislative and magisterial propositions like statements on the rights of man in the United Nation Charter would be a direct extraction from category A, i.e. community values. Most of the precepts of moral values deducible from category A are in form of proverbs and wise-sayings and hence need logical conversion to categorical propositions. Take for instance, the proverb which says, "A man who is advised and he takes it, is still a man who acts from his own freewill"[31]

[31] Okporobaro, F.B.O., and Umovon, J. A., *Nigerian Proverbs: Meaning and Relevance Today* (Lagos, Nigerian Magazine 1994). P. 134.

means that 'a man has freewill' and 'he is responsible for his social and moral actions'. These are the entailed propositions from the proverb. Another proverb says, "A man who has one finger pointing at another has three pointing towards himself"[32] means that 'we are culprits of what we accuse others' and that 'accusing others remind us of our responsibilities. These proverbs show that members of the community are endowed with reason and intuition to show responsibility in preserving the sacrosanctity of moral values and ethos of the society. From the same category A, the Kinship system or the extended family called *Umunna* in Igbo, close to *Ujamaah* in Swahili, communitarianism, the value of personal and collective responsibility in preserving family's and community's or society's name emerges. Preservation of personal, family and community name involve moral responsibility, obedience and subservience to moral, ethical and normative values which are legal rules guiding, protecting and promoting the interest[33] of the society as well as protecting properties and lives. In other words, the African communication or communitarianism reinforces social values.

African Cultural Values

It is really not necessary to get the police to enforce moral values in Igbo society since the spirit of moral responsibility and communalism or kinship takes care of deviances. For instance, the Igbo proverb that "when a man dances badly in public, it is his brothers that get the itching brow" means that unruly behaviour is a disgrace not only to oneself but to his family and community. For this reasons the Igbo society has an inbuilt mechanism for ethical and moral cohesion and stability with the communal values respected and held sacrosanct as laws. The Igbo society, therefore, maintains communal values as follows:

1. Cultural values have transcendental and theistic origin. The goddess of *Ani*, the god of the land is subserving the purpose of almighty God - *Chukwu*. The purpose is for man and man's continuation of the creative process of the Almighty. The god *Ani* oversees this process.
2. Cultural values include respect for everything done on the soil *Ani* which include planting, harvesting, building houses and social and economic transactions. These values are the dos and don'ts which aim at preservation

[32] Ibid., p. 141.
[33] Ibid.

of cultural, artistic and aesthetic heritage as well as the community and hence humanity.

3. African cultural ethical or normative values are precipitates, deductions from the communitarian philosophy which itself has transcendental and theistic origin. Some of these values can be expressed in categorical prepositional forms as follows: (a) One shall not kill or steal. Killing or taking of another's life is an abomination and contrary to the will of the goddess, Ani and the Almighty, *Chukwu.* Nemesis of death or madness normally trail after any person who commits murder. However killing in defence or in war situation is an exception. On the other hand stealing of any sort which is an infringement on someone else's right and contrary to the spirit of communalism is seriously frowned by the society. Contrary to today post colonial society, in the pristine Igbo society, the air of freedom from fear, robbery and threat to life pervaded. Stealing in the society attracted the wrath of the god or goddess or outright banishment; (b) Marriage is sacrosanct and sacred. Parties involved or the husband and wife ought to respect the sacred nature of marriage by maintaining fidelity and faithfulness to each other. Dissolution of marriage must be with the express consent of the families that gave their blessing to the marriage. The process that took place before the marriage, in most cases, must be reversed accordingly.

The first segment of the process of contracting marriage is the marriage proper called *anununwanya* which entails payment of dowry, or a token sum of money, presentation and drinking of palm wine', kola nut, etc., after the ascertainment of the character or history of each family involved by the 'go-between' of each party to avoid inheriting bad blood in the children to be born by the would-be-husband and wife. Thereafter there will be a celebration of the marriage and life called '*Igbankwu*', i.e. wine-carrying which means drinking of wine and merriment. These two most important aspects of marriage are primary while the modern fad of going to court or church to wed is secondary. Igbo people believe that in the event of dissolution of marriage, it may be easy to disregard court and church wedding but very difficult to untie the nut that was tied at the two traditional processes of marriage.[34] This accounts why the Igbo at home and Diaspora prefer contracting marriage from home. The difficult embedded in dissolving traditional marriage is to preserve the sanctity of the marriage and

[34] Laz, Ekwueme, *Junior Teasers for Schools, Poems, Proverbs and Puns* (Oko, Nigeria, Le Naus Advertising and Publishing Ltd. 1995) p. 182.

ensure stability of the society and the world at large. Writing from Ashanti (Ghana) point of view Kwasi Agyeman says: "... an authentic unadulterated African marriage is truly a social union of not only a man/woman lover affair, but more so, it is a social union in a larger sense, involving families of two lovers."[35] This gives credence to the belief that the family is the basic or atomic sense of the society. The Igbo society is patrilineal. The patrilineal culture underscore a host of other values like right of inheritance in marriage; leadership at homes and in the community and the places of man and woman in the society. The male offsprings of a couple have unnegotiable right of inheritance to their father's properties overseen on their behalf by the first son and in case of controversy, the same first son arbitrates with the aid of the wise council of the elders in the immediate and or extended family. The same first son inherits the compound/home *Mbala* of his father in the village while others are advised by traditional rules to leave the compound and establish their own compounds or homes and to continue to visit and honour their original home (their father compound now inhabited by the first son) as the 'home of homes' *Nnukwu-Mbala.*

The *Umunna* meetings are usually held in the 'home of homes' where the *Ndi-Ichie* or the ancestors are believed to congregate for their meetings too and may also be their permanent abode in the spiritual realm believed to be interposed with the physical existence of the present world.

In the wider Igbo society, men lord it over women, an ideology that has a supra or transcendental justification in the creation story of the Igbo which views woman as, inferior specie and not trust worthy. In Igbo cultural values system, 'women liberation' which is the quintessential ideology of the current social, literally and scholarly pursuit called Feminism is nonsense; it is unAfrican. This does not mean that there were no distinguished and talented women whose virtues were appreciated, recognized and honoured. There is a kind of moral equality but not ontological or physical equality among men and women.[36] Men and women have some exclusive rights respectively much as they have concurrent rights. This varies from society to society in Africa.

---

[35] See Kwasi, Agueman, "Marriage: The most important social value of all Human Relations" in Dukor M (ed) *Philosophy and Political Discovers on Values, Politics and Power in Africa (*Lagos, Malthouse Press 2002).

[36] See Dukor. M., (ed) "How not to Empower Women" in Dukor, M. *Philosophy and Politics: Discourse on Values, Politics and Power in Africa* (Lagos, Malthousse Press Ltd. 2002).

Igbo society is republican. The republican cultural values respect and promote the right of every person to the communal institutions and properties. It is nothing short of democracy. One could rise from ignoble background to nobility and vice-versa. The rise and fall of the hero Okonkwo in *Things Fall Apart* is a classic illustration of the republican nature of Igbo society.[37] A combination of communitarian philosophy and republicanship in Igbo cultural values give rise to a host of fundamental human rights reminiscent of that of The U. N. Chatter. This include: (a) The right to property; (b) The right to freedom; (c) The right to aspiration; (d) The right to religious worship; (e) The right to life; (f) The right to be king etc. In the pursuit of these rights by individuals and the society, the only inbuilt check against deviance in the individual's consciousness is the communtarian philosophy which espouses that in the pursuit of these rights there should be no excesses that impinge on other people's rights and negates the spirit of communalism. Though nowadays Kwame Gyekye could be right in arguing that "...communal relationships and kinship and extended family obligations and loyalties which characterize societies in Africa and elsewhere could give rise to political corruption simply because of social and economic pressures on the value system."[38] But in Igbo pristine cultural values there were theoretical and practical check against abuses. Igbo saying which emphasizes the right of man and extols the virtues of communitarianism goes like this: kite perches and eagle also perches; if any one says the other will not perch on the tree, her feather will be broken. (*Egbe belu ugo belu, nke si - ibeya - ebena, nku kaa - ya*). Igbo cultural values work for a particular consciousness, that is, the consciousness of the community, the society, the nation and the race. To promote this consciousness or spirit, regular meetings at age, clan, village and town levels are held at home, abroad and Diaspora. Hence, the axiological ethic that an Igboman must have a sense of belonging, i.e. one is advised to always look for an Igbo age grade, clan, village, and town associations to belong anywhere one goes and live in. This makes it imperative for every Igboman to be his „brother's keeper' which in Igbo parlance is rendered as, *Onye aghana nwannie*

---

[37] Chinua, Achebe, *Things Fall Apart*(London, Heinemann Educational Books 1958.

[38] Gyekye, Kwame, "Political Corruption: A Philosophical Analysis of a Moral Problem" in Dukor M. (ed) *Philosophy and Politics: Discourse on Values, Politics and Power in Africa* (Lagos, Malthouse Press Ltd. 2002).

All in all, the Igbo cultural values and philosophy is an adventurous philosophy that abhors laziness and promotes right conduct within the calculus of Theistic Humanism. It particularly lays emphasis on hard work and accordingly recognizes merit and achievement. The justification for hard work is in accordance with the African philosophy of Theistic Humanism, supra-empirically expressed in the adage - if you believe, your God will affirm (*onyekwe chi ya ekwe*).There is no denying the fact that most of these Igbo cultural values sometimes are absent among two or three Igbo people. There have also been palpable depreciation of Igbo values in major cities with dense population and concentration of the Igbo. This can only but simply be explained by the economic, social and western pressures and acculturation on the Igbo inquiry and adventurous mind desirous to succeed where other races have failed.

THE CONCEPT OF JUSTICE IN AFRICAN PHILOSOPHY*

The concept of justice is a substantive issue in African philosophy. The concept in the political-religious societies of the Igbo, Yoruba, Fanti, Ashanti, Akan, and so on is essentially a folk or communitarian concept of justice and somewhat close to traditional concept of justice in western philosophy. There are distinctive features of world-view, the traditional thought forms and philosophy of (West) African society that respects some conceptions of justice.

Close study shows that in pre-political African societies the concept of justice is similar to John Locke's and J. J. Rouseau's ideas. Locke's state of nature is not as violent as Hobbes'. He believes that there is no natural proclivity of men to hurt one another. For Hobbes no one steps on someone's toes just for fun but only to get an advantage: quite characteristic of his state of nature. Locke instead defines the state of nature as "men living together according to reason, without a common superior on earth with authority to judge between them."[39] This state of peace, goodwill, mutual assistance and preservation hinges on the law of nature. In J. J. Rousseau's *Emile* the idea of the „natural man' is that man is by nature good. If he is wicked it is because bad upbringing and environment have corrupted him.

---

* The concept of Justice in African philosophy was first published in *Perspective of African communalism* (Canada, Trafford Publishing 2006).

[39] John, Locke, Quoted by L. Strauss, and J. Gropsey in *History of Political Philosophy 2nd Edition* p. 453

He says: 'God makes all things good; man meddles with them and becomes evil."[40]

In his *Social Contract*, he says, 'Man was born free; and everywhere he is in chains"[41] Both Locke's and Rousseau's ideas of man's natural goodness collided with the traditional Christian doctrine of original sin and redemption and, more importantly, with the traditional African thought on man's natural goodness and initial communion with God. Various myths in Africa tell us that God once lived among the people until man misused his freewill. For instance, an Igbo myth says that God (*Chukwu*) once lived with the people. But while a woman and her children were cooking, she had a dirty hand which she inadvertently cleaned on the sky wall. God was said to be annoyed and so retired to a distant place."[42] The Mende people of Sierra Leone say that God once lived in a cave and invited the animals to come in pairs but forbade them to touch his food. Unfortunately the cow smelt the food and ate some. Immediately God seized the animal and threw her out of the cave. All the animals including man sinned and suffered the same fate.[43] These myths not only illustrate the doctrine of original sin and redemption but also show that God, like in the Roman and Greek literatures, is the author of man and law as well as the symbol of justice. The African idea of natural law and justice, as will be shown in this work, is more or less the same with the ancient Roman or Greek interpretation of the natural law and the scholastics (Thomas Aquinas and St. Augustine) treatises on Divine Laws and Justice. Hence for the African, the Roman or St. Augustine, God is the author of any law that worth that name and the precepts of law are discoverable by reason or *apriori*.

Ethical and Social Conception of Justice in African Philosophy

One of the distinctive characteristics of African philosophy is the overriding role of ethics, religion and the supernatural in the formulation and application of the principle of justice. *Ipso facto* the conspicuous and unique role of ethics of religious nature in determining the meaning and place of justice in African societies could be better captured in the folk philosophy of

---

[40] J. J. Rousseau, quoted by David, Thompson. ed *Political* Ideas (Britain, Penguin Books 1966) p. 102.

[41] Ibid, p.102

[42] See Dukor, M., "African Cosmology and Ontology," in *Indian Philosophical Quarterly Vol XVI No. 4, October, 1989* p. 537

[43] Parinder, quoted by Dukor, ibid., p. 25 and p. 237.

West African society. The Igbo or Akan folk philosophy is in accord with reason and x-rays a clear absence of Hobbesian war order. Its ethical and political dynamics constitute a check against loose control of the societal purpose. The theory of communalism is clearly applicable to different groups and norms of traditional African societies. In Igbo and Fanti societies of Nigeria and Ghana respectively, the communalistic and anti-egoistic tendency is close to natural justice which is more often than not pegged on the divine foundation that every one is his brother's keeper, and no one can do to another what he cannot do himself, expressed in Latin thus: - *nemo potest facere per alium, quod per se non potest.* Each has a right and obligation to expect help from, and give help to, his neighbour. Extended family system whereby a man's obligation extends beyond his own wife and children to his other relations and his neighbours or persons who don't have direct relation with him is meant to ensure that there be no injustice of 'have' and 'have not'. This idea is summarised in the ethical proposition of Fanti which says *Sa Amma wo nyenko centwa a kron a wo so irrentwa* du[44] (if you do not make it possible for your neighbour to have nine you will not have ten). The principle underlying this maxim is the celebrated utilitarian principle (of either Bentham or Mill) that the greatest good of the majority must always be sort. It also implies that the public necessity is greater than private necessity.

Among the Igbo of Nigeria and Fanti of Ghana, for instance, the concept of 'punishment' for 'wrong-doing', is an area where there is a manifestation of an idea justice. Punishment has a dual function of serving as a deterrent and as a means of paying the offender back in his own coin - an eye for an eye and a tooth for a tooth. There are areas of wrong doing or unjust actions that are believed to have defiled the individual and the community. In that community, propitiations for appeasing the community and the divine order are embarked upon in order for sanity and sense of justice to be restored. Here punishment is not only a deterrent or a means of exacting restitution but also a means of reforming and clearing the society. In African philosophy, morality and law have many points of interceptions. The mores and customs of the people were morals. Hence the Fanti and Igbo political philosophy rejects the doctrine of *Laissezz - faire* because of their traditional communitarian conception of justice. It is argued that the -

---

[44] Oguah, B. E. "African and Western Philosophy: A Comparative Study" in *African Philosophy, An Introduction* Richard A. Wright, p. 206.

> purpose of government for the Fante is not only to give legal protection to society but also to ensure, as far as possible, that all have and none is in need. Unless there is economic justice, legal justice becomes a problem. People can have true legal freedom to enjoy their property only if their neighbours are not hungry. At least the basic necessities of life must be provided freely for all in a free society.[45]

Also the art of consensus in decision-making or *nem, dis.: nemine dissentiente,* is a manifestation of justice at various levels of interactions in African society. There is evidence that decisions by consensus is on principles. Like Kenneth Kaunda of Zambia once wrote "In our original societies we operated by consensus."[46] An issue is talked out in solemn conclave, until such time an agreement could be achieved. Also Julius Nyerere also argued that "In African society the traditional method of conducting affairs is by free decision. Hence the elders sit under the big tree and talk until they agree."[47] Rules are absolutely essential to traditional West African communities. There are a host of rules for defining, regulating and facilitating interactions and relationships - *All laws are promulgated or acknowledged rules that are enforced or at least, intended to be enforced by a recognised authority having sanctions, usually physical force, at its disposal...But there are other more informal rules such as are prescribed by custom, tradition, convention, fashion and etiquette.*[48]

There is among the Igbo, the Akan, the Yoruba and the Fanti a category of moral rules...And morality and law intersect because some laws are simply moral rules and formalised and backed up with the authority of the state. However, moral rules have an intrinsic obligatoriness which is lacking in other kinds of rules.

According to H.L.A. Hart -

> legal rules are presented to society in quite different ways and have different functions. They provide facilities more or less elaborate for individuals within the coercive framework of the law. Such are the rules enabling individuals to make contracts, wills and trusts and

---

[45] Oguah, B. E., *Op. cit* p. 214

[46] Wiredu, Kwasi, *Conceptual Decolonization in African Philosophy, Essays,* Selected and Introduced by Olusegun Oladipo, (Ibadan, Hope Publications, 1995) p. 53.

[47] Wiredu, Kwasi, *op. cit p.* 53

[48] Ibid., p. 53

> generally to mould their legal relations with others. These rules provide facilities for the realization of wishes and choices.[49]

Such moral rules in both the African and Hart's senses are connected with principles of justice. Indeed the idea of justice could be construed as a moral rule. It is difficult, perhaps, to conceive the idea of justice without some sense of morale. In African philosophy, all that is justice is either a moral law or divine law or natural law. Hence what is moral cannot be illegal and what is illegal cannot be immoral because that which is bad from the beginning does not improve by length of time - *quod ab initio non valet, in tractu temporis non convalescit.*

METAPHYSICAL BASES OF THE COMMUNITARIAN CONCEPT OF JUSTICE

The ethical narratives about man and God in West Africa tend to show that the African lived and communed with God. Divine justice, just like that of most races, is religious and which to them is also natural law and justice, *Just naturale.* The African understanding of God, nature, man and justice could be decipherable through a number of metaphysical and transcendental macro-concepts. One of them is the concept of 'polymonotheism' which enunciates African belief in a supreme being (monotheism) and in smaller or lesser gods. In essence the Supreme Being is the creator, and the smaller gods, who were created by the same Supreme Being intermingle with mankind as the guardian of public order, morality and justice.

Polymonotheism is unity (Supreme Being) in diversity (smaller or lesser gods). It is a pragmatic and existential humanistic culture. The material universe has a spiritual underlining. Everything has a spiritual cause. It is basically because of these beliefs that Africans tend to personify nature in form of gods or spirits and this is what is called Theistic Panpsychism, another macro-concept for the transcendental explanation of African conception of justice in African panpsychism which is theistic. It is argued that, "Every thing whether spiritual or physical, flows from God. Things are either manifestation or personification of God. In other words, behind every object or phenomenon is a spiritual essence which is a part of

---

[49] Hart, H.I.A., "Separation of Law and Morale" *The Philosophy of Law,* Dworkin, R.M. ed. (Oxford, Oxford University Press 1977) p.20.

God."[50] Pansychic dimension of African culture therefore shows that every thing including what is and what ought to be has a spiritual essence. And because man has the same spiritual essence, his laws, morality and justice are transcendental. The gods were believed to check the unwanted and immoral behaviours of the people.

Another transcendental concept underlying the conception of divine justice in African philosophy is egalitarianism (the ontological equality of man) which derives its transcendental origin from the plurality of gods more or less equal in status. Philosophers have indeed traced the ancient and primitive egalitarian and democratic societies to the diversity of gods and divinities. This can be interpreted to mean that the principle that permitted the existence of diverse gods also permitted the democratic equality of man. The principle is the principle of plurality. The belief in the existence of diversity of gods instead of only one Supreme Being means plurality, equality and democracy and not monarchy and authority as symbolized by one God. It could be argued that the easy amenability of democratic socialism to the newly independent African states could be attributed to their egalitarian cultures predicated on the diversity and plurality of god.

The colligation of these concepts is what I have called 'Theistic Humanism' which is African belief in the supernatural beings and also in man. It is "principle or doctrine designating African ideas of man, God and the universe."[51] The Igbo, Yoruba and Akan, for instance, believe in the Omnipotent, Omniscience and Omnipresent supernatural God and godlings who oversee the affairs of man and see to it that man does what is good, fair and just. What is good and just though were the dictates of the Supernatural beings or Being were also good and just because they were intrinsically good and just. On the other hand, the interest in man is so salient that injustice and man's brutality to man is highly frowned at. Theistic Humanism reinforces communalism which is the social and political philosophy of an ideal African society. In other words, communalism finds transcendental justification in polymonotheism and Theistic panpsychism. The idea of communalism is a man-centred ideology which Kwame Nkrumah would call

---

[50] See Dukor, *Theistic Humanism,* P. 39 and "God and Godlings in African Ontology" *Indian Philosophical Quarterly* Vol. XVI No.1 October, 1990 p.81.

[51] See Theistic Humanism *Ibid.,* p.1 Theistic Humanism is book which exposes critically and scientifically the African world-views. It is essentially on epistemology, metaphysical and the philosophy of a possible African science. The book, in its thesis, adopts the universal norms of philosophy as well as acknowledging the philosophy in the world-view of the African.

'philosophical consciencism'. According to him the socio-political practice of consciencism ensures that -

> exploitation and class-subjection is contrary to consciencism. By reason of its egalitarian tenet, philosophical conscencism seeks to promote individual development...in such a way that the individual development does not introduce such diversities as to destroy the egalitarian basis.[52]

The concepts of communalism and kinship entail rationality. Like the classical realists, liberalists, idealists and Aristotle, the African needs the society in order to realize his capacities. According to Julius Nyerere; man cannot be separated from the society and the principle of justice, communalism and kinship system upon which it depends. The society is therefore organic in nature.[53] African conceptions of justice are captured within the framework of communalism, polymonotheistic, panpsychism and the placement of individuals in the hierarchical order of the society from the transcendental to the mundane. This hierarchical order goes in this descending order - Supreme Being, gods, ancestors, kings village heads, family heads, elders, eldest members of families down to the youngest members of families. The hierarchical order of these beings is based on their relative force and importance and has nothing to do with the ontological individuals. However that does not mean that in African philosophy the king or the elder is not ontologically equal to the youngest in the family. The point is that every man is equal, but it is achievement, age and honest hard work that give status and distinction to individuals in the community. In African community, there are the rich and the poor, but this does not influence the respect of man by man. The natural resources, including land, fruits, water, belong to no person but to the community.

Among the Igbo there is something anthropologically and ontologically common to man and objects, creatures and phenomena of the universe. The commonness lies within the fact that all are parts of furniture of universe which is God's nature. Each of these parts, of which man is one, has what is called „life' in her spatio-temporal space. The life of one may not be known by the other, but each part obeys the rhythm of nature or the mother-earth, who has judiciously assigned the respective parts, which presumably may be in billions, their respective purpose, agenda, missions and, or reasons for

---

[52] Nkrumah, Kwame, *Consciencism* (U.S. Monthly Review Press 1964) p. 98.
[53] Nyerere, K. Julius, *Ujaama* (London, Oxford University Press 1968) p. 83.

existence. The natural order is not only teleological and panpsychic, it is also a milieu of commitments and avoidances. Each object of nature desires to have a breathing place in the natural space, herself being natural too, to fulfil her innate or natural callings, to avoid threats from other objects of nature and exercise the freedom necessary for her existence.[54] To the average West African, there is natural justice for man, animate and inanimate beings and objects. This justice is viewed from the belief that the universe is spiritual and that there is life in every being and object. Some of these beings and objects have spirits or gods residing in them. So their uncanny destruction will bounce back to the perpetrator in form of nemesis. This is the reason why it is a taboo to touch or kill some trees like Iroko and some animals, much more the case of killing a man. This is a theistic panpsychic justification for some do's and donts.

The relation of man to woman in African context is cultural and metaphysical. Just like the genesis account of creation, African cosmology and ontology see the concept of womanhood as an extraction from the concept of manhood. Similarly, social and political organisations are culturally patterned to reflect the mystery and superiority of manhood.[55] Justice in African philosophy with regard to women is construed to respect womanhood as well as protect her as a weak and inferior sex.

Justice is also manifested in the communal ownership of lands and landed properties and their equitable distributions. It is also manifested in the institution of committee of elders who install and de-stool kings, and in the adjudication of disputes. The juridical actions of this committee act as checks on the power of kings. In some ancient African societies there was a tacit agreement developed over the years by the people to surrender some of their rights to a divine king who then had a duty to facilitate and protect the rights of the members of the community."[56] In practice, and in judicial sense kings could not be said to possess power but what they did possess is authority. Totalitarianism is not entrenched in the African political system but that it could have infiltrated into the exercise of authority over time cannot be ruled out. However king or ruler, ruled with council of elders, and if he abused his powers they were broken by making him perform some

---

[54] See Dukor, M., "Justice and the Principles of Necessity" in *Philosophy and Politics* ed. Dukor Maduabuchi, Nigeria, Lagos O.O. P 1998) p. 36.

[55] Dukor, M., „How Not To Empower Women," ibid., p. 89.

[56] Dukor, M., "Corruption and Social Action in Nigeria" in *Philosophy and Social Action Vol. 16,* No.3 July - *September. 1990* p.22.

action that cut him off from the ancestral forces.[57] In West African societies much as the king never dies (in the ontological and metaphorical sense) - *rex nunquam moritur* - and can do no wrong - *rex non protext precare,* yet he cannot do what is unjust - *rex quod injustum est facere non potest.* D. D. Raphael says that power is the ability to coerce people to do what one wants them to do while to have authority to do something "is to have the right to it."[58] Similarly the power of the Igbo king, if any, for instance, is a limited one and which is an authority to protect and serve the interest of the society.

The mores and customs of the society were morale. Supernatural beings like God, gods, ancestors, spirits, and masquerades act as both custodians and overseers of public morality as portrayed by 'Polymonotheism' and 'Theistic Panpsychism'. Most West African societies believe in the moral law and natural law. They believe that God punishes people for any offence committed in this life and not after death. Misfortune may be interpreted as indicating that the sufferer has broken some moral or ritual conduct against God, the spirits, the elders or other members of his society. However, in some cases appeasement or atonement can be made in form of restitution and punishment for various offences. It could be death for offences like practising sorcery and witchcraft, committing murder and adultery and it could be payment of fines in cash or kind for other minor offences. The elders deal with disputes and breaches arising from various types of moral offences against custom and ritual. Kings and rulers keep law and order and execute justice.

There are two main ways of executing justice in a typical African community. One is through the use of curse and the other is through formal oaths. The basic principle in the use of curse is that if a person is guilty, evil will befall him according to the words used in cursing him. The operative principle is that only a person of higher moral and social status can effectively curse one of a lower moral and social status, but not vice versa. Formal oaths are used as method of establishing and maintaining good human relationships. Oaths place great moral and mystical obligations upon their parties concerned and any breach of the covenant is feared to bring about misfortunes. The belief behind oath is that God or some power higher than the individual man will punish the person who breaks the requirement of the oath or covenant. The due process of African traditional law, like oath-

---

[57] Parrinder, G.E., *African Three Religious* (London, Sheldon Press, 1969) p. 93
[58] Raphael, D. D., *Problems of Political Philosophy* (London, Macmillan Press 1992) p. 68.

taking and so on, is no respecter of persons. Every person is ontologically equal in the eyes of the gods. This is based on the belief that - "The world of the spirits, human beings, and other lower organic and inorganic substances form the same totality of existing, interacting beings and reality.[59] The whole world-view with all the network of symbols and rituals seems to constitute a coherent and pragmatic system or closed logical system from where truth can emerge. I have agued that:

> the existential pragmatic culture of the Africans lies in their closeness to nature and living by the dictates of natural law and gods. The gods are guardian of societal morality, though God is ultimate. The people try as much as possible not to commit any offence against their gods or society for that would bring metaphysical evil. The gods are the watch-dogs of the societal morality and law...gods are involved as witnesses to any event, bond or agreement.[60]

A person who acts contrary to divine laws suffers a boomerang or nemesis. The gods associated with nemesis were deities of thunder and justice. The African believed there was a divine minister of justice who was the solar and thunder divinity. Among the Nupe of Nigeria the thunder divinity is called *Sokogba* (God's axe) which means that he is the expression of 'The wrath' of God. Among the Yoruba, the divine minister of justice is thunder divinity called *Sango* (polymonothistic and panpsychic element) while among the Igbo, it is called *Amadioha*. Bolaji Idowu captures the African conception of justice as follows: *The whole African concept of justice is based upon the fact that the world belongs to a deity; that the social and moral orders are his ordinance, and that he is far above all divisions into races, ethnic groups, clan differences or political* partisanships.[61]

Since African concept of justice is a divine one transcendentally erected on the conceptions of Polymonotheism and Theistic panpsychism meaning belief in the Supreme Being, lesser beings and cultic forces surrounding man. The corpus of African divine laws covers rights and wrongs, duties and obligations. Since Divine law is derived from the panpsychic and

---

[59] Okolo, C.B., "Self as a Problem in African Philosophy" *in International Philosophical Quarterly Vol. XXXII, No. 4 issue No. 128* (December 1992) p. 481

[60] Dukor M., "African polymonotheism" *Philosophy and Social Action*. Vol. 15, No. 1 - 2 Jan-June 1989, p. 27

[61] Idowu Bolaji, E., *African Traditional Religion. A Definition* (London, SCM Press 1986) P. 164.

polymonotheistic beliefs, then man, animals and objects, animate and inanimate and celestial bodies all of which constitute nature have psycho-dimensions and the Supreme Being (God) manifests His wills (otherwise known as natural laws) through them. The universe is teleological or purposive, according to God's will, in law-like manner and any contrary purpose or action to it is deemed to be against the natural law. The natural law flowing from God's will is the divine wisdom. It is, therefore, the ordinance of the divine wisdom, it is the eternal law.

The role of concepts of Theistic Panpsychism and Polymonotheism or the place of cultic forces like Supreme Being, gods, spirits and ancestors are really complex metaphysical concepts to handle in understanding the concept of justice in African philosophy. The service which these entities render in African scientific theoretical scheme is what they also do in the juridical scheme. For Robin Horton entities or forces "operate behind or within the world of common sense observation - as such a theoretical scheme is linked to the world of everyday experience by statements identifying happenings within it with happenings in the everyday world."[62] Like atoms, molecules and neutrons, "the gods serve to introduce unity into diversity, simplicity into complexity, order into disorder, regularity into anomally."[63] Robin Horton observed that both the traditional African thinker or scientist make use of theory to transcend the limited vision of natural causes provided by common sense. In understanding African divine command theory of justice, therefore, Horton's theoretical entities of God, gods and ancestors act as first level explanatory theory of justice while the concepts of Theistic Panpsychism and Poly-monotheism act as the higher level in the explanatory theory.

Philosophical Presuppositions of Divine Justice in African Philosophy

The conception of justice in West African folk philosophy is philosophically presupposed in its divine conception of natural law: natural law and justice should be construed as being the same with divine law and justice. This accounts for its concept of Divine justice in being more or less the same as that found in the Greek and Roman worlds. The concepts of Th eistic panpsychism and Polymonotheism (like Stoicism) suggest that the laws and

---

[62] Horton, Robin, "African Traditional Thought and Western Science," in *Rationality* ed. Bryan R. Wilson (Oxford, Britain, Basil and Blackwell 1977) p. 132.

[63] Ibid., p. 34

justice of nature manifest in the physical bodies, land, objects (animate and inanimate) animals and man. Hence the African lived close to nature to propitiate, appease and atone God and the godlings for their well being. The Igbo, Fanti and Akan belive that God is the author of any law since any law at all must be in tune with his divine command. However, these societies also believed in lesser gods who act as intermediaries between man and God. Any contrary action against the divine laws is an offence against God. In ancient African societies when disputes could not be resolved by man, the gods were consulted and when the gods could not resolve the issue God (Supreme Being) would be the last resort and the final arbiter. The gods and the ancestors are consulted through a complex process of rituals in the family or village temple and thereafter nemesis is expected to catch up with the wrong doer, but not after all humanly possible attempts have been made to resolve the matter. Also the gods or God could be consulted through different types of divinations from water-gazing to casting strings of bones and nuts. These societies believed that God, the author of natural law and maker of natural justice is impartial. Therefore the Divine law is impartial. Fortunate and unfortunate developments were believed to take the course of natural justice. When one party in a legal dispute swears an oath to testify to the truth of his claims, the other party will be satisfied to withdraw his own claims with utter resignation believing that God will not fall to vindicate the cause of justice."[64] For the Igbo, the divine justice knows not the rich or the poor, the privileged or the less-privileged. Every man is ontologically the same to God the maker of Divine law. The Igbo and Ashanti believe that the divine or natural justice is immutable, that is, it is timeless and changeless. According to William Amo, in opposition to the eternal law, which is totally immutable, the temporal law can without injustice vary according to circumstance of time and place.[65] Since the Divine laws manifest in both physical and non-physical entities, it means that God's will in physical and non physical entities can only be discovered. The implication of this belief is that the scientists cannot make or manufacture anything but discover it which means discovering the God's purpose in that thing.

---

[64] Okafor, F. U., *Igbo Philosophy of Law* (Enugu, Nigeria, Fourth Dimension Publishing Co. Ltd., 1992) p. 41

[65] Anthony, Williams, Amo, quoted by Eneh. J.O. "Anthony William Amo, On Jurisprudence" in Nwala, T. U. *Anthony William Amo, Treatise on the Art of Philosophising Soberly and Accurate in (ed) Nwale, T. U.* (Nigeria, *A Special Publication of William Amo Centre for African Philosophy*, WACAP, Department of Philosophy, University of Nigeria, Nsukka 1990) p. 24.

Among the Igbo, the head of a family or oldest member has a ritual staff *Ofo* as symbol of authority and is respected as a jurist and as intermediary between the family and its ancestors. The ritual staff is also a symbol of divine justice. The family head or the holder of *ofo*, politically speaking, is the head of committees which consider disputes and gives advice on customs and traditions, indicating where a proposed action agrees with or violates them.

> When decisions are agreed upon by members of judicial committees or groups, the elder strikes his staff on the ground four times, declaring that it will kill those who disobey the law and all the members of the group would respond in support.[66]

In clarifying and explaining the concept of justice in Africa, one thing anyone cannot circumvent is the ontological nature of the concept which varies from one culture to another because of different mystical and ontological givens. Here I can only use the Igbo ontological commitment to *Ofo* as an illustration of African concept of justice. The concept of *Ofo* in Igbo ethnic group of Nigeria is not only an ontological and mystical experience but also it is a symbol of justice practically manifesting as authority, honesty, and truth. So when one talks of *Ofo* it severally and collectively represents justice, honesty, authority and truth. The theistic humanistic undertones of *Ofo* are the means of preserving in total perfection and transcendence the human concepts of justice, honesty, authority and truth either severally or collectively. It is the peculiarity of Igbo philosophy that each of these concepts has its substantive subsistence as an attribute or character of man while at the same time could solely represent justice or does so in conjunction with honesty, authority and truth. Hence, *Ofo* is the concept of justice as well as the concept of honesty, truth and authority as elements of a coherent whole which can be deduced from one another. The *Ofo* in Igbo is called *aka-otule*. It can be defined as the symbol of divine spark of truth and justice and honesty which arbitrates and judges matters and issues authoritatively. Its universal appeal could be found in its cultural, religious and social manifestations among different people. It is what the Greeks call *Logos*, what the Christians call *word*, the Indians call *Akashibani*,

---

[66] Okafor, F. U., *op. cit*,., p. 43

etc.[67] The *ofor* is most of the times the properties of *Dibia* (native doctor), High priest, elders and chiefs and titled men in the society.

The concept of *ofor* means different things to different persons or groups among the Igbo. There are five different meanings of it: (1) A symbol of spiritual authority and instrument of power; (2) Proof of innocence; (3) A system of elevation into membership of the customary Bench (judges).[68] As a symbol of authority and instrument of power, it is a substance of metaphysical and epistemological reality that informs and defines all physical existence. It is the symbol of communication with the spiritual reality, the ancestors, the gods, divinities, forces and the supreme God. It is believed, by derivation, that anything that is just is a reflection of metaphysical reality and metaphysical reality is a just system. Again by implication, the instrument of power and authority is the instrument of reality or is reality in itself and therefore that of God. As proof of innocence, *ofor*, as reality and truth means equity, innocence, honesty, righteousness, spiritual equality and other attributes which moulds a disciplined and civilized society. *Ofo* is the law of nature or retributive justice, and that is why it is often said in Igbo, *oji-ofo-ga-na*, rendered as he who holds the truth *ofo*, will be free.[69] The truth or reality here means righteousness. The biblical equivalence of this is in Matthew 5:6 and 10, "Blessed are those who hunger and thirst for righteousness for they will be filled: Blessed are those who are persecuted because of righteousness for there is the kingdom of heaven."[70] *Ofo nke-onye me telu* symbolically refers to the law of karma or the law of retribution justice. It is the law of "What a man soweth so shall he reap."[71] As a system of elevation into the traditional bench *ofo* dispenses justice through judgement delivered by *Ndi-Ichie*, that is, the title men who know the customs and traditions as they relate to reality and truth. These people are the middlemen between the ordinary people and the world of spiritual reality of the ancestors, gods and God. *Ofo* also dispenses justice through judgement delivered in the court of the community deities who are superior entities in relation to the almighty God. Obedience and faith in these

---

[67] Nkwo, Nnabuchi, "*Ofo: Igbo Symbol of Authority:* in *Ogirisi - Igbo Annual Lecture, Department of Philosophy, Nnamdi Azikiwe University,* Awka, 2002. P. 22
[68] Ibid., p. 24
[69] Ibid., p. 26
[70] Matthew 5:6 and 10 cited by Nnabuchi. Ibid., p. 26.
[71] Ibid., p.26.

spiritual and religious being is in the fact that they are embodiment of spiritual realities.

Like in the western legal system or in the Greek and Roman jurisprudence, every side to a dispute is giving a fair hearing - *audit alteram partem*. Also in the West African traditional legal systems, no one can be a judge in his own case *Nemo debet esse judex in propria causa* - and no one can be it at once suitor and judge - *nemo potest esse simul doctor et judex*. The family head or the oldest member of the family is more often than not also a priest and spiritual leader in addition to being a judge in the settling of dispute. For instance, a man who commits adultery not only wrongs his neighbour but also brings upon himself a curse.

Traditionally, there is a 'reformation' and purification of the individuals involved in the adultery and a cleansing of the society by a traditional priest or the head of the family in the presence of the chief, the councillors and the offended parties. A ritual performed by the priest serves as a psychological therapy, for freeing the offenders of the feeling of guilt. The western judge pronounces the offender guilty, but does not have a means for ridding the offender of the guilt. Also a ritual "is not only psychologically therapeutic but also its very solemnity is often enough to reform the offender."[72] Among the Igbo of Nigeria, breaking of kolanut is a ritual of truth and justice. Kola-nut symbolically stands for justice and the ritual of breaking it also stands for Divine justice. In breaking of kola-nut, the head of the family says:

> we shall all live. We pray for life, children, a good harvest and happiness. You will have what is good for you and I will have what is good for me. Let the kite perch and let the eagle perch too. If one says no to the other, let his wing break.[73]

Breaking of kola-nut symbolises a cultural verdict and manifestation of Divine justice. Some deities are deities of justice.

Among the Igbo, '*Ani*' is not only ultimate judge of morality, justice and conduct, she is also the source of divine justice, public order and morality. West African societies believed that Divine law or moral law or natural justice is immanent in everything. Hence, it is discoverable by human reason.

---

[72] Oguah, B. E. *op. cit.*, p. 210.

[73] Achebe, Chinua, *Things Fall Apart* (London, Heinemann Educational Books 1958) p.14.

And when we say that the Igbo, Yoruba or Ashanti man lived close to nature, it means that he was avoiding living contrary to Divine laws.

THE CONTINGENCIES AND PARADOXES IN AFRICAN CONCEPTION OF JUSTICE

The Igbo, Yoruba or Akan certainly hold tenaciously to the Divine command theory of justice. But the unarticulated assumption of the Divine theory of justice was an incubus to the practical manifestation of the cause of justice among individuals and societies. Blind dependence on the gods and spirits (real or imagined) is the cause of most of the problems. Hence, among the Ashanti of Ghana, the ancestors were usually called upon to bless their farming seasons. The earth goddess is addressed in this manner: "Earth, while I am yet alive, it is upon you that I put my trust. Earth who received my body… We are addressing you, and you will understand."[74] Similarly, the Igbo of Nigeria make similar approach to their earth deity *Ala* during farming seasons. To Igbo or Yoruba: "All the phenomena which he perceived around him were supernatural and fearful, and the force behind them were unknown and unknowable."[75] It is indeed not surprising that there were reported cases of arbitrariness of the actions of the gods, goddesses and the spirits. And most often, the Igbo was reported to have been pushed to the point of warning a particular god or spirit against a particular injustice. The critical issue here is that some gods, goddesses and spirits may not after all be the true manifestation of the Supreme Being or polymonotheism and Theistic Panpsychism.

Also it can be argued that the existence of the weak and the strong in the pre-palaeolithic Africa, the period of hunting animals, picking wild fruits and digging edible roots or the period of primitive existence, must have vitiated the cause and conception of natural justice, and often altered the balance of communal life in favour of the strong. As a matter of fact the existence of the strong or the dominant class must have left traces of the oppressed in the primitive African with all the injustice inherent therefrom. The dominant class was said to have exploited the ignorance of the weak class and created socio-religious and socio-political myths. Commenting on this class, Awolowo rightly adverted that:

---

[74] Parrinder. E.G., *African Traditional Religion* (London, Sheldon Press 19962) p. 48.
[75] Ibid., p.13

> they created a large number of gods and made them abide in the skies, well out of mortal view... Above all, they created the institution of divine kingship. Whilst the priest was the spokesman, interpreter and appeaser of gods and spirits, the king was their divine representative on earth. For this reason, he was clothed with the same halo as the gods and spirits, and his power over his subject were absolute and unquestionable.[76]

Also the primitive background of Africa, colonialism, imperialism, disunity and lack of development militated against the realization of a social justice. In the pre-colonial and colonial eras, the minds of the dominant class were - "thoroughly wrapped, debased and imbued with callousness and contempt towards their fellow Africans."[77] This affected a departure from the communitarian conception of justice. A highlight of the salient issues in African conception of justice shows a cluster of metaphysical and socio-political concepts of West African folklore and community practices showing how traditional concepts of law, morality, social order, justice and the supernatural are linked together. The concepts of communalism, nemesis, polymonotheism, Theistic pansychism and Theistic humanism, with transcendental reality have to do with a good society and individual. Whereas the contract theorists would posit the surrender of person's rights to the king, a human person, the African traditional thought would postulate the surrender of person's rights to God, the Supreme Being. The African endorses the divine law, which he often regards as natural law, or the primary and supreme law. What is justice is what law 'ought to be' instead of what it *de facto* is. In interpreting the law, the community usually appeals to the ancestors, the gods and God as the highest reasons. While every person is given a fair hearing in any case no one including the king is above the law. However, the ideals which the divine law and communitarianism set for a functional just society are hamstrung by pressure from selfishness, greed, colonialism, modernity and arbitrary and wrong interpretations given to statements of erratic and unknown gods and forces of nature. That notwithstanding, the checks and balance of all the forces constitute a just African society.

---

[76] Awolowo, Obafemi, *The Problems of Africa* (London, Macmillan 1977) p. 9.
[77] Ibid.

THE ONTOLOGICAL FOUNDATION OF THE COOPERATIVE MICROFINANCE SYSTEM IN AFRICAN PHILOSOPHY*

Economic Predicament

Since the time of Adam Smith and the industrial revolution, the world has made giant leaps in economic and technological developments, with the West as the torch-bearer; yet the black African race was neither a leader nor a partaker in the evolution. Also, the economic recessions suffered by the West in history only made Africa sink further down the economic and social evolutionary ladder. Africa benefited from neither Western capitalism nor eastern communism. The invisible hand of the market propounded by Adam Smith,[78] much as it has brought progress in the Western economy, has made Africa the victim of economic recession, unfreedom, corruption, mismanagement and underdevelopment. The market economy has made African nations poorer and their citizens have descended further below the poverty line. The poverty rate is increasing on a phenomenal basis, even as the mortality rate is multiplying. The banking system in Africa, which follows and adopted the western capitalist traditions, has made the ordinary client in the street poor and helpless. The banks are conduits for money laundering by the politicians and the privileged. The collapse and liquidation of banks, especially in Nigeria, led at various times to unquantifiable loss of money and confidence by individuals in the economy. In each episode, a few individuals and players in the banking industry manipulate the monetary system for their selfish interests. They use the deposits of marginal and marginalised peasants and local industrialists to buy houses in London, New York, etc., as well as the purchase and use of private aircrafts. Consequently, at various times the peasants and the masses who form the bedrock of the political economy are at the receiving end of the collapse of the banking system caused by indiscretions, avarice, greed, corruption and manipulation by the dragons of the capitalist industries. The fact is that both the high and the low, the bourgeoisie and the peasants, political office-holders and the

---

* The Ontological Foundation of the Cooperative Microfinance System in African Philosophy" was first published in the *British Journal of Economics, Management & Trade,* Vol. 5, Issue 3

[78] The invisible hand of Adam Smith is his theory that the annual revenue of every society is always precisely equal to the exchangeable value of the whole annual produce of its industry. As every individual endeavours to employ his capital in the support of domestic industry, so that its produce may be of the greatest value, he generally neither intends to promote the public interest, nor knows how much he is promoting it. As he purpose his security and gain, he is in this as in many cases, led by an invisible hand in the capitalist free-market economy. See Adam Smith, *An Inquiry into the Nature and Cause of the Wealth of Nations* (1985), p. 225

masses, as well of governments of nations in Africa, suffer the economic downturn created by this roguery and theft in the banking market economy in Africa.

Also, the interventions into the monetary and fiscal policies of the African political economy by the institutions of the global capitalist economies in many subtle ways promoted graft and denied the African his personality and the *apriori* capacity to manage her own economy. The Bretton Woods lending institutions, the International Monetary Fund and the World Bank, are killer institutions in partnership with developed nations in Europe and the United States. Their interest rates and conditions for lending money to African nations are harsh and so outrageous that the African countries are made poorer instead of better off. The African is like someone who needs money; he goes to borrow it from someone else to whom he will pay interest, but whose interest is such that it alienates, reduces and diminishes the self-worth of the borrower and makes him poorer. Incidentally, this lopsided nature of the global capitalist economy and institutions against the African continent is reflected in the relationship between state financial and economic institutions and the citizenry. This led to political corruption, which Kwame Gyekye describes as "the most serious source of the financial haemorrhage suffered by developing nations in Africa, constantly gnawing at their development efforts...the greatest and most serious disease of governments in Africa."[79] In short, business management in the capitalist economies is skewed to favour the rich, to the chagrin or disadvantage of the poor, the labour.

This phase of the global capitalist machinery ensures that the labour is dehumanised, defaced, alienated and truncated by not earning his actual daily work pay, where the excess of money from his sweat is stolen by the bourgeoisie, the owners of the capital and means of distribution and production. It is a situation where profit margins in the local economies are stolen, diverted to personal accounts, where the local populations are estranged from their labour and from the intruding culture of a money economy that subsists only as nightmare, a system without any intelligible and existential meaning to them.

---

[79] Kwame Gyekye, *Tradition and Modernity: Philosophical Reflections on the African Experience*, Oxford: Oxford University Press, 1997, p. 192.

We can, therefore, summarise the following as the genuine ground for an alternative philosophy of business management in Africa to cope with not only the global economic turmoil but also as a platform of business management that is in unity with the culture and ontological personality of black Africans, where the premium of value and not money is emphasised, where human dignity is preserved and the community exalted, rather than the individual:

1. Hunger and poverty caused by the mental disequilibrium of the post-colonial African in determining her destiny has resulted in lack of focus and vision on management;
2. Corruption as a result of poverty and disordered personality has left indiscipline, graft, avarice, lack of probity, governance and unaccountability in the social and political turf of the enculturised African society;
3. Money, though a veritable, measurable scientific means of exchange and value, has certain material estimations that deified it as a god over and above human dignity;
4. The ontological value of man and the universe is lost in money market economy and despicably treated the African as a means instead of as an end. The consequences of this are money-oriented actions and inactions such as roguery, bribery, brutality, graft, avarice, unaccountability, theft, etc.;
5. The post-colonial African political economy, which is artificially money-market-oriented, has caused triple alienations to the African peasant and labour. One, he/she is alienated from the capitalist system, because he is not one of the owners of the means of production and distribution; two, he is alienated from his labour because of incommensurate pay; and three, he is denied the fundamental human right to self-determination, especially in the banking system, where he is again alienated because of inadequate interest rates for his deposits and gross abusive interest rates for his loans;
6. The global capitalist system has consistently dictated the tunes of the banking system in Africa, resulting in profit maximisation, without care for the poverty level of ordinary Africans on the street, who need to save their money without arbitrary and inhuman bank interests;
7. Corruption and money laundering in African political economy was largely the result of imperialist and neo-colonialist economic presumes on both the African mind and non-scientific communalistic social

economy and management. The clash of cultures of management of Anglo-Saxon and African tradition, on one hand, and that of the Francophone and the African, on the other hand, has resulted in loss of an authentic African philosophy of management;

8. The banking system of money market capitalist economy is not comprehensible to a communalistic psychic and is, therefore, prone to abuse and dilapidation in practice. Money laundering, embezzlement and stealing associated with banks in Nigeria, for instance, are the results of the collapse of management ethics in the face of a clash between western management ethics and the African communalistic management ethics;
9. Absence of good governance in Africa is a consequence of lack of necessary symbiotic relation between the ruling elites and the average and poor masses whose ontology is communalistic, who live out their lives in self-pity while viewing and patronizing the bank as another foreign gold;
10. Trust is the ontological underpinning principle behind the pooling and leasing of funds in a rational society and among rational independent persons. While this element is still subsisting among local folks, workers and peasants, it is conspicuously absent in the money market economy being operated by the African governments of today.

Methodology

In view of the above backgrounds impinging and eroding the money market banking system in Africa, there is need to philosophically seek out a latent and insipient alternative in African culture, which, although it is being practised by workers in governments and private establishments and among local folks, needs to be globalize. This is the African co-operative microfinance, whose uniqueness is its ontological communalistic foundation.

The African traditional microfinance system is a cultural *cum* anthropological saving method for varied prospects and business ventures carried out by different groups of peoples of different social strata, namely:

1. Club or association members, who are naturally of the same social and economic class;
2. It could be initiated by an individual in a community who is the collector and had the sole responsibility of enlisting trust worthy and socially and economically suitable members;

3. Group of friends could come together for the purpose of pulling funds for individual social and economic interests.[80]

With regard to the first one, i.e., the club or association members, there is no number of members required, as it is usually referred to as cooperative society meant for people in the same workplace, social clubs or in a particular community. In this type of microfinance, an individual decides on the amount that would be convenient for him to pay monthly or weekly. The money contributed is shared at the end of the year, depending on the amount of money each member contributes to the system. Members have access to loans from the contributed money with minimal interest. In a large cooperative society, they do not share their money at the end of the year. It is allowed to grow through investments and acquisition of properties, which are made on behalf of members of the society. However, members are required to obtain loans from the society, which are usually determined by the amount they contributed.

The second type, which may be initiated by an individual who is the collector, is usually for small-scale businessmen and women or petty traders. The fact that the collector goes around to collect money from interested members and to give them back their money with interest could be what earned the business the nickname 'merry-go-round' in Kenya. The collector goes around every day or weekly to get contributions from members. The money collected is recorded in the cards of members and at the end of the contributions tenure, which is usually one month, the saved amount is given back to the individual contributors, sometimes with more money to lend for business. This money is usually less a day's contribution, which is the collector's charge at the end of the month for coordinating the business. One of the main objectives of this type of traditional microfinance is to help petty traders in the market save their money.

In the third type, a specified amount is agreed by a group of members on the amount to be paid by each person. A person is assigned the responsibility of managing the contributions. The contribution period could be six months or one year, which also depends on the number of people interested. At the end of the month, each member pays his contribution to the contribution manager, usually on an agreed date, beyond which a penalty

---

[80] I credit this idea to the discussion with my wife, a production pharmacist, who is also a practitioner of the informal traditional saving and credit promotion method called *Esusu*.

will be paid. The first person who will collect or the second, third, etc., is usually determined by ballot. In the ballot, the month an individual picks will be the month he or she will collect his money. Where the number of contributors is large, two or more people can be paid in a month.

All three types of African traditional microfinance system are varied strategies of poverty reduction systems. It is an inductive and participatory method of nurturing partnership. The process of nurturing partnership in an African traditional setting usually takes three structural and cognitive steps: identifying potential partners in terms of whom one can work with; defining areas of common interest marked by holding meetings in which partners respective agendas are delineated and underlined by concessions and recognition of one another's strength and weakness; and joint programme formulation and implementation with concrete results of resource investment.[81] Graphically, the partnership nurturing process can be seen clearly as shown below:

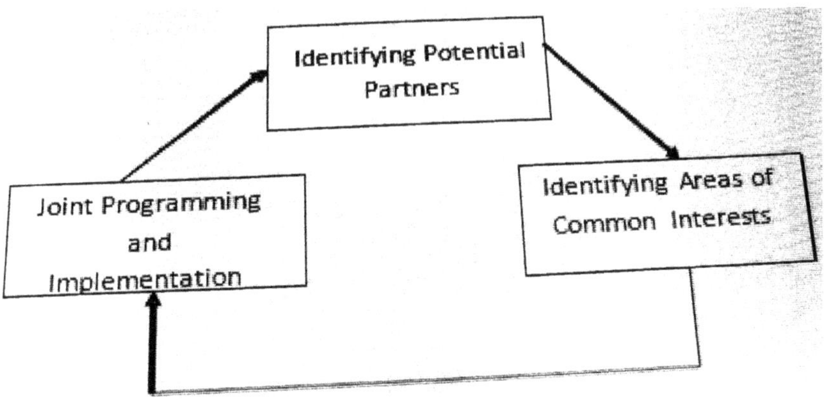

The cardinal ethical principle of this participatory process is a philosophical consciencism which treats "each man as an end in himself and not merely as a means. This is fundamental to all socialist or humanist conceptions of man."[82] In traditional African society: "We were individuals within a community. We took care of the community,

[81] See O. O. Ladipo, "Participatory Development and Project Success" in *Journal of the Administrative Staff College of Nigeria*, Vol. 23, No. 1, April 2003, p.

[82] Nkrumah Kwame, *Consciecism* (U.S. Monthly Review Press, 1970), p. 95

and the community took care of us. We neither needed nor wished to exploit our fellow men."[83]

The African *Esusu* (Yoruba) or *Isusu* (Igbo) is a sort of an unfree market enterprise that seeks to promote the entrepreneurial ingenuities of members of the folk business circle under the ontological umbrella of a universal moral order created by a deity. African Igbo or Yoruba universe is a teleological order that brooks no disobedience, injustice, unfairness, inequity, lawlessness, cheat, corruption, avarice and as such the parishioners of this folk and egalitarian business enterprises operate under the burden of an awesome power that has be capacity to kill in the invent of disobedience to the principle of justice. A teleological and moral order the *Esusu* or Isusu business enterprise is under the ubiquitous universal police man or principle of order which in

Yoruba society is called *Esu* or *Ani* in Igbo (the earth goddess). This is the power that makes it possible to for us to achieve order and peace in an otherwise chaotic and disordered universe.[84]

In an African microfinance system, interpersonal interaction and relationship is one of the bases of a solid business cooperation, sustenance and growth. It is a situation where X, Y, Z, etc., know one another, see one another, or call one another on telephones in a dialogic manner. On an interpersonal note, they engage in a continual business struggle and learning process motivating or motivated by a saving mechanism variously called *isusu* in Igbo culture, *osusu* in Yoruba culture, or what Kenyans call a *merry-goround*. This concept, as it is variously conceived and understood in African cultural settings, denotes some form of interpersonal touch, an element which is objectively lacking in the western-oriented impersonal and institutionalised banking and finance system. The impersonal and institutionalised nature of banking, guided by Adam Smith's invisible hand, allows channels and avenues for abuse by the privileged class and those in power.

Since it is depersonalised, reified and disembodied, anarchy can be introduced by contrary ideas, unlike the objective and interpersonal dialogic interaction that practically goes on in *isusu* or *osusu*, where ideas are in

---

[83] Julius Nyerere, *Ujamaa* (New York: Oxford University Press, 1968), pp. 6-7.

[84] Wande Abimbola, "An Appraisal of African systems of Thought." *The Arts and Civilization of Black and African peoples, volume two, Black civilization and Philosophy* (Lagos, centre for Black and African Arts and Civilization, Lagos, 1986) P.17.

constant interaction with questions and answers, critic and revisions and agreement. It is not that interpersonal relationship is totally lacking in western banking systems or that it is not advocated institutionally, but the peculiar feature of microfinance system in Igbo or Yoruba philosophy is the binding force of the interpersonal relationship, which is animistically based on mutual respect for one another and fear of being accused of dishonesty, fraud and financial incapability.

African traditional community was a mutual society. According to Aylward Shorter, "human need was the criterion of behaviour. Members of the community acted always to fulfil a human need, their own and that of others. They co-operated because there was strength in numbers and this as the only effective way of supplying the need."[85] An African business community is a human community built around a network of interpersonal relationship and interaction.

Linked to interpersonal relationship and interaction is the binding force of trust, which is the lubricating oil of not only the relationship but also the business. Without trust in the business and financial relationship, X, Y and Z could not have sat at the table to fashion a common business vision. In accordance with the supernatural and animistic order of the African world view, the concept of trust is both a meta- and a second-order concept. It informs and strengthens the financial business roundtable. The social contract for the microfinance is first based on moral and financial trust. With respect to every individual in the business partnership, the subjective and objective criteria of eligibility are trustworthiness, naturally capacity and financial liquidity. In an African microfinance system, the element of trust operates functionally on interpersonal, animistic and ontological framework, while in the western banking system the element of trust is heavily loaded in one impersonal institutional entity under the control of the capitalist monopoly. This 'unique trust' in African business management smoothens the vertical integration of the partners in the microfinance.

It must be pointed out that this 'trust' is accompanied by the ontological and emotional concept of 'love', which in Léopold Sédar Senghor's *Négritude* is described as true to African mind and personality. *Négritude* is "the whole complex of civilized values, cultural, economic, social and political – which characterize black people – these values are

---

[85] Aylward Shorter, *African Christian Spirituality*, London: Geoffrey Chapman, 1978, p. 27

essentially informed intuitive reason, because this sentiment reason, the reason which comes to grips, expresses itself emotionally."[86] Trust is based on an African philosophy born out of an" apprehension of the unity of man as a whole self, of man at one with his fellow man, of man at one with nature and God."[87] The element is predicted on a set of moral tenets or "spiritual moral order in which man is surround by a lost of spiritual powers."[88]

The god of *Esu* in Yoruba from where the business enterprise *Esusu* originated stipulates that each individual is expected to cultivate the gods and the positive which imbibes the principle of trust. According to Wande Abimbola, "A man who chooses good character will be rewarded by the benevolent supernatural powers" and he will achieve a state of harmony with his neighbours. The state of harmony is the unqualified presupposition of "Trust"[89] in a company of *Esusu* or *Isusu.* Secondly, this animistic or theistic humanistic element of trust also presupposes that a man "is in the final analysis the architect of his own fortune and misfortune."[90]

But western philosophy of capitalism has tended to create distrust and artificial dichotomies between man and the other, "between man the knower the known and man the doer, between the subject and the object, between the freedom of the individual and the demands of the common good and society, between the technology dominated welfare of man and the respect for and harmony with nature."[91]

Interpersonal relationship and trust are always subjective and objective factors, upon which the element of moral and financial credibility of members is ascertained. Vertical business relationship is the financial liquidity of the individual members, which often are based on self-assessment and subsequent declaration of interests. Hence the credibility of members of *isusu* or *osusu* is based not only on financial liquidity, but also on the subjective moral quality. Credibility here is reduced to a moral, ontological and objective concept, yet which is undergirded by an Africa animistic worldview. This animistic confidence of members in the business is based on the belief in gods and God of retribution when one is guilty of

[86] Léopold Sédar Senghor, "What is Negritude" in *Readings in African Political Thought*, ed. D. M. Mutiso & S. W. Rohio, London: Heinemann, 1975, p. 83.

[87] J. A. I. Bewaji, "African Philosophy some comments" in the Nigeria Journal of Philosophy Journal of the department of philosophy University of Lagos Nigeria Vol. 3, No 1 and 2 p. 112

[88] Wande Abimbola *op.cit* P.23

[89] Ibid., P.24

[90] Ibid.

[91] Bewaji, "African Philosophy, some comments"

dishonesty and fraud. Therefore, credibility is ascertained from objective financial capability and sustained on the superstructure of fear of the unknown.

The philosophy of management behind the African microfinance system is to exploit the financial liquidity at a maternal particular for personal and a positive capacity and profit-utilisation and maximisation. This is encoded as futuristic mission, in a well-packed vision of business and self-development, without any costs or expenditures inherent in liberal capitalist ownership and process of production and distribution. Coded in qualitative calculus, it is like financial liquidity X in a maternal particular Y is made to yield capacity Z and profit utilisation S and maximisation T. This is the conceptual picture of the mission of an average participant or the African microfinance system called *osusu* (Yoruba) and *isusu* (Igbo) or the Kenyan merry-go-round. Therefore, the economic objectives of an African Microfinance Bank can be illustrated graphically as follows:[92]

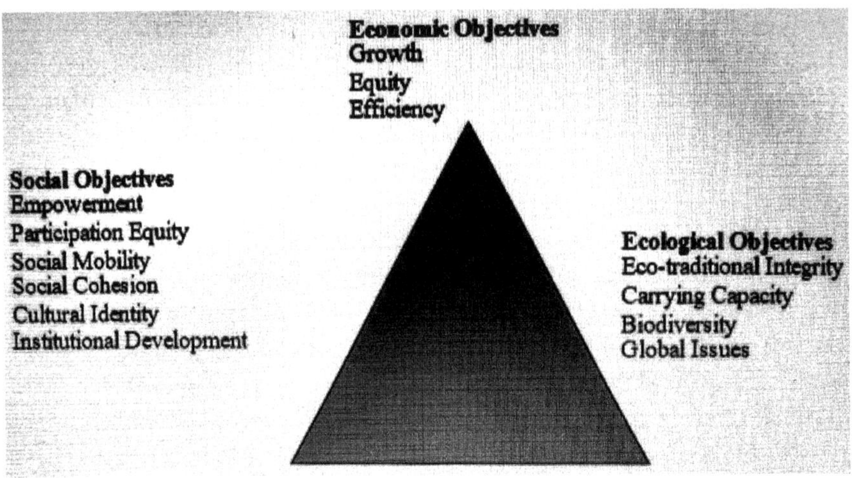

As reiterated earlier, the overall mission of an African traditional banking mechanism is focused on economic growth, equity and efficiency. This is erected on the vision of accomplishing social empowerment,

[92] Ladipo, *op. cit.* p. 4.

participation equity, social mobility, social cohesion, cultural identity and institutional development. The ecological objective might have been identified in a pre-colonial African setting but subsumed under the general communitarian social objectives. It is important, therefore, in this global and scientific era to highlight ecological objectives like eco-traditional integrity, carrying capacity, biodiversity, etc., along with the social concerns.

The African Microfinance System has over the years exceeded from cowries as a means of exchange to use of money which is associated with modern banking system. In spite of social change that has taken place and the new Western type of currency in the exchange, the value and function of money remains the same in African traditional and Western economic. Money is used to purchase commodity which in turn produces money again. It is not only an orbit of market forces; it is also an indicator on wealth reward and blessing in African traditional society. In African religions universe, the gods would reward any person who follows their ways with *aje* (Yoruba) or *ego* (Igbo). For the Igbo and the Yoruba's, money is considered to be a sacred entity as a means of exchange and as a valuable agent in the socio-economic process. For Wande Abimbola, this money concept call *Aje* in Yoruba "has been elevated to the status of a Yoruba divinity the Chief Priestess of which is a woman[93] who has distinguished herself in marketing. Money is important to both man and gods without which the former would be incapable of fulfilling his spiritual obligation to the late who in turn owns the former her continual blessings. Money is therefore the motive for business enterprise and the associated profit.

The undergirding principle behind the zeal to exploit the financial liquidity of participants in the microfinance ring is not only to make a profit, but also to promote sense of saving and hard work among members who are more often of middle or low economic class. It is predicated on the belief that if the saving mechanism successfully goes around the members in six months or one year, it will go a long way to promote business incentive and hard work among the participants. It spurs up the business potentials of members and awakens innate and latent capacities in them to enable them to live fulfilled and happy lives. It widens their social circles through the benefits of liquid financial purse, steady income and economic self-reliance and independence. The evidence of economic independence is mostly

[93] Wande Abimbola, *op.cit* P. 26

pronounced in the capacity for self-fulfilment, self-determination and self-realisation.

The African microfinance system, apart from promoting the individual's economic social interest, has altruistic, communalistic and holistic forebodings that presuppose the general welfare of members and stakeholders above selfish inclinations and strivings. In the microfinance, general welfare is predicated on commitments on the following grounds:

1. An agreement arising from this kind of partnership is rooted on the ontological foundation of the equality of man;
2. Justice is to be administered without fear or favour;
3. The animistic foundation of justice and agreement under girding the business is one predicated on the fear of the unknown and the law of retribution;
4. Profit-sharing is equitable and proportional relative to one's contribution; and
5. There is love of one to another or everyone loves everyone in the business circle. This kind of ethical disposition is only possible where every person has animistic and theistic commitments.

In the centre of the interlocking social and economic considerations and network of ontological foundations is the spirit of communalism. It is community planning which is a "device for allowing many people of moderate skills to contribute to wise decision making rather than leaving it wholly to the great skills of a small group of leaders."[94] Communalism is the social philosophy of collective ownership of land and properties in an ancient African philosophy. This philosophy is erected on the foundation of kinship relationship among members of a pristine African society where everyone has a blood tie with everyone else and where everyone is his brother's keeper. The animistic forces are the fundamental categories of African ontology and communalism. On the principle of participation, it is by participating that the active side of animistic forces engage in functional belongingness, harmony and communalism. The principle of manipulation in the idea of belongingness also relates to the sharing which the ideas of participation project too, though not explicitly. Both ideas equally relate to

[94] E.A. Ruch, OMI, "The power of ideology" in E.A. Ruch, OM Iand K.C. Anyanwu, *African Philosophy: An Introduction to the main philosophical trends in contemporary Africa*, (Rome: Catholic Book Agency, 1984),p. 70.

the principle of solidarity among forces (entities) so as to maintain the integral wholeness of the system.[95]

African communalism can be viewed as similar to but not the same as communism in being public, populist and community-centred, but is different from the latter, which is said to be scientific. It is unscientific and emotional, since the binding force is love of one another based on the humanity of man in one God. "The unity of the self-world, one-much individuality-universality, freedom-necessity is based ultimately on religion or faith."[96] It is rather closer to the communalism which was practised by the disciples and followers of Jesus Christ. The primitive nature of Christ's communalism, one could argue, is as undiluted as the African communalism. Communalism is, therefore, the ontological foundation of modern African age-group, peer group, 'workers'' associations or union coming together for thrift business with the objective of saving their money for business and better life in what is called merry-go-round in Kenya, *isusu* in Igbo and *osusu* in Yoruba of Nigeria. Beyond the spirit of kinship or blood relation as the binding force of African microfinance communalism, one of the social tentacles is theistic panpsychic animism:

> The spirit world (theistic panpsychic animistic world) is peopled by the ancestors. The 'living dead' greatly influence the living. Their presence in the community of the living is always felt and they are capable of participating and sharing actively in the daily affairs of the living.[97]

For instance, in Chinua Achebe's *Things Fall Apart*, an epic story of the fall of Igbo African traditional culture, Uchendu, an epic character, prayed for Okonkwo and his family when he "broke the kola-nut and threw one of the lobes on the ground for the ancestors."[98] The African people are a religious people, remarked John Mbiti. Anything they do, whether singing, dancing, cultivating, painting, doing business, etc., they do religiously, having at the veneer of their mind that the Almighty God through the

---

[95] Maduabuchi Dukor, "Theistic Panpsychic Animism of African Medicine." *Essence Interdisciplinary International Journal of Philosophy* (Philosophy and African Medicine) No. 3.2006, p. XVIII

[96] K.C. Anyanwu, "The African world view and theory of knowledge" in E.A. Ruchi Onu and K.C. Anyanwu, *African Philosophy* (Rome: Catholic Book Agency, 1984) p. 93

[97] Ibid., p. XII

[98] See Chinua Achebe, *Things Fall Apart* (London: Heinemann, 1958), p. 117

intercession of the ancestors, gods, goddesses and animistic is overseeing them.

Theistic Humanistic Communalism

The belief that God and all these lesser forces places man on constant surveillance explains the fear of the unknown to which every participant in any social and business engagement is subjected. Africans believe that God created man and gave him authority to have dominion over all other objects of nature, while allowing the existence of gods, goddesses and ancestors as intermediaries between Him and Man. Man in Africa is not religious for nothing, but trusts and believes in God who gives life health, wealth and glory. This explains why the African worldview is worldly and other-worldly, thereby substantiating the African traditional philosophy of theistic humanism. It is, therefore, within the superstructure of theistic panpsychic animism and theistic humanism that the African microfinance system or *osusu* or *isusu* is embedded.

Chapter 2

THEISTIC PANPSYCHIC RATIONALITY

Theistic Panpsychic Rationality of African Literature and History*

There is need to rethink the question of rationality and rationalization processes amidst structural functionalism, system theory, enthno-methodology, hermeneutical and phenomelogical sciences, positivism, enlightenment modernity, critical theory, and add to its lexicon what I call Theistic Panpsychic rationality, a pristine category of African philosophy and a paradigm of truth. The contributions and triumphs of the Enlightenment philosophy, the Frankfort critical school and the Marxist dialectics proceeded exclusively against the otherwise closed critical, transcendental and hermeneutical African rationality theory. A theory of rationalization is not only "the elaboration of categories and concepts for a systematic examination of the character and different modes of rationality, but also an explanation of how they are concretely embodies in social and cultural life."[1] In African philosophy, Theistic Pansychic rationality is the rendering of the cognitive, subjective world in terms of transcendental and animistic foundations and how concepts and categories are employed symbolically and synchronically in the understanding of social life through literature and history. With the disenchantment of the world that results from the ineluctable processes of modernization which destroys functions of traditional world-views, Theistic Panpsychic rationality provides a rational justification for community normative standards in accordance with the principles of relativism, divisionism, or emotivism which hold that ultimate norms are arbitrary and beyond rational warrantability. But for Habermas and the enlightenment modernity the mission on the human emancipation depend on a rational justification for a universal normative standard. This

* "Theistic Panpsychic Rationality of African Literature and History" was first published in *US Open History and Culture,* Vol. 1, No. 1, March, 2014

[1] Bernstain, Richard. .J., *Habermas and Modernity* (MIT Press, Cambridge, Massachusetts) p.4.

thinking belongs squarely within the enlightenment tradition of oppressive, monological reason. In modernity, self-transcendences are replicated in absolute spirit' of Hegel's theory of the model state.[2] Hence, the crisis of modernity informed by the monotheistic reason of Hegel left the world without soul, and the search for alternative worldviews led to plurality of views either as relativism or emotivism.

THEISTIC PANPSYCHIC EPISTEMOLOGY

In the challenges of epistemological nature, generated by the crisis, African philosophy as Theistic Panpsychic communicative rationality provides a veritable alternative framework of understanding, yet distinct from the anti-humanist discourses of Nietzsche and Heidegger. Faced with the crisis of cultural modernity that destroyed European society and the world, what has become relevant, as an alternative methodology yet to be subjected to scientific appraisal is the communitarian animistic form of understanding which, like Freudian or Marxist analysis, is called Theistic Panpsychic rationality. Hence, we think that the philosophical and social lexicon has to be updated with Theistic Panpsychic analysis which hitherto has been a missing link in the genealogy of knowledge, and which could be vital tools of rational communication in a globalized world. Theistic Panpsychism as applied in African philosophy is a rationalization process that underlies every sphere of the African activities and actions, immanent and extant in their culture, literature and history. These subjects epistemologically have a theistic Panspsychic overtones and undertones. They are god oriented and determined. There are no general laws governing historical or literary explanation. It is rather a speculative and providential meta-subject. In other words, African philosophy of history could be a purposive will of gods or God. Therefore, theistic Panpsychic rationality of African literature and history is a methodology outside the framework or paradigm of modernity that can best capture the African mind in the postmodern science and value system.

Achebe's *Things Fall Apart* is the African novel from whose literary perspectives the African experience in culture and philosophy will be analysed. However a critical approach will be adopted because of our epistemic and ontological interest in an art, that "uses the resource of

2 Habermas, and the unfinished project of modernity: critical essays on the philosophical Discourse of modernity "Introduction" (eds) Maurizio P and Seyla B (U.S.A. Mitprers 1997) p. 6.

language to shape experiences, communicate meanings, and express emotions."[3] In this work there is little or no relevance attached to any biographical information about Chinua Achebe or any of African writers for want of any information about their lives as they bear no epistemic or cognitive imperative to a disinterested philosophical study. Most important is the historical interest in which the novel, *'Things Fall Apart'* is enmeshed, which this work value immensely because it "provides a context of background information necessary for understanding how literary works were perceived in their times...show how literary work reflects ideas and attitudes of the time in which they were written."[4] But the psychological interest is not much of value, aesthetical, literary or otherwise save the fact, that the subjectivity and psychology of the epic character in *Things Fall Apart* may be intermittently resounding as a pointer to some African values. This invigorates the historical and the philosophical import of this analytical work in not being isolated from the social contexts in which they are embedded. Hence on this work is the mythical character, the relevance and import which is recognized in so far it represents common, familiar subjectivity even universal human experience such as being born and dying, God, growing into adulthood, society, man, etc. Like deconstruction and historicism, a philosophy of culture involves multidisciplinary perspectives which studies ways of life, customs, beliefs and attitudes. We shall employ the objective and subjective theory of art,[5] in line with the thinking of M.H. Abram and hence concentrate on *Things Fall Apart* with allusions to values it generated.

Examination of Theistic Panpsychic rationality of African literature and history is an exposition of the uniqueness of African values planted naturalistically in the superstructure of African oral and modern literature and history. The interest and importance of this enterprise is therefore predicated on: (1) the uniqueness or Africanity of Black man's epistemology, metaphysics, ethics and methodology from which their values and the ones they share with other races emanate, i.e., there is a commonality and universality of values and philosophies; (2) the need to unify human races, globalizing universal, enduring and progressive values from the centre and

3 Diyanm, Robert. Critical perspectives; Approaches to the Analysis and Interpretation of Literature (New York, McGraw-Hill, Inc. 1995(p. 14.

4 Ibid., p. 23

5 See *Olorun*leke, Ojo. "Approaches to Literary Criticism in The 20th Century in Ojo Olorunleke, *Materialist Essays in Literature* (Ibadan, Olu-Akin Pub. 2004), p. 6

distant corners of the world by tracing back cultures through philosophy, literature and history. In other words, there is need to go 'beyond culture' to 'convey the idea that there are beliefs, perceptions, outlooks, values and practices that are not features or properties or characteristics of a particular culture...[6] (3) the fact of history that in the evolutionary ladder, the African was advertently or inadvertently left out in history, exalted the Renaissance Enlightenment Modernity and the Development in Europe exclusively and above the African being. Hence Theistic Panpsychic rationality of African literature and history is a search for Africanity with the objective of re-launching it back to world civilization.

THEISTIC PANPSYCHISM AND THE AFRICANITY OF LITERATURE

It is necessary to determine the definition of African literature and history as theoretical and methodological tools of this enquiry. Debate on what constitute African literature has vacillated between writing in African languages and using English or French as meta-languages, writing by an African or the African writing on Africa. I would agree with Ezekiel Mphahlele that African literature is "creative writing in which an African setting is authentically handled or to which experiences originating in Africa are integral."[7] For instance Chinua Achebe's remark in *Things Fall Apart* that proverbs are the "palm oil with which words are eaten" is an Africanity and as such applies not only to the Igbo but to all other tribes in Africa. According to R. N. Egudu, proverb constitutes a significant dimension of African traditional literature and is as important as palm oil is for seasoning and making meals attractive.[8] Chinweizu and others pointed out some elements in Okot P'Bitek works, which like Achebe's *Things Fall Apart* are most consistently influenced by African literary traditional and vernacular modes of expression. These elements are "African imagery, proverbs, laments, invocation and curses."[9] Egugu has added folk songs which are used by these to create comic effects, reinforce points and generate humour. Oral literature as it concerns African philosophy and development is a very important vehicle of thought transmission from one age to another and the mirror of Africanity or African civilization. Theo Vincent rightly captured

6 Kwame, Gyekye, *Beyond Culture: Perceiving a Common Humanity* Ghana Academy of Arts and Sciences Accra, 2000. p. 19.

7 Maphahlele, Ezekiel, quoted by Egudu R.A., "Africanity in Modern African Literature" in *The Arts and Civilisation of Black and African Peoples; Vol. 3, Black organization and Culture*, p. 20.

8 Egudu. R.A, ibid., p.21

9 Chinweizu, quoted by Egudu. Ibid., p. 23

oral literature as the "rich, orally expressed and transmitted literary inheritance of African societies comprising the folklore, legends, myths, songs and praise songs, heroic recitals, festivals and ritual enactments based on their world view. It is an articulate medium for expressing the people's idea of society and human relations, aesthetics and philosophy. This literature is communal, is still vibrant. The significant fact about the historicity of the oral literature of Africa is its paradoxical antiquity and contemporaneity, for these reasons, it has remained a problematic part of reference in determining the character of the other literary activities."[10] African literature, in terms of metaphysical superstructure because of its religiosity or ontotheology, is theistic humanistic and panpsychic. It expresses an Africanity, a unique cultural and metaphysical type. Developing from a theistic humanistic and panpsychic nuomena, Africanity expresses the cultural synthesis and unity of Black Africa. It is both a mysterious and empirical essence. In terms of ethics and public sphere, it is the attitudes, ideas and behaviour arising from life experience in small aggregating communities which coalesce into communicative and political rationality of Theistic panpsychic type.

Theo Vincent isolated three dimensions of Africanity in African literature; one is those common features of the cultures and customs of Black African peoples which signify their cultural unity in the Theistic Panpsychic elements in the works of Haile Selassie, Wole Shoyinka, Chinua Achebe, Elechi Amadi, J P Clark, L.S Senghor, and Efua Sutherland. Another feature is the language of modern African literature which is English and which as a meta-language has been adapted and given local flavour adequately capturing local nuances and rhythm of speech:

> The bending of the English Language to express African ideas and experiences goes beyond the manipulation of syntax. It also has to do with the use of imagery in literary works. These images which are based on the landscape as well as the wisdom of the people and which try to recapture the poetic and picturesque manner of communication among Africans are important aspects of the African flavour of the language of modern African literature.[11]

---

[10] Vincent, Theo, "Africanity in Modern African Literature" in *The Arts and Civilisation of Black and African People; Vol. 3.* Ibid.

11 Ibid., p. 42

Another feature is that "the ultimate as far as the Africanity of African literature is concerned is the discussion of general human conditions through an acute analysis of particular African experience."[12] The African artists speak to man and humanity and deals with the wider issues bordering on cosmic optimism and communalism. From particular African experience, African literature deals with general human condition for instance Ngugi's treatment of the enormity of guilt and expiation, Soyinka's allegorical exploration of the myth of Ogun in *The Road* and *Idanre* and Okigbo's Spiritual Odyssey in *Labyrinths,* all attesting to the collective unconscious and metaphysical reality of Theistic panpsychism, the spiritual and empirical humanism of African philosophy.

Finally there is feature enthroned by the contemporaneous nature of African society whereby foreign values, education, technology and religions have changed the face of traditional African society. The emerging modern African society informed the adaptation and welcome of techniques and motif of western literature to grapple with the literary imagery of the indigenous aesthetic and artistic hoops and warts. For instance the urban novels of Cyprian Ekwensi, Chinua Achebe, Peter Abraham, the violence of Yambo Quoloquem's *Bound to Violence* and Kofi Awoonor's *The Earth My Brother Poetry.* "As a philosophy, poetry is the description of a particular thing...The poet described those things in the radiant atmosphere produced by imagination..."[13] As a mode of literary regression, African poetry was a highly developed art in traditional African societies. There were lyric strain and penchant for bold imagery in traditional poetry, which with the employment of some elements of oral tradition of African literature is to underscore the Africanity in modern African poetry. There is the element of song-praise, songs elegies and so on in the poetic practice of the oral tradition in African literature. Song as a poetic mode in African literature is seen in the works of Kofi Awoonor and Okot P'Bitek.

The poems of Awoonor will portray this idea.

> When our tears are dry on the shore and the fishermen carry their nets home and the seagulls return to bird island and the laughter of the children recedes at night there shall still linger here the communion we forged, the feast of oneness which we partook of.

---

12 Ibid., p. 43
13 Critchley, Simon, "Philosophies As Poetry" in Havi Carel and David Gamez, *What is Philosophy* (London, Continuum, 2004) p. 185.

> There shall still be the eternal gateman who will close the cemetery doors and send the late mourners away. It cannot be the music we hear that night that still lingers in the chambers of memory it is the new chorus of our forgotten comrades and the hallelujahs of our second schaes.[14]

African poems have this philosophy of Theistic humanism and Theistic panpsychism being re-echoed in every one of them because it is the philosophy that informs and controls existence generally whether individual, human, object or the natural. In the poem, above, there are elements of providence, creation, creator, life here and there after, the sovereignty of God and salvation. African poems also dwell on issues and facts of life like, feminism, man and woman, righteousness and communally based lyrical songs that portray the finitude and mortality of man, etc. Below are some of the song poems of this nature which I translated and composed from my community and cultural background.[15]

Gift of the garb

My man, I greet you,
I say! Everything you do
Will be well for you.
My prayer for you
in this world is good
health and long life.

Speech is in my mouth,
Walk is in my leg,
How can you be eating
one food and be looking
at another?
Use money to know me
because I am rare commodity.

There is a question which
I will question you
and I hope you will answer
the answer
I am asking you:
Egg and Chicken, who is older?

---

[14] Ibid., p. 50.
[15] Dukor, M., "Guest Poet" in T*he Post-Express on Sunday May 12 2006*

I will tell you
They are twins.

Do you know that
A scheduled and agreed war
Cannot consume a cripple?
Instead of a scheduled
And agreed war will
Consume a cripple
It will be better we go
And find out why.
Do you know that
A he-goat does not
Climb a tree?
If he does, he will fail
Is it not true?
Do you know that
Killing a he-goat is annoying
To she-goat?

Have you heard
That an old woman
Is angry Because a baby is
Sucking her breast?
But a man who is impotent
Who knows whether?
He can have a child?
(Dukor, May 2002:18)

Vengeance (Igbo-Africa)
Once upon a time,
Tortoise gathered all the animals,
Enroute to debt recovery,
The earthworm to clear the road
The cock to do the talking,
The lion to do the collection
of money,

The hunter to lead them all,
The sun will look after them.

On that day when the earthworm
Was clearing the road
The cock ate her into the stomach

Are they still on course?
Then the lion ate up the chicken,
Then the hunter killed the lion,
With the hunter only alive,
What will happen to the money?

Hard Choice (Africa-Igbo)

If you take your child,
Your wife and your mother
To the bush for firewood,
And you finish collecting the firewood
And you go to swim in the river
And the water drowned
Your wife and your mother,
Who are you going to rescue?
Your wife or your mother?
(Dukor, May 2002:18)

Disobedience (Africa-Igbo)

Do you know that My father says:
I should not go to church
With mat,
And my mother says:
I should not go to church
With mat
I did not obey and
I went to church with mat.
And they did not care
And used rope to tie me down
If a child carelessly
And brazenly goes to a ...
To a big masquerade
Then he will be beaten brazenly
(Dukor, May 2002: 18)

Son of God (Africa-Igbo)

Sunday morning, the angelus rang,

Church I went with the he-goat
With the sheep, the he-goat came
With all pleasure, the sheep followed,
In the church the Rev. father
Declared the sheep is the son of God
And the he-goat left the church in annoyance
Oh, the 'messiah' and 'The son of God'
That led to the crucifixion of
Jesus Christ.
(Dukor, May 2002: 18)

Men's Chauvinism
To a woman I went one day,
To my surprise the old woman
Was frying beans
When I expressed my hunger
Then she said it is for sale;
„Ten, ten naira' to tantrum I flew;
Hence I took the fried beans
And ate them and took
The frying oil in the frying pan
Poured on the woman..
(Dukor, May 2002: 18)

Women's Chauvinism
When a man earns money
The woman is the spender
But when a woman earns
Money
It goes to her maintenance.

Hippopotamus (Africa-Igbo)
My friend hippopotamus,
I am for everybody and the community,
Not for you or any gang or group,
We cannot move and advance,
With no love lost,
Life is short.
I cannot realize myself

By following you or your group sheepishly.
God and not you or your group
Is the author of life,
I am for everybody global village and God
(Dukor, February 2003: 21)

My Woman (Africa-Igbo)
Speech is in my mouth,
Walk is in my leg,
I have to be going
Because my wife is
Pregnant for eight months,
If she does not deliver today,
It will be tomorrow
If I touch her
She will deliver prematurely
(Dukor, May 2002: 18)

Like the aboriginal African poems above, the subjects of African drama are "human nature, life and death, fate and its operation, and conflicts that dominate and give meaning to human life. African dramatists use African social circumstances and myths to give universal implications to these themes."[16] The myths in African drama also relay the message of Theistic humanistic communalism and Theistic Panpsychic rationality.

The African character in African novel is also in question as it is undisputably one of the means of promoting the Africanity of African literature. Achebe's *Things Fall Apart* is a good attempt to render in fictional prose materials, history, cosmology and metaphysics extant in African-Igbo communal culture as a novel and as a philosophy, as Africanity and as a Theistic humanistic and panpsychic rationality.

META-HISTORY IN ACHEBE'S *THINGS FALL APART*

The title for Achebe novel originated from the following poem by the Trish poet William Butter Yeats (1865-1983). Although Yeats poem is symbolic most philosophers should be able to analyse the narrative as well as the significance of Achebe's Choice of a Title?

The Second coming (1921)

[16] Vincent, Theo, *op. cit.* p. 54

Turning and turning in the widening gyre
The falcon cannot hear the falcones;
Things fall apart; the center cannot hold;
Mere anarchy is loosed upon the world,
The blood dimmed tide is loosed, and everywhere
The ceremony of innocence is drowned;
The best lack all conviction, while the worst
Are full of passionate intensity.

Surely the re-elation is at hand;
Surely the second coming is at hand,
The second coming! Hardly are these words out
When a vast image out of spirit as maidi
Troubles my sight: somewhere in hands of the desert.
A shape with lion body and the head of a man
A gaze blank and pitiless at the sun,
Is moving its slow thighs, while all about it,
Reel shadows of the indignant desert birds
The darkness drops again, but now I know
That twenty centuries of strong sleep
Were vexed to nightmare by a rocking cradle
And what rough beast, its hour comes round attest,
Slouches towards Bethlehem to be born.[17]

In human developments progress without traces of the past is very difficult. Historical reflection remains indispensable in the life of Man. According to George Santayana, History repeats itself and, "the knowledge of history helps man to come to self-realization. History is also the subject of philosophical study."[18] "It was Plato who in *Charmides* defined Philosophy as "the only science which is science of itself and of other sciences as well."[19] "As such History is included in its scope of study. Hence, there is Philosophy of History with great Philosophers of history like Kant, Hegel, Schelling, Fitche, Karl Marx, etc. Besides, the Jews, Christians and Medieval Philosophers like St. Augustine also contributed to the interpretation of history. As usual they brought the idea of God in historical interpretation.

---

[17] William, Butter. Yeats, The *second coming*
[18] C. Santayana, Encyclopedia of philosophy
[19] Plato, *Chamides*

Their own view was a providential view. This view holds that history is the working out of divine providence. Similarly, the providential view exists in African Philosophy of history. This view was portrayed in the novel *"Things Fall Apart*" written by Chinua Achebe. It was expatiated in the epic story of "Okonkwo" who was a major character in the novel. The historical background is a providential view of history. Hence we are interested among other things in the relationship between providential view of history according to medieval philosophers and the one in African philosophy of history as explained in the novel as well as African folklore, poems and history.

The term "philosophy" was etymologically derived from two Greek words - "*Philo"* (love) and *Sophia* (wisdom). Literally, it means the love of wisdom. There is no universally accepted definition of philosophy as there are philosophers. However, an attempt can be made to define philosophy as the objective and subjective science that studies the existence of reality. Philosophy is an art of reasoning which provides a critical and intellectual weapon for analysing and synthesizing the basic problems of man, society and nature through literature, history and Science. On the other hand, history is the recorded narratives of past events especially those concerning a particular period, nation, individual, etc., it is a written account of past events. This study of the past has important contributions to make towards the attainment of the basic goals in the society. It is very difficult to imagine what life would be like in a society without history. Philosophy of history has to do with producing of the actual interpretation of the actual cause of events showing that a special kind of intelligibility could be found in it. Philosophy of History aims at not only giving a narration of what happens but also why such a thing happens. According to the idealists, Philosophy of history is primarily concerned with the activity of human beings.[20]

In *Things Fall Apart* Chinua Achebe looks at the Igbo society specifically at the period the white man broke into it as missionaries, traders and administrators. *Things fall apart*" is about a clan that shared a common awareness and acted like one.

The white man came and his coming broke this unity. In the process many were killed and, new words, new usage and new applications gained entrance into men's minds and the old society gradually gave way for the

[20] For a good example of an Idealist Philosophy of History see R.G. Collingwood, The Idea of History. (Oxford 1943).

new society. This lesson in *Things Falling Apart* is pointed out by Obierika in his accusation of the white men: Now he has won our brothers and our clans can no longer act like one; He has put a knife on the things that held us together and we have fallen apart.'[21] Furthermore, the book, *Things Fall Apart,* is an apt recognition of Okonkwo's role in the war against imperialism. One can see Okonkwo as one who fails to hold the shared response of his clan and as a result of which the clan like him, break apart. Hence, clan and hero are symbolically trapped in a dance of destiny. The novel opens at the height of Okonkwo's fame, which he won through "solid personal achievement" like when he beat Amalinze the cat in a wrestle at the age of eighteen. From then on it was clear that he was destined for great things. He was a renowned wrestler, a wealthy farmer with three wives. He had courage, reputation and was wealthy.

Achebe has this to say of Okonkwo:

> his life has been ruled by great passion to become one of the lords of the clan. That has been his life spring. And he had all but achieved it, then everything had broken, he had been cast out of his clan like a fish onto a dry, sandy beach, painting. Clearly his personal god or chi was not made for great things. A man could not rise beyond the destiny of his *chi.* [22]

The narrative novel shows that subsequent developments in the society of Umuoha are contradictions and enculturations. The tradition and the custom of the land is no more, the missionaries had come to Umuofia and established a church with a hand full converts amongst who are Nwoye Okonkwo's son, as Christianity has settled among Umuofia. A man can now leave his father and his brothers. He can curse the gods of his father and his ancestors.

Consequently Okonkwo revolted against the church, but flabbergasted by the assault of the religion on the tradition of the land he went to exile. On returning, he saw that the white missionary has captured the 'heart' of his people and things have really fallen apart. Now the clouds have gathered and there is nothing more to expect but a storm. In the grand old manners, Okonkwo tries to rouse Umuofia to act as one in the face of treachery and violation, He fails and nobody follows him. He is let down and he goes on to commit suicide. In the dance of destiny which Okonkwo was a hero and

[21] Achebe, Chinua. Things Fall Apart (Heinemann Ibadan 1958) pp. 124 - 125
[22] Ibid, p. 92

symbol, enculturation overshadowed acculturation, a superculture imposed herself upon an inferior culture as the local one give way to a universal one.

Okonkwo's tragic end began with a series of providential episodes. He was one of the great elders and title holders in Umuofia. In a somewhat ironic fate, he was assigned to take care of the lad, Ikemefuna. Ikemefuna, along with a young virgin was sacrificed to the people of Umuofia by Mbaimo people. This act was to appease them for killing their daughter, the wife of Ogbuefi Udo. Ikemefuna was later executed according to the wish of the Oracle of the hills and caves - Okonkwo defied all the warnings of the Oracle and partook in the killing of Ikemefuna. He latter started to feel restless about the act. Consequently, in Ezeudu's funeral, Okonkwo's gun exploded and a piece of iron from it killed the sixteen-year old son of Ezeudu. Okonkwo was banished from the land of Umuofia for seven years. He then fled with his family to Mbanta. His house was burnt down to cleanse the land he has polluted with a clansman's blood. Okonkwo settled in Mbanta among his mother's kinsmen.

While in exile, Uchendu and the elders encouraged and consoled him. Regrettably again for him, Okonkwo's son, Nwoye was captured by the new religion in Umuofia and Ibe joined missionaries as evangelists. Okonkwo felt humiliated by his son's act. In Mbanta, the new religion had been introduced by the missionaries. The folks did not give a serious thought to the stories about the new religion. They were not concerned at all with white men's government or the consequences of killing the Christian's. The reasons were that the new converts were their people and clansmen and the missionary, Mr. Kiaga was harmless. Okonkwo counselled his maternal people, that until the gangs (Christians) were chased out of the village, there would be no peace. However, some saw the situation differently from Okonkwo. He consoled himself that this clan was a womanly clan. As soon as Okonkwo entered his last year in exile he sent some money to Obierika to rebuild his two huts in his old compound. He also had a feast to thank his mother's kinsmen for hospitality given to him. Finally, they thanked him for that and he went home to Umuofia.

Okonkwo returned home to Umuofia only to find out that things had really fallen apart. Both low-born, outcasts and even titled men like Ogbuefi Ugonna had joined the Christians. The white men had also brought a system of government. Under the leadership of Mr. Brown, the Christian Church restrained excesses and were able to avoid provoking the wrath of the clan. Mr. Brown's successor, Reverend James Smith was over-zealous and differed greatly from his predecessor, Mr. Brown. He provoked the wrath of the clan unmasking the *egwugwu*, the unknowable masquerade, symbol of panpsychic and animistic infinity.

Okonkwo returned again to momentary glory and a position of influence when he met with the elders in market-place. They planned and carried out the work of destruction of the church building. After what seemed to be a peaceful discussion with them, they were arrested and imprisoned. The only condition given for their release was the fine of two hundred bags of cowries. They were given nothing to eat or drink for three days. Okonkwo persistently decided to avenge himself even if others choose to be cowards. Hence, the next meeting they had in the marketplace was interrupted by the appearance of five court messengers whose leader Okonkwo beheaded. Instead of taking action, the clansmen broke into tumult. So they let other court messengers escape unhurt. Consequently the district commissioner arrived in Okonkwo's compound to arrest him and found out he had committed suicide. Tragically Okonkwo could not be buried like any other man in the village of Umuofia because he committed an abomination by killing himself. It was only the strangers that could bring him down and bury him. It is an irony that the strangers Okonkwo died opposing are the people who came to bury him.

HISTORICAL OBJECTIVITY IN *THINGS FALL APART*

This book reflected the history, culture and philosophy of the pre-colonial Igbo society. And in it are many signs of history, values and cultural identity otherwise, known as facts in history which constitute historical objectivity.

First, town crying in *Things Fall Apart* is symbolic of communicative rationality and the acceptable medium of mass information in Igbo villages. The town-crier called a meeting of the whole Umuofia village to let them know that the people of Mbaino had killed their daughter, the wife of Ogbuefi Udo. Town crying is a system of communicative rationality transcendentally justified but specifically in a theistic animistic and panpsychic sense.

There existed the Oracle of hills and caves who ministered to the clan god of Umuofia: And in fairness to Umuofia, It should be recorded that It never went to war unless Its case was clear and just and was accepted as such by its Oracle - the Oracle of the hills and caves.[23] Consulting of oracles was and is a tradition and a religion among Igbo society.

Human sacrifice was common among the pre-colonial Igbo society. Ikemefuna and a young virgin were sacrificed to Umuofia by the people of Mbaino. This act was to appease them for killing their daughter.[24] However; the modernizing value that Christianity brought to the African society is the abolishment of human sacrifice which is a local primitive culture of anti-humanity.

There were certain things considered as abomination *Nso-ani* in Umuofia village. Okonkwo beat his wife in the week of peace and committed a great evil against the land.[25] In other word, peace is recognized in the society as both a universal absolute but also intrinsic in its ontology.

Wrestling March was also common in Umuofia village.[26] It is a symbolic game and ritual for unity and communication among the people. It was not bloody and suicidal like the modern European wrestling.

Ekwefi suffered a great deal in her life.[27] She had borne ten children and nine of them died in infancy. It was the Oracle who confirmed that she had been giving birth to *Ogbanje* children. The pre-colonial Igbo society believed in *Ogbanje* reincarnation. Okonkwo was told that the child was an *Ogbanje* one of those wicked children who, when they died, entered their mother's wombs to be born again."[28] African traditional religion has some cardinal structures of which belief in spirits is one. Every object or structure has a spirit *Ogbanje* spirits are "born-to-die spirits. The belief is that they are wandering mischievous panpsychic animistic spirits who find their way into the wombs of women in order to die immediately or later after birth. It is believed that there is a league of spirits (panpsychic animistic kingdom) whose real pre-occupation is to undertake this bad assignment.

There was *egwugwu* a kind of masquerade or spirit.[29] There were no courts and lawyers. The only way of dispensation of justice among the Igbo clans was through the gods of the land like *egwugwu*. Judgment here is based on true evidence. Hence Igbo African traditional justice system is based on

---

[23] Ibid, p. 12, p. 75
[24] Ibid, p. 43
[25] Ibid, p. 21
[26] Ibid, p. 34.
[27] Ibid., p. 54
[28] Ibid., see pp. 50 -60 for the tortuous ritualistic animistic process of breaking the chain of rebirth
[29] Ibid., p. 62 - 66

natural law and justice reducible to the Theistic Panpsychic animistic truths and asymmetrically deducible from them.

We leant that Ekwefi and her son used to gather and tell each other stories.[30] Story-telling was common in pre-colonial Igbo society. There was no radio or television to relate during their leisure time. So they turned to the act of story telling, as one, an oral tradition and communication and two, as an instrument of communicative rationality. The art of story telling or oral tradition in ancient Africa carries along with it the aura and conscience of animism and panpsychism, ancestorship and the ever presence of God.

During funeral in traditional Igbo society, guns were fired or shot.

In one occasion Okonkwo's gun exploded and killed a young lad. It was during the funeral of Ezeudu, a titled man of Umuofia.[31] Gunfiring is animistic - it must be heard by the living and the dead. Besides, it is a means of communalistic and communicative action.

The village had a forest called evil forest. The evil forest was inhabited by the evil spirits. It was also inhabited by lepers, smallpox victims, evil medicine-men, and outcasts,[32] etc. Python was also venerated and not killed in Umuofia. In the animistic cosmology and ontology, forests are abode of departed spirits in form of pythons or familiar spirits - forms into which human spirits transmigrate.

Education was introduced by the missionaries in Umuofia. It was not initially valued.[33] The people of Umuofia sent their children to school as a punishment. It was only the slaves, the weaklings and the children of foreign wives that were sent to school. Hence, most of the educated and liberated in the postcolonial Africa were the early Christians.

Okonkwo committed an abomination by committing suicide. Suicide was greatly abhorred in the primitive Igbo society. So, Okonkwo despite his fame and position was not properly buried because of this abomination he committed.[34] Suicide, even in the animistic panpsychic culture is illegal, unjust and antihuman.

---

[30] Ibid., p. 67
[31] Ibid., p. 86
[32] Ibid., p. 110
[33] Ibid., pp. 128-129
[34] Ibid., p. 147

PROVIDENTIAL VIEW OF HISTORY IN ACHEBE'S *THINGS FALL APART*

Philosophy of history, especially the providential and cyclical views of history are extant and immanent in '*Things Fall Apart*'. The providential view of history holds that history is the working out of divine purpose. This view was held by the Jews, the early Christian, St. Augustine and the medieval church. In his *City of God* Augustine says that history is the revelation of God's purpose. It explains the drama of salvation from the creation through the fall and the redemptive process to the end of the world and eternal reward and punishment. There are two cities existing side by side in the world. They are *City of God* and *City of Man.* The *city of God* includes all the souls predestined to be saved, that is those saintly men of old as well as the faithful of today who live closer to God. The *"City of Man"* on the other hand refers to the earthly cities of Satan. It includes those devoted purely to worldly pursuit and who are impious and corrupt. History is then the scene of conflict, between these two cities, these two moralities, two orders of life which are dramatically opposed. When the Lord appears the blessed will receive their reward and the wicked their punishment.[35] For the African every blessing is a sign of God's kindness. History whether good or bad is providential.

There is also evidence of providential view of African Philosophy of history. In *Things Fall Apart* it is remembered that for many African people God's active part in human history is seen in terms of his supplying them with rain, good harvest, children, cattle (animals), health, etc. God makes his presence felt through natural objects and phenomena in theistic Panpsychic and animistic sense. Another aspect of this view is that God intervenes in the affairs of men. He intervenes to bring changes in the society. Ikenga Metuh noted, "Man remains bound to God by ties of creation and by God's divine providence over the world of which man is part."[36] Hence, people constantly turn to God in various acts of worship which in effect constitutes man's response to God's interest and active part in human history. According to J.S Mbiti, "God is not divorced from this concept of history because it is His universe. He is active in it and apparent silence may be a feature of his divine

[35] See St. Augustine, e.g. City of God, vii. 24: xiii, 16: xvi 2

[36] See Metuh, Ikenga, *African Religions in Western Conceptual Schemes: The Problem of Interpretations* (Pastoral Institute, Bodija, Ibadan.)

activity."[37] The perceived silence of God is the epitome of his infinitude, awesomeness and power.

The philosophical interpretation -of history in things in Things fall Apart is significant in the sense it was a necessary requirement in any solution of the general metaphysical problem of evil. The issue in *Things Fall Apart* is an obvious metaphysical evil because, a clan that once acted as one, shared things together, spoke as one was later turn to shred by the coming of the white men. The whole chaotic state and evils in the land of Umofia could be traceable to the speculative view of history. Moreover, the whole story and events, in the *Things fall Apart* is a speculative treatment of detailed historical facts and as such partly belong to metaphysics and theory of knowledge.

There is the view that in the cause of history that there are periods of progress and decline, period of ascension and dissension. History according to this theory moves in a cycle like but over long period of time, there is a series of changes leading back to a starting point or the original process repeats it's self. In *Things Fall Apart,* History is also cyclical in the sense that the whole event marked progress and decline. The Umuofia clan was graphically moving from one development to another till the traditional ways of behaviour paved way for European way or Christianity. Finally this type of history marked a turning point in the following line, *Things fall apart; the centre cannot hold; mere anarchy is loosed upon the world.*[38] However, this is also a providential view of history as the working out of a divine purpose, i.e., the cause of events and all that happen is out of divine essence and purpose. In *Things Fall Apart,* the epic tragedy of Okonkwo could be ascribed to the providential view of history in the sense that all that happened to him could be as his "*Chi*" made it to be, thus: "A man could not rise beyond his destiny..."[39] but if a man said yes, his *chi* also affirmed.[39] Here was a man whose *chi* said no despite his own affirmation.

A German philosopher, Immanuel Kant gave a lineal account on the interpretation of history; as either progressive or digressive. According to him, history could be seen as a continuous thought not perhaps straightforward progression towards a better state of affairs. Such a progression can not be seen as real if we conform our self to looking at historical happening solely from the point of view of individual concerned;

---

[37] Mbiti, .J., *African Religions and Philosophy*, Heinemann Educational Books, Ibadan

[38] Aigboje, Higo, Introduction P.V. in Achebe, ibid.

[39] Achebe, ibid.

there we meet with nothing but a chaotic aggregate of apparently meaningless and unconnected event.[40] In *Things fall apart,* the whole event could be seen as linear history. This is because right from inception, we see a community or clan which was traditionally dependent on the custom of the land, be benevolence of the gods and observe all laws of the ancestors not knowing that their whole event is linear and progressive. This later gave way or resulted to society where old tradition gave way to a new tradition of Christian belief and faith, where war and strife gave way to peace and order. The issue of slavery is no longer the order of the day because human right and dignity of man has returned to the entire society. Furthermore, the linear and progressive history of Kant as seen in the *Things fall apart* is from the old practices of exile, sacrifices, killings, etc., to a free society where the dignity of man is improved.

According to Hegel, philosophy brings to the study of history the concept of reasoning. Reason is the Sovereign of the world. Reason here is not the rationality of external causation but a philosophical account of history whereby history is a concerned with the life of spiritual beings, i.e. the religious notion of a process controlled by a divine providence. Hence rationality of history is a realization or plan. Hegel's general thesis is that reality is spirit manifesting itself in nature, in human history and in the action of man. History is the development of spirit through successive stages.[41] The Hegelian explanation of history may be amenable to the epic story of Okonkwo in *Things fall apart* because it is the spirit that is manifesting the whole events in the story. It is the *chi* or gods that are behind the event. The question is whether the story is causal or accidental. The Umofia clan believes in the strength of gods that could be the cause of their predicament and evil that befalls them.

The clash between the African and European cultures in *Things Fall Apart* yielded some conclusions. Before the arrival of the Whiteman in Umuofia, the people had shown that they were religious people. They had a clan god and other divinities whom they worshipped. They even had some people who were dedicated to the worship, of those gods, deities, priests, oracles, etc. In this book, we saw the long discussion between the missionary Mr. Brown and one of the elders of Umuofia clan, Akunna. Their theme was the right religion in practice; and whether it is the religion of the church

---

[40] See Emmanuel, Kant, "The Idea of Universal History with cosmopolitan Intent" Poem.

[41] See Hegel, George, *Philosophy of History*, Trans. J. Shree (New York, Dover, 1956) Introduction, pp. 78 and 209

missionary or the religion of the clan of Umuofia. Although they could not convert each other, both of them learnt a great deal about each other's religion. Okonkwo and some elders remained adamant and continued to fight against the new religion.[42] The new converts won by the missionaries were included in this group that constituted the church which is the visible representation of the *city of God.* This period was actually when God manifested himself to the people of Umuofia in a special way. The *City of Man*[43] includes those that are purely devoted to worldly pursuits, were impious and corrupt. They were supposedly the majority of Umuofia people who out rightly rejected the new religion and opposed the missionaries. They, perhaps, chose to follow the religion of 'darkness' practised by their ancestors. They could have indulged in many hideous practices in the name of tradition and religion. The evil practices included killing of twins, maltreating the widows, human sacrifice, having outcasts like slaves, *osus,* etc. All these were checked by the new religion and salvation was brought to them. Hence, these two cities were in conflict. The "*City of God*" visibly represented by the church worked towards converting the sinners in the "city of man" opposed to this new change as they chose the way of their ancestors. Okonkwo being an arch enemy of the church missionaries fought against the Christians. He did everything he could but failed as some of his clansmen were converted to the new religion. The scene of this conflict is described as the dance of history and destiny; good and evil are followed by reward and punishment respectively, the Christians and missionaries were promised eternal life, they were greatly blessed by God whom they served.

Education was also introduced in the land of Umuofia. There was civilization and development as a result of the white man settling in Umuofia. All these are the rewards of the few who welcomed the missionaries and embraced the religion. In other words, there were punishments awaiting the majority of the people of Umuofia who rejected the missionaries and the goodness of salvation. The promise of heaven (paradise) had eluded them for choosing to remain in darkness. A lot of good things brought about by this new religion wouldn't have reached them. Those evil practices would have continued as a punishment for them. Similialy Okonkwo the arch enemy of this new change (new religion) fought against the missionaries to the extent of committing suicide His punishment

[42] Achebe, Chapt. 21
[43] St. Augustine, op. cit.

was failure and death-a shameful death. The trend of the history of Umuofia and the story of Okonkwo could therefore be explained by the Kantian or providential views of history.

The novel *Things Fall Apart* is not a factitious novel but it has a solid historical background. It is remarkable to note that African people believed in gods who were different from the God preached about by the European missionaries - Christian God. This is predicated on the providential view of African philosophy of history. Their "god" or 'gods' provided for them just as Christian God Almighty provided for him Christian. The Europeans advanced in both science and technology as a result of divine providence. The Almighty God they worshiped and preached about provided for them. On the contrary, African people were said to be backwards in everything because their 'god' is, perhaps, not like the Almighty God. African people would equally become like their European counterparts when they wholeheartedly turn to the Almighty God.

Time is a condition; it is a period, situation of duration. Time has the status or a condition of a being in potency in so far that such being is in potency. In Africa the measurement of time is cyclic and polychromes, that is, different to European and American concept of time, i.e., linear and monochromes. To say that a time is cyclic is to say it moves round and round. To say that times is polychromes is to say that time is dynamic i.e., it involves so many events in a period. It is obvious that the whole event in the tragedy story of Okonkwo in *Things Fall Apart* is caused by the cosmology of cyclic and polychromes concept of time which is that the whole event and story is caused by the fact that the Umoufia clan and community had been so static that they depended entirely on the old and outdated system of living such as sacrifices, slavery, taboo and tradition which is highly static and underdeveloped. This conception of time which is immanent and holistic makes them to view the white and the missionaries as intruders to their custom and tradition without having any knowledge of the impact of social change, progress and development such coming would bring. Thus, they view the whole situation of light and progress brought by the white to their community as stated below: Turning and turning in the wilding gyre. The Falcon cannot hear the flamer, Things fall apart; the centre cannot hold, mere anarchy is loosed upon the world.[44] To say that a time is linear is to say that the time goes straight and stretch, i.e. it involves only one thing in time.

[44] William, B., Yeak, *op. cit.*

The motive and aim of the European, the white and the missionary to African land is total transformation and development but the Igbo people (Africans) see it as worst things that could ever happen to their customs and traditions. "Our clan can not longer act like one. He has put a knife on the thing that held us together we have fallen apart."[45]

THESTIC PANPSYCHIC ANALYTICAL FRAMWORK OF *THINGS FALL APART*

Literary criticism will help bring out some ideological elements in *Things Fall Apart* African literature can be described as the one that is peculiar to the modern African which comprises of their belief, attitudes, origins, their nature, structure of organizations and interaction in the world. As well as their conception of the physical and metaphysical world. This literature or philosophy of the African is derogatively called an Ethno Philosophy, folk philosophy in the sense that it has to do with dogmatism. It has low level of respectability.

African literatures as seen in *Things Fall Apart* are basically traditional, in the sense that it is limited by nature. It is not something arguably revealed to the African such as Islam or Christianity. This is why the Umuofia clan vehemently refused the coming of the white. This African literature is largely seen in the people's myths, proverb, riddles, in their songs and their liturgies. Furthermore, African literature is primarily mythical. This is quietly understandable because the people have no other way of preserving their insight and view about reality. Also the African (Igbo) man has myth regarding the origin of the world, myth about the origin of the time, existence of God and his attributes. When we say that the African worldview is mythical, we mean that myths are means through which such a worldview is transmitted. But it is properly theistic panpsychic.

African literature is a anthropocentric in the sense that it is centred on man and theistic Panpsychic because God is at the apex of being. Man is important and indeed central in African world view but he is by all means a measure of all things or created things. Man is likely to claim a central and strategic position in the hierarchy of beings in the interaction and intercommunicative actions between the visible created order and the invisible world of gods, *chi* and spirit of ancestors. It is right to hold that African literature is centred on man because the spirit of the dead ancestor is

[45] See Nwoga. "The African Imagination" *Research in African Literature* Vol. 12 No 1 Spring, 1981, pp. 43-45

in contact with the living and to continue living on earth. As we can see in the book *Things Fall Apart,* the whole literature is dangling between the Umuofia people and their *chi* or gods. Man is at the centre of the created order, the focal point of the universe, the ontological mean between the visible and the invisible.

Indeed myth is mythical but it contains wisdom. The story in *Things Fall Apart* contains wisdom which serves as eternal legacy for the African. Professor Nwoga argues vividly that myths contain some truths. According to him, "mythology of a community contains those stories which represent the underlying truth behind the life of the people and which will be a good source from which to establish the people's concept of causality, their belief system as they relate to deity and the relationship between man and other beings." [45] It mirrors the reality and the metaphysical beliefs of the people. Metaphysics can be defined as that branch of philosophy that studies reality. It is the science that tries to determine the real nature of things. Here metaphysics subject matter are God, freedom and immortality. It could be recalled that the whole episodes in *Things Fall Apart* or the epic story of Okonkwo and the destiny's of Umuofia clan is highly metaphysical in concept. It could be recalled that the episode that reflected on the death of Okonkwo is immersed in a spiritual theistic animistic world. The war against the coming of the missionary is related to the protection of their animistic ideology and philosophy for the protection of their land which they claim is the domain of their ancestors. Like the Bantu people, Igbo soul hankers after life and force. It is all about deity as it relates to ontology, wisdom and ethics.[46] It is precisely a theistic panpsychic cosmology.

The first major deity in the Igbo land is *"Ani"* or *"Ala"*[47] and minor gods are "Amadioha" - god of immediate punishment and *Arusi* another minor god. Things fall apart is all about gods. They believe in God as the author of their existence, their destiny and their life. They depend solely on the direction of gods for their well being. The gods prescribe and direct their entire affair. There is a general belief that when a person dies, he merely changes life, for he goes to a place of rest where he will occupy a vantage point to supervise the affairs of his children or family which he left behind. No wonder then that Achebe says, the land of the living was not far removed from the domain of the ancestors. There was coming and going between

[46] See Placide, Tempels. in English Parker and Kalumba M., Kibujjo, *African Philosophy: A Classical Approach* (New Jersey Prentice Hall, 1996) p. 19-26

[47] Achebe, *op. cit.*, P. 21

them, especially at festival and also when an old man died, because an old man was very close to the ancestors.[48] Life and death is a continuum in theistic mystical infinity

In *Things Fall Apart* is discussion about the existence of man and god and consequently death. Cosmology here is to be understood as a philosophical science which studies the material world as regards its origins, its characteristics and ultimate end. It is distinguished from the metaphysical that is concerned with immaterial reality, belief in the existence of the physical and spiritual worlds. In *Things fall Apart*, there is the belief in this world of phenomena and the spirit world of immaterial things which can be described as Theistic Panpsychic animistic phenomenalism.

In the epic story of Okonkwo there is the belief that man lives in a genuinely spiritual/ and temporal condition which is directed towards what really is still to come. The Igbo man believes that he continues to live after this world of phenomena. Consequently, he has a strong belief in life after death, i.e. doctrine of re-incarnation and immortality of the soul. For Igbo people death is a transition, it is a gate valve; a means of joining the ancestors in the world.

One of the requirements of "civilization" is that a nation must have a history. But Unuofia seems to lack one. From European point view. Gikandi suggests that the beginning of *Things Fall Apart* is an "imaginary response to the problems of genealogy and cultural identity that have haunted Igbo culture…"[49] This according to him, is the story of Okonkwo, prominent man in a small village of the Igbo area in Nigeria. The story takes place in a time not quite decipherable, but just at the period of White Christian missionaries, British Government and law. Okonkwo is the son of a lazy father named Unoka. Given his boyhood experience, Okonkwo rises from his status as a poor kid to becoming one of the most honoured in his village; Achebe portrayed a total paragon of virtue in him in order to build a one-sided case. While Okonkwo has many fairly universally recognized virtues of honesty, handwork, loyalty to the group, courage and so on, he is also very quick to anger, a relatively brutal husband and father, a man who carefully shut up any emotions of love and care lest he show some weakness to his concept of virility Therefore for Gikandi *Things Fall Apart* is the story of uncivilized people, which, however, is false.

---

[48] Achebe, ibid., p. 85

[49] Gikandi, Simon, *Reading Chinua Achebe; Language and Ideology in fiction; An Antholoty of Critical Writing* (Black Orpheus 1991) p. 29

Umuofia is on a collision course with the western world. Christianity is first introduced to this village and the surrounding neighbourhood by a relatively kind and understanding missionary that preached his new gospel with fervour, but approaches the Igbo with understanding and gentleness. This approach works and before long a significant number of the people have been converted to his religion, sent their children to his school and embraced the western medicine at his clinic. At the background, comes the British system of government, law and courts, supported by a military with weapon far beyond anything the Igbo could challenge. Consequently, the life of the Igbo, their entire cosmology and structure of life, simply fell apart when faced with the invading British colonial religion and administration. The novel is a carefully detailed account of Igbo society, centring on the rising fortunes of Okonkwo and how life battles are played out within his family of three wives and many children.[49] as well as the sustenance and collapse of African cosmological empire.

Achebe can be said to have undertaken the writing of *Thing Fall Apart* out of awareness of a primary connection from the indigenous background that he seeks to explore in the novel. Commenting upon his own work forty years ago after its appearance, "the story of Okonkwo is almost inevitable; if I hadn't written about him, certainly somebody else would have, because is already the beginning of our story."[50] This observation concerning his fictional creation draws attention to the allegorical significance that Okonkwo has assumed for the African imagination: he is not merely a character in a novel but the representative figure of African historicity. An important element in the novel is the way the story is embedded within an elaborate reconstruction of forms of life in the traditional, pre-colonial culture, specifically, that of Achebe's own people, southeast of Nigeria. Indeed, significant is the very tenor and warmth of Achebe's presentation of the traditional world, especially in thirteen chapters that form part of the novel, with there elaborating representation of setting. The Igbo tribal world emerges here in all its specificity, its daily routines and seasonal rituals attuned to the natural rhythms (panpsychic animism) of its living environment and ultimately the theistic humanistic panpsychism of African culture. The even cadence that epitomises the collective life in its normal course is summed up at one point in a simple but telling way "in this way,

[50] Ibid.

the moons and the season passed."[51] The moons and season are historical signs of progress and decay or theistic animistic historiography.

Achebe, according to Gikandi, presents us then with a dynamic framework of social interactions and interpersonal relations that lay the effective foundation for what, in the language of Durkheim, we might call a collective consciousness, one that is properly commensurate with a sphere of existence and an order of experience that, by the very fact of their being rigorously circumscribed, conduced to its institutional strength. "Okonkwo was well known throughout the nine villages and with which the narrator indicates the outer limit of Okonkwo's fame, reflects the tribe's limited awareness of its location in space, of its specific place in the world. This accord with the curious indefiniteness of its name, Umuofia or "people of the Forest,"[52] a name that also doubles as that of the novel's locale, designating a community firmly situated within the natural world. Globalization for this African community then means the space and location determined by the sight of the sky rising and falling in another village, that is, the falling of the sky in a distance means the end of the world.

The tribe's myth of origin sets the keynote of its entire mode of self-apprehension and structure of knowledge which Gikandi has called "the Igbo epistemology".[53] The myth of origin also ensures that time is experienced not as a static category but lived continuously and intensely in the mode of duration. This consciousness of time permeates the collective life, so that the worldview involves a ceaseless procession of life, in an interpenetration of time and space that is ensured by the eternal presence of the ancestors. The land of the living was not removed from the domain of the ancestors as there is a panpsychic animistic continuum. There was coming and going between them especially when an old man died, because an old man was very close to his ancestors. A man's life (birth to death) was a series of transitional rites, which brought him nearer to his ancestors.[54] The culture of Umuofia and the system of belief derived from it as experienced at every level of rationality serves as the measure of social control, as demonstrated by the role of the *Egwuwu* (animistic symbol) incantations of the ancestors, in the administration of justice, a role that endows the laws and customs of the land with a sacred sanction. As a culture of Theistic humanistic Panpsychic

---

[51] Ibid., p. 39.
[52] Ibid.
[53] Gikandi, *op. cit.* p. 31-38.
[54] Achebe, *op. cit.*, p. 8.

communicative rationality 'dialogue' such as the one engaged with throughout the novel points to the processes by which the principles governing the world concept and value system of the tribe are constantly debated, remained and in this way, retrospectively rationalized commonly.

Thus, as represented by Chinua Achebe, Umuofia the primordial Igbo village emerges as a locus of the immediate context of the novel. Unoka's refusal to conform to the prevailing ethos of the tribe is considered in wholly negative terms. More importantly, his son, who wills himself into becoming the antithesis of all that Unoka represents, opposed modernity, modernization and by implication Christianity: "He was a man of action, a man of war, unlike his father; he could stand the look of blood. In Umuofia's war, he was the first to bring a human head home. That was his fifth head; he was not an old man yet. On great occasions, such as the funeral of a village celebrity, he drank his palm wine from his first human head."[55] This symbolic and ritualist action, however, represents the crisis and decadence dimension of African tradition which indeed could be separated from the pristine world view of theistic Panpsychic rationality. It is this portrayal of Okonkwo that prompted Thomas Melone to propose, in his pioneering study devoted to the first four novels of Chinua Achebe, an evaluation that both captures him as a "complex and unsetting personality.[56] Okonkwo certainly is, but not exactly complex; given his delineation in *Things Fall Apart.* One would be inclined rather to consider him a "flat" character, to use E.M. Forster's term. It is true that, in the particular context in which we encounter the character, the novelist nudges us to the edge of what could have been a powerful psychological portrait considering his problematic relation to his father, who throws a long shadow over his life, yet Okonkwo's character portrays him as a true republican Igbo man who is born and determined to succeed in life in a puritan republican, individualistic, humanistic animistic theistic environment and society.

BETWEEN THEISTIC PANSYCHIC ANIMISM AND LITERALLY CRITICISM

It has been argued that *Things Fall Apart* can be summed up as largely the narrative of the process of self-fashioning by which Okonkwo is transformed into the sombre inversion of his father. But the mental condition into which he falls as a result is not really explanatory, to make a statement about inner

[55] Ibid.

[56] Melone, Themas, 1973, p. 64

working of his mind as a fully realized individual. Even at his moment of greatest mental turmoil (in the immediate aftermath of his killing of Ikemefuna), we are provided with hardly any insight into the happenings within his troubled soul. The point here is that, despite the occasional glimpse, the narrative affords us into the states of mind that are also occasions for introspection on the part of the character, it narrows our gaze, to focus upon what is presented as essential to his make up: "Okonkwo was a man of action not of thought."[57] The ambivalence by which the novel is governed inheres in the portrayal of Okonkwo. We must go further to observe that the largely negative thrust of this portrayal comes close to undermining the polemic intent of the novel. The ironic devaluation of the character and the ethos he embodies suggest a profound sense of unease on the part of his creator regarding many issues of moral import raised by the habits of mind and social practices that define the traditional of life and expression, there is then a sense in which the Achebe's novel begins to tend towards a subversion of its ideological premises. It is as if Achebe's intellect, sensibility and his sense of artistic integrity had entered into contention with his primary affections for his cultural identity. What he is indeed doing is a panpsychic animistic analysis of his culture.

Achebe's novel is not the expression of a repudiation of the tribal ethos, or a form of recoil from the tribal universe, but to consider the text in light of its ambivalence is to recognize it for what it is: an uncompromising reappraisal of the tribal world. We are made aware of the inadequacy of the ethos, by which the past was regulated, its limitations as embodied in historical forms, and of those questions arising precisely from their mode of insertion in the world. Moreover, as Piere Nora has pointed out, the phenomenon of memory exceeds the purview of history.[58] In this particular context perhaps more than in any other, the dynamics of cultural memory involves much more than the reaching into a past; they also engage the present, insofar as the traditional culture upon which they are focused remains a vibrant contemporary reality. While it continues to exert its force upon minds, the question remains how far the past can be invoked to legitimize the present, how far it is capable of functioning as a practical reference in the contemporary circumstances of African endeavour. These, then, are some of issues raised by Achebe's work. The point is that the novel

---

[57] Achebe, *op. cit.*, 48

58 Nora, Pierre, *Great Introduction, Between Democracy and History*, 1989

genre serves Achebe as a mode of reflection upon the nature and significance of the African past, and its relevance to the African present. In *Things Fall Apart*, this reflective tone is made evident in the conversations and dialogues he attributed to the elders of the tribe, who are thereby presented through the course of the narrative as minds engaged in a sustained, rational deliberative and communicative process. The novel takes on a discursive character as it stages a running debate on customs and practices, on institutions and values, on systems of belief: a debate that is in reality conducted as an interrogation of the human possibilities offered by the material world and mental landscape that together compose the tribal culture and stamp it with a distinctive quality.

But although this interrogation is presented as internal, it amounts ultimately to an objective scrutiny, in the light of an alternative set of values that, in the nature of things, were not available to the subjects themselves. This scrutiny forms a part of the implicit communicative panpsychic ideology of the system of ideas presiding upon its organization, for which the Euro-Christian system of values begins to function as touchstone and measure. This is not to imply that the emphasis on Christianity as a factor of liberation authorizes us to read the work as a justification of the new religion, much less of colonial imposition, but rather as a mirror held up to African society, enabling a process of self-apprehension. In other words, a new African consciousness emerges through the mediation of the Christian/Western vision of the world, yet against the heavily densed monotheistic Panpsychism.

The contradiction generated by the fundamental ambivalence of the novel's propositional content can be grasped at the level where the process of self reflection manifested in the novel is traversed by what one might call a deep cultural anxiety. The need to validate the tribal culture in some emotionally satisfactory way runs up against the question of value, a question that is central to the order of meaning proposed by the novel. It is in this light that Obierika, who stands as the manifest antithesis of Okonkwo, can be said to function as the moral centre of the novel. He comes closest among the novel's characters to a representation of what Valdez Moses has called a "modern sensibility".[59] It is perhaps, not far-fetched to suggest that we have in Obierika not merely the one character with which, as Jeyifo points out, but rather a subtle projection of the critical consciousness that Achebe

[59] Valdez, Moses, The Novel and the Globalization of Culture 1995, p 113

himself brings to the imaginative conception of the novel.[60] The evidence of the novel lends such weight to this view as to make it a matter of more than mere speculation.

Whatever the case, the debate enacted within the novel gives the work an analytical bent to which its initial ideological inspiration is ultimately subordinated *Things Fall Apart* testifies to a clear recognition of a decisive break in the African experience of history occasioned by the colonial fact. It hardly needs to be stressed that this recognition is far from committing Achebe to acquiescence in the methods of subjugation employed by colonial agents and the humiliation described in the latter pages of the novel, in which the historical grievance of Africa is vividly represented, dramatized in the martyrdom of Okonkwo and the Umuofia elders. The pathos of their situation resonates through the entire society, takes on wider meanings including the suspension of the entire energy, systems, poetic rational and aesthetic life in Umuofia. All these portend the stifling of the tribe's spirit by a collective trauma: "Umuofia was like a startled animal with ears erect, sniffing the silent, ominous air, and not knowing which way to run."[61] The dearth of a society is a signification which beckons a call for a restitution.

The anti-colonial thrust of the novel is evident but this is not all there is to the story of Okonkwo and Umuofia, as recounted by Chinua Achebe. The novel ended with the hero's suicide. This marks the end of the struggle and the beginning of a new and unpredictable future for the Umuofians and for the continent of which they form an integral and indeed representative part. The import of the novel arises from this intimation of which *Things Fall Apart* registers ultimately as an acute consciousness of historical and cultural discontinuity occasioned by the colonial encounter in Africa, and of its ontological implications; the necessity for a new mode of being, of relating to the world.

It is one of the novel's peculiar traits that the historical realism that directs the narrative progression or providentially historical progression harmonizes readily with the panpsychic animistic mood that serves as its ground base, or communalistic animistic ideology which is registered in one of the most remarkable passages in the novel:

---

[60] 60.Jeyifo, Biodun, "Okonkwo and His mother - Things fall Apart and issues of Gender in the constitution of African post-colonial Discourse" *Callalloo* Vol. 16 No 4 on "Post-Colonial Discourse" A Special Issue (Autumn 1993) pp. 847-859.

[61] Achebe, *op. cit.*, 139

> that night the mother of the spirits walked the length and breadth of the clan, weeping for her murdered son. Not even the eldest, Umuofia had ever heard such a strange and fearful sound, and it was never to be heard again. It seemed as if the very soul of the tribe wept for a great evil that was coming - its own death.[62]

The epochal significance of the passage is intensified, assumes cosmic resonance, in the lament that pours out of one of the characters, Okika, at the final meeting of the clan: "All our gods are weeping. *Idemili* is weeping. *Ogwugwu* is weeping. and all the others…"[63] Okika's lament directs us to the heart of Achebe's novel: It is as an allergy that incorporates a tragic vision of history that *Things Fall Apart* elicits the strongest and deepest response. *Things Fall Apart* is an imaginative delineation of those significant moments in the African colonial experience. The novel is therefore a work on African philosophy, African colonial history and cultural experience. It is a significant work of philosophy that acutely address the metaphysical and ontological world view of Igbo people and the Africans generally, and the one that represents Immanuel Kant synthesis, on idealism and realism in the didactic reference to the roles objective and subjective life plays in the philosophical and economic history of Igbo people.

This stylistic evolution of the novel may be interpreted as the scriptural and historical sign of a corresponding readjustment of the writer's vision, reflecting his sense, as it begins to develops, of the pressure of history as it begins to exert himself upon the community. This seems to accord with a Hegelian conception of history as the unfolding spirit of modernity, with the modern novel as its imaginative equivalent. Modernity is a historical phenomenon arising primarily from the Western experience and as the paradigm that informed the writing of scientific history, and, the emergence of the novel, the literary genre that is thought to be most closely associated with modern culture. In this view, the novel as a specific modern genre affords a new medium for the construction in aesthetic and moral terms of a vision of a totality no longer immediately available to consciousness in the fragmented, reified world of modern civilization.[64] Yet the objective truth is that *Thing Fall Apart* is an unconscious elevation of theistic panpsychic animistic vision of Igbo society.

---

[62] Ibid., p. 132

[63] Ibid., p. 143

[64] Lukas, 1977 quoted by Abiola F. Irele, *The Crisis of Cultural Memory in Chinua Achebe's Things Fall Apart* (New York, Anchor Books 1994) or www.africa.ufl.edu

On the conception of history that underwrites the status of the novel, the society depicted in Achebe's novel, along with the culture it sustains, appears as prehistoric, subsisting, as far as the record of its existence is concerned, on mythical narrative orally transmitted. *Things Fall Apart* challenges this conception, for the whole purpose of Achebe's novel is to bring the existence of this culture into view as a historical reality, one that bears witness to the human world realized within it. The narrative mode, in both its epic aspect and at the novelistic level of articulation, affords Achebe the means of restating the grounded historicity of the African experience, in a creative reconstruction of stages of the collective being. The sequence of events narrated, and the society and culture represented, are products of an individual imagination, detached from any function of pure predication; the narrative unfolding of events conducted along a definite plot line is thus sustained by an aesthetic faculty. *Things Fall Apart* as a work on philosophy of African history propounds a theory of objectivity and subjectivity of History dealing with real events in the past, featuring real historical personalities as characters. Hence, the need for a more inclusive conception, such as the one propounded by Hayden White, which posits a fundamental relationship between fiction and history as modalities for the signification of narrative as a universal phenomenon. The collapsing or unification of narrative historiography with literature and myth should provide no reason for embarrassment because the systems of meaning production in *Things Fall Apart* is a distillate of the historical experience of a people, a group, a culture.[65] This suggests that the assimilation of fiction to history is authorized not merely in formal terms but also in content, insofar as in both cases, the real world of concrete experience features as referent of the narrative. In the novel there is a special notion of fiction, deriving from its enhanced value as symbolic representation of experience. Hence, "the narrative figurate the body of events that serves as its primary referent and transforms these events into intimations of patterns of meaning that any literal representation of them as facts could never produce."[66] Achebe's work registers on the other hand a recognition of the compulsions upon the human estate of the historical process itself (what he has called 'the power of events)a compulsion that admits of only narrow margins for the play of human agency. This is what Ahiola Irele calls the "humane pessimism"

[65] Heyden, White. 1987 44-45 quoted by Irele, *op. cit.*
[66] Ibid., p. 45

which he believes Achebe shares with Joseph Conrad.[67] However, this pessimism is not by any means a disabling one, for it does not imply a resignation born out of a passive suffering of events. According to him, it calls rather for a purposive adjustment to those great shifts in the structure of the world that destabilize established constellations of thought, initiating a new historical process and enforcing therefore a new adventure of mind.

It is most likely that what cultural history delivers in Achebe's first novel is not so much of a revealed past, recollected in a spirit of untroubled celebration, but ultimately opening out of the African consciousness to the possibility of its transcendence, to the historic chance of a new collective and existential being. The sense of the tragic clings nonetheless to this consciousness, for Achebe is aware that this historic chance, if real, is at best limited and fragile. His vision is probably best expressed by the voice of the "Oracle" in his poem *Dereliction* in the volume *Beware Soul Brother*, inviting his worshippers to a form of action, perhaps a collective affirmation, in the precarious space constituted by the, strip of dry land between sea and shore at the ebbing of the tide*; Let them try the land where the sea retreats, Let them try the land, where the sea retreats.*[68] Achebe's tragic vision of history is presented in these lines in tension with his utopianism. But to invoke the tragic dimension of Achebe's first novel is not merely to seek to uncover the full scope of its statement of the colonial encounter in Africa, but also to reach for its contemplative character of the general human condition. For Abiola Irele It is this sense that is conveyed by Roland Barthes's summation of the *tragedies of Recine* as the aesthetics of defeat.[69] There is this aesthetics of defeat in the social and cultural condition of Umuofia and as is portrayed in the rest of Africa then. The description applies equally to all the great tragedies of world literature, among which *Things Fall Apart* must now be seen to occupy a distinctive place. Beyond its reference to the personal dilemmas of *Racine's* characters, Barthes's phrase points to the apprehension of the tragic imagination of the essential fragility of our human condition. The deep insight that tragedy provides into this condition may well shake our being with fear and trembling, but it is the illumination and psychic release it generates that enable humanity to keep going. As a necessary component of its exploration of the African experience, *Things Fall Apart* embodies this fundamental truth of the imaginative vision.

---

[67] Irele, ibid., pp. 32-45. or see Joseph Conrad, *Heart of Darkness*

[68] See Achebe, Chinua, Dereliction

[69] Bathes, Roland, (1963), Mythologies or the Death of Darkness p. 61 quoted by Irele, ibid.

NATIONALIST LITERATURE AND LIBERATIST PARADIGSM

Things Fall Apart by Chinua Achebe is, to use his Igbo concept 'Town Crier', a communicative or literacy instrument, to call on all Africans, laymen, statesmen and nationalists to come out and see what the white has done to the culture, philosophy and history of the Africans, and a call for national re-awakening, restoration of their values that have been trampled upon, and if need be a revolt against colonialism, neo-colonialism and imperialism. The response to this incipient degradation of African dignity and the dignity of man is what entailed in the essence of nationalists struggles championed by Julius Nyerere, Kwame Nkrumah, Nnamdi Azikiwe, Leopold Senghor among others whose mission was not only political freedom but the preservation of African personality. *Things Fall Apart* by Chinua Achebe is, therefore, an agenda setting novel for the nationalists and the progressives in black Africa. In order to achieve liberation of African countries from neo colonial slavery, African leaders attempted to restore traditional values, communal, social practices, and above all, the traditional African socialist/communalist values. These values and social practices of traditional African include communal spirit, hospitality, hard work, generosity, acceptance and practice of egalitarianism, communal ownership of land, and equality of opportunity for all and so on. The concept of brotherhood is expressed in Zik's communalism, Senghor's negritude, Nkrumah's consciencism and Nyerere's *Ujamma* (socialism), African literatures and so on. Nnamdi Azikiwe widely held to be a prophet of African and Nigerian nationalism did not really say much on brotherhood, but this could be inferred from some of his teachings. He speaks of African communalism in the general sense of kinship relationship. This corresponds with J. Nyerere's concept of African brotherhood. Azikiwe argues that the renascent African must be reckoned with as a factor in the peace of the world. He described the Africans as those that believe in the universal fatherhood of God and those interested in the affairs of other.[70] Their mission to the world appeals for collection security, respect for others and international brotherhood.

Leopold Sedar Senghor, the former Senegalese president is a renowned poet and philosopher. He is one of the contemporary African philosophers who had an ardent desire to regain what Sartre called "existentialist integrity" which he paraphrased as "the original purity of his (black

[70] Azikiwe, Nnamdi, "Africa in Renascence" *Reading in African Political Thought,* Gideon-Cyrus *et al.* (London, Heinemann, 1975) PP. 166-167

Africans) existence."[71] Senghor's drive was not just for social progress, economic consolidation and stability, but above all, for the black man to be in rapport with himself. African culture, he said has strong roots in the literal and cultural movement of what is today known as *negritude*. In its historical beginning *negritude* was more of a literal or sociocultural movement. It has the vision of African personality. African identity and personality, which is completely overshadowed by the Western civilization was what led to Senghor and his contemporaries into rejecting the western worldview and thus calling for a return to African socialism. Senghor saw socialism as essentially a vision of the world in the African way, at least, the Senegalese way to socialism. It intends to be a harmonic democracy, in both the political and economic sociocultural field. African brotherhood, he argues, means that traditional African society is based on both the community and on the person and which was founded on the dialogue and reciprocity. The group had priority over the individual without crushing him, but allowing him to blossom as a person. Like others, Senghor explained African brotherhood in an appropriate manner by insisting that: African society puts more stress on the group than on the individual, more on the solidarity than on the activity and needs of the individual, more on the communion of persons than on their autonomy.

Considering the historical elements of 'belonging', Senghor likened it with brotherhood. The elements of this belonging worth mentioning are particular values and cultural virtues like group solidarity, commitment, hospitality, patriotism, and participation.

'Oneness' in Africa, according to him, is the sharing togetherness, which provides foundation for their continuity. Each member of the community is constitutively involved in the course of the community both individually and communally. Members do not merely exist; they are also the performers of duties. Leopold Senghor expresses in general terms what is synthetically conceptualized as the principle of belongingness thus: the African (Negro) society is a collective society, more precisely communal, because it is formed by a communion of souls more than of aggregation of individuals.[72] Furthermore, the strongest feature of Negritude upon which Senghor built his African brotherhood is derived from the phenomena of collectivism. According to him, the collective setting of African society is

---

[71] Leopold, Sedar, Senghor. "What is Negritude?" in *Reading in African Political Thought*, Gideon-Cyrus *et al.* (London, Heinemann, 1975) p. 83.
[72] Ibid.

constructed on several integrating forces (panpsychic and animistic) such as the ancestors of the clan, members of the large family, play or work-mates conceived as one. This oneness manifests itself in the activities of production (and consumption) particularly in social and economic activities. Senghor specifically emphasizes economic activities and productive relations as manifestation of the brotherhood of Africans. Labour was not seen as a source of personal profit and if it was ever so conceived, it was only "when the vital maximum"[73] of the collectivity has been obtained and always with the express authorization of the family and societal head. African society in the Senghorian conception accepts some of the main features of classical socialism and rejects others. It is based on social philosophy which according to him, rests on the belief that man is not an individual entity but part of the society or community into which he is inseparably bound. The African brotherhood, which is founded on animistic theism, is also a form of humanism which aims at the material well-being of man, the improvement of the conditions of production and the equitable distribution of resources. It is a humanistic ideology, which seeks to do away with racism, nationalism, tribalism and religious antagonism. It is important to stress that the objectives of re-awakening the spirit of African brotherhood in Senghor's thoughts and literatures have a great deal to do with the predicament of a people with a colonial history. One of such objectives is thus the liberation of the mind of the colonized, to scrape off the scales of colonial values and substitute them with the original values of pre-colonial Africa.

Kwame Nkrumah (1909-72), was a socialist revolutionary philosopher who was very critical of capitalism, which according to him, is a refined form of feudalism, and slavery. As a political philosopher, in one of his major works *consciencism* he tried to restore traditional values, communal social practices and above all, the traditional African socialist mentality. His list of the basic value and social practices of the traditional African includes the spirit of brotherhood. According to him; they express this by the gesture of communal spirit, hospitality, hard work, generosity, acceptance, and the practice of egalitarianism. He likewise traces the genesis of socialism advocated in Africa by Africans to "brotherhood" which they practice through their communal life. According to him, "any one who seeks the socio-political ancestor of socialism; he or she must go to communalism.

---

[73] Nkrumah, Kwame, *Consciencism: Philosophy and Ideology of Decolonization* (Monthly Review Press, U.S.) p. 73.

Socialism has characteristics in common with communalism just as capitalism is linked with feudalism and slavery…"[74] Nkrumah states that traditional African institutions, values and attitudes have been greatly disrupted by foreign importations. He thinks that we are so affected by these foreign influences that we are left with no choice other than to recognize and reckon with their presence. Nkrumah however admits that a great deal of what was traditionally Africans still lingers on. He expresses the view that the communalistic nature of African society meant no class antagonism or exploitation. He claimed that these features, which have now become part of contemporary African society, were introduced by western industrial society. However, Nkrumah does not seem to be consistent in his classless nature of African society because according to him, class struggle and tension are universal laws of progress.

Furthermore, traditional Africans according to Nkrumah are not individualistic, but communalistic. Individualism is irreconcilable with brotherhood in traditional African society. African nations should reject the inequality, individualism, imperialism brought into Africa by the European imperialists. He admonished African nations to go back to the brotherhood, egalitarianism or traditional African society. According to him, the developed form of African communal life is socialism, and by so doing, Africans nations would not only be going back to their roots, but would be adopting it in its developed form.[75] Finally, Nkrumah sees traditional Africans as being selfless and they see every other as brother. This is what he meant when he argued that originally, Africans lived communalistic lives, and everybody worked for the common good of all. The society for him was characterized with virtues like mutual sympathy and empathy, which certainly point to a peculiar mode of existence, that embrace the 'I' and 'others' and their concerns. This mutual concern of the African society certainly expressed "brotherhood" in traditional African society.

Ujamaaism was authored by the former President of Tanzania Julius Nyerere. It is in his conviction that it is only through socialist principles embedded in the African way of life that Africans would hope to build a truly human and equitable society free from the ills of colonial capitalism, namely, exploitation, injustice, class struggle, discrimination, poverty of the masses, etc. It is therefore, in the interest of human society where the individual is

---

[74] Ibid., p. 74

[75] J.K. Nyerere, *Ujamaa* (Oxford University Press, London 1968) pp. 2-12

seen and treated as an end in itself, and not solely as a means, that made Nyerere to opt for socialism based on brotherhood.

Moreover, Nyerere agreed with Nkrumah and Senghor that capitalism and individualism are alien to African society. Conflict and tension is just as foreign to African society as capitalism and must be rejected. Here, Nyerere disagreed with Nkrumah who sees class struggle, conflict and tension as universal laws of progress. The traditional African society, Nyerere argues, is not based on conflict, struggle and tension, but on brotherhood. Nyerere's notion of brotherhood is that type experienced in the "Ujamaa Village". His socialism revolves round the concept of *Ujamaa.* This is Swahili (African) word which literally means *family hood* and is employed by Nyerere to portray his meaning and notion of brotherhood in traditional African society. Thus, he opined that he was the first to use the word *Ujamaa* in order to explain the kind of life they wish to live in their country. The word " *Ujamaa* according to him denotes the brotherhood of a man and his family and towards neighbours. For Nyerere, society is made up of atomic family units in a country made up of *Ujamaa* village, a kind of village with mutual co-operation and collaboration. Such a nation would be basically family units extended to embrace the whole society. The capitalistic spirit of acquisition, individualism, the exploitation of man by man, class struggle and conflict will all be excluded from the society, which according to him does not express brotherhood.

Thus, *Ujamaa* or family hood is opposed to capitalism, which seeks to build a society on the basis of exploitation of man by man. Therefore, *Ujamaa* (Nyerere's pet programme of *villagisation)* shows his own notion of brotherhood. Thus, *Ujamaa* represents rural economic and social communities where people live and work together for the good of all; their governments are chosen and led by the peasants and workers themselves. Thus, *Ujamaa* is predicated on the simplicity, egalitarianism and freedom that were the hallmarks of traditional African society. For instance, the organization of communal societies especially the production and distribution of social produce, was such that there was hardly any room for parasitism in the traditional African society, an individual takes care of the community and the community in return takes care of the individual. All felt secured and worked for the common welfare.[76] In the word of Nyerere, brotherhood in Africa is based on the principle of co-operation. People must

---

[76] Ibid., pp. 107-144

work co-operatively for the common good rather than competitively for individual gain. This, according to him is the best way to enhance productivity, ensure fair distribution of goods and eliminate exploitation of man by man. The important thing here is that the community would be farming as a group and living as a group and investment in the community would be investment in the farm of every member, investment in the village such as clean water supply, would be of benefit to every member. The return from the produce of the farm and from all the other activities of the community would be shared according to the work done and to the needs of the member.

This brotherhood as exemplified in Nyerere's Ujamaaism however, does not only limit its literally meaning (i.e., persons who are members of the same family, who have blood relationship) it also extends to neighbours, villagers, and others around. This inspires a feeling of oneness and belongingness, which is not limited to blood relatives. It suggests above all, a motive of action. It is not just a sense of civic relationship or social solidarity, it is also similar to the devotion that a person would naturally feel towards a blood relation, except that it is not limited to any particular group of persons or community.[77] Finally, the relationship that exists in *Ujamaa* village becomes for Nyerere the foundation of the brand of African brotherhood which aims completely at welfare and progress. Thus, brotherhood is love offered to individuals in the society as members of the same family. There is a thread that runs through Nkrumah, Senghor, and Nyerere in tacitly accepting socialism as a sophisticated version of communalism simply because of the criticism that communalism offers no room for the expression of individuality. It has to be pointed out, however, that the argument is *non sequitor* as in African philosophy of culture, the community is the individual *writ-large,* hence, according to Kwame Gyekye, and communalism manifests features "of both communality and individuality". It must be noted that the social order cannot and does not go beyond outside the immanent and transcendental superstructure of theistic humanistic panpsychic rationality.

The African father's *gong* (Town-cry) or rather to speak in the popular political parlance, 'nationalism', is predicated on those literary and historical values diachronically and synchronically transcendent and immanent in the subjective values and objective symbols represented by theistic pansychic animism. Such necessary symbolic objective-subjective reality as God is the

---

[77] Achebe, *op. cit P. 127*

Referent of all objective beings. African poems and literatures advert generously to this superstructure. The Igbo people in Nigeria as encapsulated by Achebe would argue:

> We make sacrifices to the little gods, but when they fail and there is no one else to turn to we go to *Chukwu.* We approach a great man through his servants. But when his servants fail to help us, then we go to the last source of hope. We appear to pay greater attention to the little gods but that is not so...[78]

The Value in belief in gods, theistic polytheism or theistic panpsychic animism) is in the democratic communalistic public sphere in African society, it is the philosophy of pluralism and democratic truths and individuals as enshrined in post modernism. Again, political concept such as common good, human dignity, togetherness or collectivism and kinship morality or communalism are legacies here and beyond, but generated and preserved by African literatures and history. The African in *Things fall Apart* speaks,

> a man who calls his kinsmen to feast does not do so to save them from starving. They all have food in their houses. When we gather together in the moonlight village ground it is not because of the moon. Every man can see it in his compound. We come together because it is good for kinsmen to do so...But I fear for your young people because you do not understand how strong is the bond of kinship. You do not know to speak with one voice.[79]

As the progenitor and bedrock of the ideological manifestos of African nationalism, the above line from *Things fall Apart*, suggests freedom, rational free actions on the part of the kindred, common good in space and time and communalism and respect of one another in one voice. Not less exciting is the logic of equality in the purview of the moon from every man's compound.

In African tradition, there is the cognition of peace as not only an ethic or morality but also as a universal law, hence the sanction on Okonkwo who committed a sacrilegious act by beating his wife during the week of peace. The chief reminded Okonkwo that he has committed offence against the law of the land. "You know as well as l do that our forefathers ordained that before we plant any crops in the earth we should observe a week in which a

[78] Ibid., P. 118
[79] Ibid., P. 22.

man does not say a harsh word to his neighbour. We live in peace with our fellows to honour our goddess of the earth without whose blessings our crops will not grow."[80] The week of peace is a week of festivity to celebrate life in African way. But Okonkwo turned it into a week of crises and wailing. The consequences are grave; "The evil you have done can ruin the whole clan. The earth goddess whom you have insulted may refuse to give us her increase, and we shall perish"[81] These statements of natural law are logical reasonings that respect the hypothetical syllogism and *modus ponems* argument in the following ways.

1 Breaking the Peace is evil,
The evil ruins the whole clan,
Therefore breaking the peace ruins the whole clan

$\mathbf{P > q}$

$\underline{q > r}\quad p > r$

2 If the earth goddess refuses to give us increase we shall perish.
The earth goddess refuses to give us increase.
Therefore we shall perish

$P > q$

P

q

The value in African philosophy whose existence and inculcation has been the preoccupation of African literature and history is rock foundation in the subconscious subjectivity and objective reality of African mind. The inter subjective objectivity of cognitive insight into the culture and tradition passed down from generation to generation through oral tradition is an epistemological matrix whose reference point is the transcendental unity of apperception. Unlike the objectivity of modernity that destroyed the soul of one humanity by the self transcendence of reason and the Habermas subjective incursion into the vein and arteries of modernity to give it a human face, African philosophy is not simply a subjective capacity and an objective rational principle but a dimension presupposed by both which allows for their final reconciliation in Theistic panpsychic animism.

---

[80] Ibid.

[81] Bernstein, Richard. .J., (ed) "Introduction" in *Habermas and Modernity* Cambridge, Massachusetts, the MIT Press) p.18

THEISTIC PANPSYCHIC COMMUNICATIVE RATIONALITY*

Thesitic panpsychism as communicative Action

The difference between a scientific system and the non scientific system is only a matter of forms of rationality: so also the difference between empirical system and non empirical system explainable in terms of the kinds of rationality systems in their structures. Similarly, the classification of civilized cultures and primitive cultures or the black civilization and Western civilization is all about forms of rationalizations. That is because the form of explanation of European Society is different from the form of explanation of the Black African animistic society. The traditions of Kant, Hegel, Schelling, Marx, etc., are forms of rational enquiries into particular socio-political for mations of their respective cultures. The American pragmatic thinkers like Pierce, Meed and Dewey had the vision and understanding of radical participatory democracy. Horkhemer, Adorno, Marcus and other members of the Frankfurt school formed a rational system antithetical to the methodology of modernity and the Enlightenment Europe. The history of Western philosophy is indeed the history of rational explanations and communications.[82] Yet in the ancient Africa (uninfluenced by western tradition) there is a peculiar and unique form of rationalization process in form of oral tradition that is animistic but symbolically and philosophically described as theistic panpsychic communicative rationality and its antithesis theistic panpsychic literally criticism.

Until the emergence of the critical theory, it was not obvious that the soul of humanity was being desecrated by modernity. Consequently recreating the world from the battered assault of modernity becomes the preoccupation of Habermas and the Frankfurt school even as the pristine African consciousness holds tenaciously the lubrics of the universe which the former failed to recapture. African society is a fallibillistic critical community whose perception and utilization of society is partly a function of transendentalism and inter-subjectivism, yet based on Theistic Humanism. However, Habermas sought the Kernel of what he was to later call 'Communicative action'. For him,

> communicative action is a distinctive type of social interaction the type of action oriented to mutual understanding. It must be distinguished from other types of social action and non social

* First published in Open Journal of Philosophy, USA.

[82] F. David, Martin. & Leo, A. Jacobus. *The Humanities Through The Arts*, 3rd ed., (USA, McGraw-Hill, 1983),p. 452

> action which are oriented to success, to the efficient achievement of ends. These later action types exhibit the form of purposive rational action where we seek to achieve an end or goal by appropriate means.[83]

However, communicative actions which are in form proverbs and prayers or liturgies which in African philosophy are based on Theistic Psychic rationality is a kind of purposive rational actions. Purposive-rational actions, according to Habermas, can be treated under two different aspects, the empirical, efficiency of technical means and the consistency of choice between subtle means. The rationality of means requires technically utilized, empirical knowledge.

The rationality of decisions and goals requires the application and inner consistency, of value systems and decision maxims, as well as the correct derivation of acts of choice. Theistic Panpsychic rationality not only emphasizes decisions that requires the understanding and consistency of value systems and decision maxims, as well as the correct derivation of acts of choice but also the rationalization of empirical knowledge as a secondary quality in African philosophy. Rational purposive actions which is the inner consistency of value systems and decisions maxims have transcendental claims and justifications and the rationality is what I call Theistic Panpsychism which ethno-methodologically and unscientifically is an animistic thought process and actions. Animistic philosophy is a pervading and immanent philosophy that underlay socio-political and techno-empirical actions in Black man's universe. The ultimate justification or foundationality which is Theistic Panpsychism and Theistic humanism theoretically manifest in a host of symbolic interactions, arts, aesthetic monological regularities and empirical analytic hermeneutics in all spheres including the aesthetics, the cultural, the political and the technical. Unlike the theistic panpsychic philosophy, modernity disintegrated objective reason into partial moments, scientific-technical rationality, practical moral rationality, and aesthetic rationality. Like Adorno, a post-modernist, African philosophy of Theistic panpsychism rationalizes aesthetic production so as to achieve a sublation of instrumental rationality into a non repressive form of reason. African philosophy with its metaphysical rationality rescues the arts, painting, dancing, etc., from the metaphysical and aesthetic hiccups of

[83] Reading the full text on Aristotle's position on literature may enhance proper understanding.

instrumental rationality and provides a framework of theistic panpsychic rationality for instrumental reason to be sublated into a field of forces which is ruled by logic higher than that of identifying instrumental action. Through the metaphysical foundation of Theistic Panpsychism, African philosophy distils out a non repressive instrumental rationality and achieves an aesthetic unity out of a manifold of its individual elements. Authentic work of art in African philosophy supported by the metaphysical foundation of Theistic Panpsychic rationality exhibits a resemblance of reconciliation and achieves a non repressive form of social and spiritual integration.

ARTS AS COMMUNICATIVE ACTION

Generally, when we think of art, what may first come to mind is „beauty', intrigue, imitation', festivity', and so on. Plato's states that "art is the imitation of sensible things by means of a copy at lower level of reality."[84] Here, imitation is used to suggest a similarity in appearance between art and object of the material world. On the other hand, material objects are perceptible to our sense, thus we are aware and certain of them. In other words, artist actually endeavours to imitate all that is visible, and in essence, immaterial objects of our sense. This is contrary to Plato's notion, which is embodied with elements of idealism, which is that the artist imitates sensible thing, which are but faint shadows of reality. The social, spiritual, artistic or aesthetic integration in Igbo African philosophy, independent of instrumental reason, is nomological, theistic panpsychically communicative, interactive and idealistic. Art, in this sense, endeavours to depict the features, qualities, facts, and character of the original. In this sense, art can never be the genuine but a copy or specimen, which is made to look like the original. Thus,

> Aristotle rightly states, that it is „natural for man to delight in works of imitation"[83] For communicative actions reasons, 'delight', 'beauty', or 'pleasure' is paramount to artistic representations. This view may have been initiated by Santayan's notion which states that beauty, which can only be found in the sensory appearance of things, is pleasure objectified. Implicitly, pleasure is actually cast as a quality of the object resulting from natural impulse, which appear to us as beautiful. Santayana, argues that," The beautiful is itself an essence, an indefinable quality felt in many things, which however disparate they may be, otherwise receive

---

[84] J.O. Urmson, *The Concise Encyclopaedia of Western Philosophy and Philosophers.* New ed., S.V. "Aesthetics"

> this name by virtue of a special emotion, half wonder, half love, which is felt in their presence."85[84] In aesthetic communicative interactions and actions the beauty of something which one sees or hears lies in one's whole attention centring on loving care and on the precise character of that with which one is confronted. In doing this, one is really not concerned with the irrelevant factual context in which this thing is embedded. What is found to be beautiful then is a given essence, not the physical things. Basically, the essence attracts and holds the interest of the viewer when it is beautiful and charming. Typically, this leads one into aesthetic contemplation. Further, art gives a unique quality of pleasure, which appears distinct from the pleasure derived from the satisfaction of any of the instincts. Such a pleasure can be derived only from art, which is pure and worthy in itself. This is typically hedonistic, in view of the fact that beauty lies in the ability of an object to please, when in aesthetic contemplation.

In addition, both the expression of art and the contemplation of beauty are activities of the self. Art can be interpreted as a free expression. Generally, art portrays freedom, frankness and independence, especially, of the artist. In light of this, 'artist' may suggest an individual, who can flourish only by becoming free of all collective entanglements and commitments in the external world; just like the spectator is entranced by the beauty of artworks. Similarly, the artist is entranced by the beauty of material object; he dissociates himself from elements of his immediate surroundings but surrenders himself to the trance of tranquil state of aesthetics. In other words, the artist endeavours to acquire full mental and steady concentration on the object of aesthetics which in turn, enables him to express himself fully in his art, otherwise his art does not assume art of the highest standard. In fact, such an art will be no more than a mere imitation of nature, or an expression of the tastes of the public whom it may aspire to please.[86] Art organizes, and endeavours to be orderly, like it is in nature. Also, art is brought into being not only by its physical appearance or the material component, but most importantly, by the beauty it embodies. In fact, it will be consistent to state that since art is an imitation of the material world, then beauty may well be an extension of the beauty embodied in all original and natural materials, objects, and events such as stones, water, colours,

---

[85] Gretel, Adorn, Adorno and Rolf, Tiedemann, "Art, society, Aesthetics" in *Aesthetics Theory*, ed. Trans. C. Lenhardt (London: Routledge and Kegan Paul, 1984), P.21 - 22.

[86] Egonwa, Osa, D., *African Art* (Edo; Nigeria; Edo State house of Assembly Printing Press, 1994) p.0.14.

animal, wood, vegetation, language, sound , movement, and so on. In other words, beauty is a nature given essence embedded in all that is nature-created. All art forms come to being as a result of nature given aids. For instances, dancing involved the human body and movements. Music is complimentary to dance; it involved human body (as in gesticulation), language, and action.

Art is universal and phenomenal. It is not and cannot be the exclusive culture of a particular race, class, or era. Also, beauty is pure, distinct and penitential as well as universal means of communication. Nevertheless, most troublesome and inconsistent is the notion that primitive societies embody such production (of art) without values. This is completely unintelligent, unphilosophical, ridiculous, and prejudiced. Art is universal and phenomenal, thus, its aesthetic value or beauty cannot be determined by race, class or individual taste. Art lies in all corners of the universe, and beauty is an inevitably universally eternal embodiment of art. So, African individual who has been called primitive, has a taste for, and sense of art and beauty, which in its unique and metaphysical sense is called Theistic Panpsychic animistic art and aesthetic dance and painting, etc.

In the advent of colonialism, *African* cultural institution was relegated. This led to the imposition of western communicative culture. Since then, African aesthetics culture suffered misinterpretations. Yet African art cannot be denied of its status and of its communicative value. It will be an inconsistent view to express 'art' as an exclusively western idea. Art is universally evident in and common to all people. African art is a genuine indigenous art, which is not influenced by foreign ideas and culture. It is a art, in its pure Theistic Panpsychic animism. However, according to Osa D. Egonwa, "African art could be defined as the Creative objectification of Africans, which bear the imprints of African aesthetics in their styles and subjective contents…"[87] African aesthetics is technically displayed on the African artwork, verbalized by the African in the evaluation of objects of aesthetic and communicative experience, and is rooted in the collective views of the people. African cannot be understood without its culture, without its aesthetic expressions and belief system, without the thousands of hectares of fertile lands where all variety of fruits precious minerals, forests, rivers and stones such as crude oil, gold and diamond are found. In fact, one, inevitably, becomes completely lost in deep aesthetics contemplation within

[87] Ibid., pp. 35

a mysterious halo or theistic panpsychic communicative transcendence and animity.

Perhaps, the high esteem and deep veneration, which the traditional African attached to the Supreme Being and the gods informed the production of animistic panpsychic aesthetic expressions. In fact, the priest, diviners, and herbalists, who were also craftsmen, rationally communicated, conceived and produced most of the artist works such as carved masks, sculptural world of human and animal figures, bronze and brass objects in Igbo-ukwu, Ife, and Benin among others. Perhaps, this is why it was only in the shrines that we have an abundance of carved figures and other aesthetic objects, Thus, our art forms such as architectural works, painting, drawing, sculpture, dance, music, poetry, clothing and body designing carry theistic panpsychic symbols. It is pertinent to point out that religion and aesthetics cannot be completely divorced from the African culture. To the Africans, art belongs to the world of creativity; the autonomy of artworks of the men and women are given the blessing of dexterity for manipulation and sensations.[88] One readily appreciates the architectural beauty of traditional Africa. In providing shelter for himself, the African evolved a design composition that is not only aesthetic, but also rationally communicative. Socio-political and economic considerations determined the nature of traditional architectural designs. Basically, while the town people build simple structures, the nobles preferred elaborate forms, rationally communicating to the high and the low. There exist a mixed use of shapes such as rectangles, cylinder, square and cone with which buildings are composed, and the resulting forms represent the way the African seeks to achieve delight and beauty with art as a vital part of the design process and communicative rationality. For instance, in the coastal forest belt, buildings are completely constructed with timber, the walls are carefully woven in wood, and roofs are of wood covered with thatch. Dramatically, these building are rested on poles raised above the level of high-tide water. Secondly, the courtyard design is basically found in the region of open tropical animistic forest to the rich grassland large cities of Yoruba, Benin, and Ashanti. The number of courtyards varies with the status of the head of the household, and family life is held exclusively private and with convenience. The courtyard mainly surrounded with a wall made of red earth is as hard as bricks. But within the courtyards, verandas and rooms are artistically created. Again, in the Mousagoum and Massa

[88] Ibid., pp. 39-55

communities of Cameroon, the building complex is a large space enclosed by a wall made with panpsychic animistic beads in necklaces drawn on the ground in a circle formation.

The African believes the inanimate but animistic objects have essence, which is spiritual. Only this 'life force' makes some of these objects suitable for certain functions, determines their physical qualities, accounts for the choice of materials such as gold, bronze, brass, wood or clay for artistic creations and the high panpsychic and animistic symbolisms and metaphors. For instance, among the Yoruba, a four-sided shape refers to the four powerful deities: East represents Sango, West represents Ifa, and North represents *Oduduwa* and the south represents, perhaps, the *sumpem* deity God *Otadumer/ or Oloriun.* A sense of uniqueness and style is revealed in traditional African painting. The first style used was the application of carefully outlined dark shadows to capture descriptive scenes of animals and human in motion. This style of *silhouette* isn't only beautiful and elegant, but it is also original to the African. Also, there were the realistic representation of figures, and polychrome tendency. In fact, in the attempt to capture realistic images, natural colours, such as copper, red, brown, ochre, and Kaolin white were obtained from minerals such as iron, hematite, chrome and lime among others and bound with a variety of adhesive agents. Painting and drawing were used for decorative, magical and preservative purposes. In fact, in ancient Egypt, the belief in after death gave rise to realistic emphasis on painting and drawings of kings and nobles, used to ensure that they continue to enjoy all that they had on earth even after death.[89] These kind of animistic Panpsychic sculptures serve as aesthetic communications. The richness of the facial expressions in some of the stone sculptures suggests that they may have been idealized portraits of people. Also, there are evocative stone monoliths with engravings metal work with ritual symbols, stool, and staff's office, some form of animal and human figures. The blacksmiths were talented and well skilled as they produced exclusive aesthetic communicative designed works, especially for religious purposes and for the royal class. African wood sculpture is predominantly naturalistic representations of human figures usually in African regalia, especially if the figure depicts a chief, animal figures or decorative motifs. African objects of art, especially the wood sculpture, are meant to be perceived, appreciated and relished, but except in cases when members of

[89] Steva, Vago. *Social change (USA, Prentice Hall, Inc 1996) P. 84*

secret cults or groups used them. However, the African sculpture is simply a folk expression of folk-people as diverse as the traditions of Africa. The intricate designs, which are some of major characteristic of African sculpture, suggest the great talents, dexterity and craftsmanship in traditional society.

Africa also produced dancers' musicians and poets. In traditional society, every event such as war, marriage, birth, death, ritual, initiations, and festivals is celebrated in public sphere accompanied with songs and music. Music is a means of theistic humanistic communication. In its rhythm, melody and harmony music is blend in such a way as to evoke theism, animism, emotion and ecstasy. There are many musical instruments particularly drums of different kinds; it is this that gives our dances a communicative animistic spirit and variety. The emotional responses to the inspirational quality of the theme, vocals, the power of its story and the vividness of its characterizations are the communicative actions of African music and poetry. Poetry is recited or sung orally. Studies of the traditional literature of many societies such as Igbo, Swahili, Yoruba, Uganda and Kenya, have shown that African communities have always had their own ideals of the nature and function of poetry. Traditional poems are a serious art and communicative action for dealing in a wide range of human experiences in rich figurative languages, presenting beautiful pictures in words and certain deep reflections about the world and man's place in it, and treat the relation between man, his environment and nature, all of which are theistic Panpsychic animistic in nature. Traditional oral poetry is composed as religious songs, and lyrics, dirges, praise-poetry, prayers, proverbs, myths, and so on. Also, the emotional facial expression by poets and dancers enhances the aesthetics and beauty of traditional songs and poetry.

Also, beauty, sensuality, artistic sensitivity, and a taste for spectacle suggest already existing aesthetic culture in Africa. For instance, in the West African sub-region, the clothing of both genders is almost the same. Generally, it ordinarily consists of a long piece of cloth wrapped loosely around the body. However, the lengthy job of adding finishing touches to pieces of clothing with an aesthetic arrangement of multi-colour paintings, dyes, embroidery and breads are delicately and artistically done, especially for ceremonies, festivals or for royalty.

The African women dressed in colourful attires and make-ups are the real queens of festivities. For the Igbo the natural beauty of a woman might be heightened by various hairdressing styles and the use of indigo and red cam-wood dye to decorate the body and face. Also, like Nuba in New

Guinea, people decorate themselves with beautiful feathers, animals' furs, paint, leaves, and grasses especially during colourful ceremonies. But, in many parts of Africa, body scarification and cicatrisation are practised, and these last the life-time of the individual on whose body we admire the aesthetic appeal of these ornaments. Also, it is usually the womenfolk who spin and weave cotton, which they afterwards dye and make into garments. However, it shouldn't come as a shock to discover that our principle luxury was perfumes, especially among the Igbo they were basically two types: an odoriferous wood of delicious fragrance which is beaten into powder and mixed with palm oil, and secondly, the kind of earth, which when thrown into fire, diffuses a very powerful fragrance. Both men and women perfumed themselves.[90] But in some African societies women were more inclined to aesthetic make ups because beauty is highly cherished.

Theistic Panpsychic Animistic Arts and Literally Criticism

Theistic Panpsychic rationality as the underlying principle of African philosophy points to some element of the universal in the communicative epistemic actions of African art. This presupposes a position that refuses to create mutual exclusiveness between western and African aesthetics except the difference in the underlying cultural principles that separately informed both. African arts and aesthetic as modes of communicative rationality have sacred and ritualistic superstructure, the reason for which I have described theistic Panpsychism as a mode of rationality.

This Panpsychic and animistic nature of African art and aesthetic sensibility gives it uniqueness, yet as an art and aesthetics in continuum with civilization of humanity. It is neither Platonic nor Kantian in methodology but the same as a mode of intellectual appreciation of nature. Hence Eugenia collier critical theory that treats African art and aesthetics and western version as mutually exclusive is a disservice to artistic and aesthetic humanity. The background to this position is the truncated invention and methodology of J.R.O. Ojo:

> I have indicated earlier that European artists recognized African sculpture as an art form. This is rather a pity because many of the objects which European artists regard as works of arts were not conserved as such by their creators. Many of these objects, which Euro-American aesthetic sensibility classified as works of art are in

[90] Collier, Eugenia, "The African Presence in Black American Literary Criticism" in *The Arts and Civilization of Black and African People, Vol. Three, Black Civilization and Literature*. P. 114.

> fact sacred and ritual objects, objects whose forms are dictated partly by tribal convention, technical instruments each of which has its own well defined functions. But the religious and spiritual backgrounds which brought them into being are not often considered. It is not realized by many that art in the phrase 'African Art' is an unsatisfactory term and that when used, aesthetic analysis based on either Platonic or Kantian definition of beauty is unapplicable.[91]

Art as an intellectual appreciation of object and as a means of social and cultural communication is a universal value. But aesthetic valuations differ from one race to another and that of the African is sacred and ritualistic. The meanings attached to art by the Africans may be different from the meanings attached to it by the Europeans. However Collier rightly stated that "African art grows out of a concept of the universe which holds that man and nature are one: that the spirit world and physical world are equal realistics; the past, present and future exist together and that man is in harmony with his world."[92] This is a monistic or naturalistic conception of art that explains African cosmology; there are, however, other conceptions that caters for other segemental realities without a total bifurcation of the ultimate principle that underlie everything that bespeaks of Theistic humanism or Theistic panpsychism in Africa. Though God created man to have dominion over nature, the African maintained dominion at animistic and ritualistic level conditioned with theistic panpsychism: while the western dominion of nature takes on a scientific and technological dimension that subsists outside the confines of nature and spirit and the turns against it. Western metaphysical and social dualism presupposes a human that emphasizes the person as an individual.

Western humanism claims a schism between man and nature. The central assumption of this humanism is a dualism of man and nature. On the other hand, African unity of man and nature and its dualism of soul and spirit underlies a special form of humanism that is obedient to (and not against) nature, a humanism that is derived from the gods and God, a humanism that is artistically and aesthetically amenable to the objects of nature in the name of Theistic humanism and panpsychism. It is therefore false for Collier to assert that "humanism is the antithesis of the unified view

[91] Ibid., pp. 114 and 115

[92] Ibid., p. 115

of Africans."[93] This is because the Western form of humanism is different from the African humanism. While the western humanism is scientific and technological the African humanism is metaphysically theistic humanism, an amalgam of the spiritual transcendental and regrettably crudely inchoate scientific animism that subsists at the level of subliminal existentialism. The western aesthetic humanism operates with an instrumental rationality that pits man against nature, an offspring of the hollowness and destructive ontology of the modernity, while Africa aesthetic humanism is coherent specie of the holistic, communal, social and monistic world view superimposed in the ultimate universal principle of theistic panpsychic superstructure of transcendental unity of apperception in African philosophy.

Rational aesthetic communication in African philosophy activates the sensibilities that produce sculptors, proverbs myths, tales, songs poems dance, tragedy etc. that relates man to subterranean objects and entities that pronounce the dependence and mortality of man and his limitations in the face of the infinite and immortal creator perceived as synonymous to nature. In this sense, the African art or aesthetics is a deeper reality than the Western understanding of art, though the difference borders at the level of culture, the former is Theistic humanistic and panpsychic while the other is scientific and technological. Eugenia Collier captures the substance of African culture as follows "Art is like a pebble dropped in water...individual, family, community, universe, spirits world, all brought into meaningful relationship through art. Thus art is functional and highly disciplined, serving purposes that are social, political and psychological."[94] In African philosophy art is participatory being rational instrument of communication and dynamic, realistic and concrete means of realizing the society's moral, social, spiritual and economic goals. As a moral vehicle, "it is committed to truth and ultimately to the sacredness of the human spirit."[95] There is the element of Puritan view of art in African philosophy as much as in Plato's conception of Art. Plato's view of art as much as that of the African is both relevant to the political welfare of the state and the religious or spiritual salvation of the individual soul. For Plato, "lyric poetry is an utterance of the gods through the medium of the poet conveyed through virtual 'possession'".[9695] This

[93] Ibid., p. 117.
[94] Ibid.
[95] Plato, quoted by Collier, ibid.,p. 119.
[96] Ibid., p. 117

view by definition has moral and African theistic animistic implication. Hence African art and Plato's art coincide in their spiritual, political and moral interests in the society.

African aesthetic communicative rationality presupposes African forms of political organization and government as well as the totality of individuals' cultural and behaviouralistic manifestations and as directed by Theistic humanistic and panpsychic tendencies.

In the art there are both Egoistic and altruistic conceptions and in some cases outright conceptions of pleasure. In African artistic and aesthetic conceptions there are material and emotional elements as shown in carved figures which contained the spirit of an ancestor, a praise song to a chieftain, in a dance to thank the gods for a beautiful harvest, etc. I agree with Prozirimu that African art is different from the art of the whites:

> The authentic critical standards must be born from the works of specific societies and their representative creators. That is where it all begins, criticism. Not in Aristotle's Poetics. The Poetics were written from Greek dramatic performances and experience, it was a distillation and a summation of what appeared to be operating principles from observed plays. Our plague has been to think that Greece was the universe and Aristotle the world oracle.[97]

In terms of literally criticism, writers must not study African arts and aesthetics from the mind set of white standard but from the fundamentally metaphysical theistic principles that form the superstructure of blacks' world view, as "black aesthetics is an outcome of black societies."[98] African art is a Theistic panpsychic art that reflects the values of communalism and community, and communicatively and rationally functions as a means of sustaining the society or the community in aesthetic and public spheres. "It was art in which beauty and function coalesces, art rich in archetype, myth and symbols, and in which the creator was honoured as a carrier of the culture,"[99] but more fundamentally a Theistic pansychic humanistic art that is a supra-foundational absolute. It is communicatively rational within transcendental connectivities among God, gods, ancestors, spirits and man. Communalism as the extension of the fundamental category of Theistic

[97] Ibid.
[98] Ibid.
[99] Ibid., p. 124.

humanism in the public sphere is a means of communicative rationality and functionality. Drama, poetry and aesthetics in African philosophy are supposed to be metaphysically and ontologically true as they are the passions of moral thoughts and actions with emotions channelled to the working rationality.

The Plato's view that lyric poetry is an utterance of the gods through the medium of the poet, conveyed through possession coincides with African aesthetics and poetry, which is metaphysical. The fundamental metaphysical supra -structure of Theistic panpsychism informs the archetypal primitive African arts through the medium of prophets, chief priests, poets, gods and masquerades. Emotion is also part but not the core of African arts. Puritan morality as an aesthetic and emotional cognitive rationality is present in African art but not as the repressive monotheistic rationality of European modern or enlightenment art. Just as the African art is not only emotional but also cognitive, it is also not mainly concerned with pleasure but with metaphysical and epistemological realities of black workaday world. Plato's crude or primitive communism resembles in many ways the African concept of a communal based art erected on the superstructure of Theistic panpsychism. In African philosophy, there may be no professional dichotomy between a philosopher and a poet. While in Western philosophy there are crematoria segmentation and individuation of objects, groups etc. In African philosophy, there is a tendency to see the world as monolithic.

African aesthetics and arts is also mythical and could be analyzed and understood at metaphysical level because of the people's collective unconscious based on the supra-natural Theistic panpsychism. African arts, therefore, has what one can call communal archetypes and myths reinforcing the entire worldview. African literature, aesthetics and poetry is fundamentally couched in mythical planks underlying the mysterious and supernatural nature of the universe, and its creator, for which in many ways it differs from Freudian and Marxist analysis of arts. African poetry is, in the same sense, in search of the ultimate in the mythical universe; it is both an expression of ultimate reality and the emotional phenomenal nature. The African would agree with T.S. Eliot that "Poetry is not a turning losses of emotion, but an escape from emotion: it is not the expression of personality."[100] African aesthetic experience is a response of sensitivities to the supernatural and the natural, the Theistic humanistic structure of the

[100] *Webster's Third New International Dictionary, Volume 3* (Chicago, William Benton 1971) p. 242.

universe, created, static or dynamic, but which represent or articulate essential archetypes, symbols and attitudes of the community and uncreated.

Orality and forms of communication

Oral tradition is one of the theistic animistic elements of African folk literature which serves as vehicle for historiography, and communicative actions consist of folk tales, ballads songs, epic narratives, myths and legends, riddles, proverbs, recitations and chants, orations, festivals, drama and ritual performance. A tradition is oral if it has no written literature or sacred scriptures. *The Webster's Third New International Dictionary* defines oral tradition variously as follows:

> the process of handing down information, opinions, belief and customs by word of mouth or example, transmission of knowledge and institution through successive generations without written instruction. Cultural continuity embodied in a massive complex of evolving social attitudes, beliefs, conventions and institution rooted in the experiences of the past and exerting a normative influence on the present. Something existing only in popular belief inherited reputation or memory.[101]

In order for a thing to be regarded as traditional, it must be widely understood and practised in a society and it must have been handed down for at least a few generations. Unfortunately, the term is misapplied to represent just anything anyone wishes to give legitimacy. Strictly speaking however, oral traditions are those recollections of the past that are commonly or universally known in a given culture. Versions that are not widely known should be dubbed testimony while those that relate to recent event belong to the realm of oral history.[102] As a coherent communicative network of theistic animism oral tradition consists of myths, legends, stories, proverbs, belief, folktales, songs and dances, liturgies and rituals, pithy sayings, riddles and adages, social attitudes, conventions, institutions and customs. Some of these communicative symbols and actions appear in work of arts and crafts, symbols and emblems, names of people and places, shrines and sacred places. Works of art are not merely for decoration. They usually convey religious feeling, sentiments, aesthetic feelings ideas and truth.[103]

---

[101] Henigo, D. *Oral Histomography* (London, Longman 1982)
[102] Ajayi, S.A. *West African Traditional Religion* (Ado-Ekiti, Omolayo Standard Press, 1981) p. 2.
[103] Aderibigbe, I. *Religion, Study and Practice* (Lagos, Almon School Press Ltd. 1997) p. 157.

Oral tradition involves the handing down of a thought system from one generation to another by word of mouth or by practice. The elderly and the wise men are regarded as the purveyor of the thought system. Oral traditions can be described as testimonies of the past which are deliberately transmitted from mouth to mouth. These traditions are neither rumours nor sensational stories but eyewitness accounts that have been passed from generation to generation. The absence of the art of writing in traditional African societies has made it necessary to employ oral traditions as a means of preserving and transmitting African religious beliefs and practised. These oral traditions constitute the scripture of African traditional religion. They are mirror through which the religion of African is known.[104] However, the reliability of the various form of oral traditions as vehicle for the authentic beliefs of the people varied. For example, the condensed, and memorized forms like proverbs, names and pithy sayings, which are said to be memorized as they were handed down from the time immemorial, are certainly more reliable than myths, legends, folktales and daily speeches which are susceptible to changes and sometimes have distorted version. Oral tradition is both an art and an instrument of communicative action in African philosophy with its epistemological foundation in the unity of apperception consciousness or Theistic Panpsychism. No human face is exactly the same as another human face, but it is like many others in having two eyes, a nose, two lips and two ears. In the same way, no two people even respond to God's presence in exactly the same way:

> Similarly each particular religion has a particular character because of the particular people who practice it. For example, Islam grew in the Caravan Cities of Arabia, Hindus developed in India and African religion in the indigenous religion of the Africans. It is the religion that has been handed down from generation to generation by the fore-bears. It would be seen, therefore, that in one form or the other every person in the world over seems to have in him a force that links him with the "Ultimate reality" called God.[105]

The force in African philosophy is Theistic Humanistic Panpsychic animism. It should be noted that the absence of sacred literature and also the absence of imposing sacred buildings like mosques, churches, cathedrals and

---

[104] Aderubugbe, ibid., p. 156
[105] Ibid., p. 157

temples should not be interpreted to mean that African religion cannot be known. The history of religions the world over testifies to the fact that the societies from which these religions emanated were backward and pre-literate and the revelation given to them existed in oral form before being committed to writing at a much later date. In the same way, Africa religious ideas or Theistic Panpsychic animism exist largely in oral form. Thus, in spite of the fact that Africans have no written records, their religious beliefs and practices can be known and revealed.

African Panpsychic animistic philosophy is mirrored through some institutionalized devices. Some of these devices are both oral and non-oral. The oral devices include myths, proverbs, theophorous names, everyday speech, pithy saying, liturgy and songs. The value of proverbs as a reservoir for religious beliefs and customs of non-literate people derives from reportorial communicative value of proverbs in most African Societies. These proverbs reveal a lot about African philosophical belief, especially ideas about Theistic Panpsychism. From some of these proverbs, we learn of the following attributes of God: Creator, omnipotent, holy, compassionate, omnipresent, self-existing, accessible and determiner of destiny. Some of the proverbs also describe his power, his transcendence, his mercy, his care for his creature, his lordship over the universe and his divine providence. Proverbs are natural to the people. They are the rational voice of the people in the profound sense and are accepted as a true index of what a people regard as true and are interpretative of the principle of life and conduct. Among Africans, the use of proverbs is cultivated as an art and cherished as an instrument of rational communication. The Yoruba say that proverbs are horses for retrieving missing words. The Zulu also assert that "without proverbs, language would be but a skeleton without flesh and to a body without soul."[106] The Igbo have it that 'a child who knows how to use proverbs has justified the dowry paid on his mother's head'. The same could be said of most African peoples.

Most of these proverbs refer to Theistic humanism as the spiritual, physical and moral principles of African philosophy. For instance the power and reliability of God are expressed by some African proverbs. The Bangerwanda (Rwanda) say "The tree set up by manna (God) cannot be

---

[106] Jacobs, A.B., *A textbook on African Traditional Religion* (Ibadan, Aromolaran Press Ltd. 1997) p. 10-16

blown down by the wind."[107] Similarly the omnipresent of God is expressed by this Akan Proverb: "If you want to tell God, tell it to the wind." Again, the Lordship and providence of God over the entire creation are expressed in proverbs like, "God drives away flies for a cow which has no tails" (Yoruba). "What a frog will eat, God do not put it on top of a tree" (Igala). An Igbo proverbs says, "God has both the yam and the knife, only those whom he cuts a piece can eat."[108] Other proverbs affirm some attributes of God, his mercy, his goodness, his justice, and his up rightness. A Yoruba proverb say that an enemy may sound the drum of someone's down fall, but God will not let it sound. Another Yoruba proverb advises the powerless to leave one's fight to *Olodumare* (God) and look on for He is the defender of the defenceless. There are hundreds of such proverbs in different African Societies and they carry with them theistic panpsychic instructions, moral teachings, and metaphysical significance.[109]

Oral traditions have played important roles in revealing both the ethical as well as the communicative rationality of the Africans. They serve moral purposes. Some of these oral traditions, e.g. proverbs reveal the value judgment and morality of the people. Good character is cherished in such a way that everyone is expected to cultivate it. According to the elders, good character is the king of medicine for fortune. Proverbs project the belief that the entire world is a stage, as we have our entry and exit. Consequently, life itself is transitory and ephemeral. Hence the slogan "As I watch through this span of life, what name, what image do I have behind, what hope and what thought for the future, preoccupies their minds."[110] Therefore, according to the African, man should do good and hate evil. Thus, for the Igbo good character is the key to success and that good name is better than riches. The Yorubas believe that character is a god; it supports one according to manners and the way he behaves. Consequently, "whatever one sows he shall reap."[111] Hence, the watch-word is that good character is the adornment of man.

They also stress the fact that worthless people are so many as the grass while good people are dearer than the eyes. From the foregoing, one cannot but agree with the view that proverbs as oral tradition are used to emphasize the importance of good character among the Igbos and Yorubas. The

---

[107] Ibid.
[108] Ibid.
[109] Ibid., p. 16
[110] Isaac, O. Delano. *Owe Lesin Oro Yoruba Proverbs* (Ibadan, Oxford University Press 1972) p. 11
[111] Ibid.

following could be considered as among the proverbs which deal with the moral value of the Yorubas. For instance, when the earth worm pay respect to the soil, the soil opens for it.[112] The proverb serves as an advice to the experienced people that if they accept their position and give honour to those who are superior to them, they will receive favour and help they need. With this proverb, it is necessary to state here that the African greatly believe in the saying that if youths could give respect to the elders and listen to the advice and the dictate of the elders, they believe that their ways will be straight in life. There are some proverbs which serve as warning to our future living. For instance, if a kinsman is not warned in time when he eats poisoned insect, the resulting itch will keep the whole family awake.[113] The proverb is pointing to us that the actions of those near to us may affect our ways of life and so it is wise to warn them if they are acting imprudently so as not to suffer with them in the very near future. For instance, if a man had developed the habit of stealing right from the youth, if this habit is not checked in the early stage, the result may be very disastrous to the entire family. In order words, the bad eggs within our society need to be checked so as not to suffer with them in the very end. This proverb as a form of oral tradition and communication is pointing to us to love our neighbours as ourselves and maintain good relationship with them. On the other hand, it is logical in the sense that the first premise is the fact that your neighbour is eating a bad insect which indeed is harmful; the second premise is that you refuse to warn him.

Oral tradition reveals the moral aspect of the Yoruba people through proverbs which include the following. The dress does not meet up '*Omoye*' since she had gone naked to the market.[114] The proverb shows that the Yoruba dislike the practice of going about nakedly. '*Omoye*' a typical girl of fashion moved out of the household nakedly and suggestion to pursue her with a dress to cover the shame of her nakedness was made impotent by reply that the secret was already publicized, since '*Omoye*' had reached the market place typically of any congregation of people or the public at large. It is however pertinent to mention here that through oral traditions, the Africans uphold dearly the spirit of unity and togetherness which is not only fundamental but also instrumental in living a progressive and peaceful life. This conception is well conceived in proverbs. Consequently, the proverbs

---

[112] Ajikola, J.O., *Owe Yoruba* (Ibadan University Press Ltd. 1974) p. 60
[113] Odujinrin, J.S.A. *Modern Lessons in Yoruba* (London Waterloo Press Ltd 1984) p. 80
[114] Ibid., p. 98

such as "the decease which troubles forty also torments three hundred and when the right hand washes the left and the left washes the right, makes both hands clean, do not only encourage the spirit of unity and togetherness but also stress its importance."[115] This gives incentives to mutual help which is beneficial to all parties concerned for instance. "The child's hand cannot reach the shelf; the elder's hand cannot enter the gourd." Oral tradition through proverbs recommends cooperation between the young and the old. It points out that the old need the young and the young need the old conversely.

It could be used as a rational communicative instrument whenever there is a quarrel between young and old people. It would suggest that the old and the young are dependent upon one another and that cooperation between them will be mutually beneficial for it is stated that one good turn deserved another. If you do good, you will always expect good things in life. To the extent that this idea is true, it is also true of the contrary that one bad turn deserved another, because if the hen wasted my medicine, I will in turn break its egg. However, the relevance of the story is that the bad deed of one of the friends is reciprocated by the other. But the first bad turn they say is not always as bitter as the return of it. The proverb, "It is only in the mouth of the elder that kola is ripe"[116] shows the place of elderly man in African tradition in general. It reflects the customs of the Igbo as to deference often given to age from a sense of respect. Whenever there is a gathering of people and the kolanut is broken, an elder is first to chart it. Thus, an elder would be the person who would comment on the ripeness of the kolanut. Similarly in a debate or at an assembly for arbitration, the final say is always given to the eldest person in authority. It is up to him to pronounce the verdict and decide the case. This proverbial expression is used to invite the eldest person in authority to bring discussion to an end by pronouncing his opinion on the subject. It would be used after a full discussion has been held and all views heard. The elders' decision would be final. The proverbs expressed esteem for the elders' wisdom and respect for his authority.

Oral traditions are mirrors through which the religion, the history and philosophy of Africans are known. The elderly and the wise men are regarded as the purveyors of the thought system. In the African pre-literate society, when there were no means of communication either by writing or

---

[115] Ibid., p. 81

[116] Ajibola, *op. cit.,* p. 24

reading books, the pre-society gave expressions to their creative instinct, feeling and imagination through oral tradition. While the modern writer may turn to his novel, pen and paper to communicate his ideas artistically, our fore-fathers who were not educated had no other means but to turn naturally to the spoken words which provide the means whereby he can communicate his feelings effectively and recall history. Among these spoken words are myth, proverbs which are forms of oral tradition.

Proverbs are wise sayings; simply expressed they are the words of elders, which are words of wisdom. A wise man has it and get wiser, while a foolish man hears it and becomes more foolish. The ideas expressed in proverbs are generally regarded as truisms truths, which cannot be rationally disputed because they express certain truths about value and reality. The elders say proverbs are the horses of speech, if communication is lost; we use proverbs to retrieve it. Generally, proverbs are employed by elders in a discussion of importance. The more an elder can appropriately use proverbs, the more he is regarded as a man of wisdom. Like a proverb: "The drum sounding a message of war is beaten in critical manner, only wise men can dance to it, and only experience men can understand it."[117] The value of proverbs lies in what it reveals of the thoughts of the past, expressed of the present and speculated on the future as well as on the facts of being a model of compressed and forceful language. Apart from drawing on it for its words of wisdom, the speaker or user of proverbs takes interest in its verbal technique, its selection of words, and its use of comparison as a method of rational communication.

However, proverbs are not only a body of short statements and insight of a community into problem of life, but also a technique of verbal expressions. It is a traditional saying which expressed the basic common truth of a people. According to Oladele Taiwo, oral traditions deal with all aspects of life. They are used to emphasize the words of the wise and the stock-in trade of old people, who use them to, convey precisely moral lessons, advice and warnings, since they make a greater impact on the mind than ordinary words. The judicious use of proverbs is usually regarded as a sign of wit.[118] Proverbs as oral tradition form the main structural materials of the language of communication.

---

[117] Oladele, Taiwo. *An Introduction to West African Literatures* (Hong Kong, Thomas Nelson Ltd, 1967) p. 26

[118] Akinlade, Kola., *Owe ati Humo* (Ibadan, Abiprint Publishing Company Ltd, 1982) p. 20

Appropriate and correct usage of proverbs is important among the users. Oral tradition through proverbs is constantly pressed into the service of the elders during deliberations in council and at home when settling disputes. It is generally believed that a relevant proverb if mentioned throws light on the subject and drives points so vividly home that the impact enters very fully into their feelings. Consequently, one can be allowed to take part in communal discussions if he is considered to be versed in the use of proverbs.

Oral traditions are found all over the world and their comparison provides insight into the effects of cultural conditions, consequences and local variation on expressions. For instance, it is argued that the Yorubas are well-known for their love of diplomacy. In their social exchanges, they believe that it is very bad to speak with the whole mouth. It would for instance be indelicate to reprimand directly a friend who has committed an offence. The Yoruba would, through well considered references to what the sages used to say, make the offender realize the wrongness of his behaviour.

Epistemology of Proverbs

A general epistemological survey of some African proverbs will tempt one to conclude that the Africans are also empiricists. Knowledge to them is sometimes based on experience. Elders say "experience is the content of wisdom," we do not stay away and claim to know what a particular soup tasted like and news is not as reliable as personal witnessing. In other words, seeing believes. The Yorubas have it that it is the eyes that can assess the quantity of food that will satisfy the stomach, the navel is the middle of the body', they also believe that it is "the face of the plate that is used to take food, not that of any one else, because 'nobody tested wine with the mouth of another person.'" Moreover, it is often said that "no one stays at home and claims to known who will die in the war." All these proverbs cited so far, readily reflect the epistemological and panpsychic animistic proposition that knowledge is derived through experience. Under this situation, if something bad happens to someone, for instance, if one looses a job, the fact that one has personally experienced that danger of unemployment makes him to know the evil effect of unemployment in the society.

The African also through proverbs express the view that knowledge is a universal phenomena, hence the proverb 'wisdom is not an exclusive possession of any one and does not belong to any individual'. This proverb is similar to Yoruba proverb; "the young man is wise and an elderly man is also wise as a result of which Ile-Ife was founded."[119] This proverb concerns Ile-Ife which is regarded as the cradle of Yoruba land. The proverb arose from the story of Oduduwa who was the founder of Ile-Ife. He was a warrior who was said to have travelled all the way from a place around the present day Mecca. He eventually got a piece of vast and plain land where a young man suggested to him that they should settle and which he readily accepted. Hence, they settled down and agreed to call the place Ile-Ife, which simply means a plain land or an expanded of land. The proverb is epistemological and rationally communicative in the sense that knowledge is not restricted to the elders alone; although an elder could be more knowledgeable, knowledge is also extended to the youth. In African tradition, it is believed that the elders are wise but at the same time, the elders could sometimes tap from knowledge of the youth.

Another proverb on knowledge is "we know nothing of the life history of the gorilla but as for that of the ape we know a little."[120] This is used to give emphasis to knowledge of one's subject and ignorance of another. Even though we do not know much of something around us, we still have rational knowledge of other things, for there are many ways through which we acquire the knowledge of other things around us. For instance if a man's attributes are given or his personality being described, this is believed to be enough for other people to recognize the man in question. If somebody is still not aware of the man being discussed, then this proverb replies to his ignorance. One's achievements are being narrated and his praises sung, yet, you do not recognize who the deceased was." The point being raised is that the descriptions given are sufficient for one to know the person you are speaking about.

Furthermore, there are some vital issues which a man ought to discuss with the members of his family but which he fails to do but prefers to discuss it with outsiders. Therefore, if the man should get involved in a problem, his people might feel unconcerned. This is because 'pad-locks do not know inside of one another' People within the same circle are expected to understand one another. The above proverb is similar to the following proverb: "A single hand cannot lift the calabash."[121120] This is reminding us that one should always seek help in doing a task which cannot be done single-handed: There are many things which two can do better than one.

---

[119] Ajibola., *op. cit.,* p. 82
[120] Isaac, Delane, *op. cit.,* p.5
[121] Ibid.

"For he who walks slowly (acts intelligently) will bring the title home: and who runs (acts recklessly) missed the chance of enjoying a title"[122] This proverb is pointing to us that it is unwise to make hurried decisions on important matters of which we have little or no knowledge, for one should think clearly and weigh the consequences with others even if it takes time before acting: for "if night does no fall in one's presence, it will be difficult to walk in its darkness."[123] This proverb is reminding us that one should not interfere in matters where one is not conversant with details. Hence, it is dangerous to get involved in matters in which we were not initially concerned.

Another proverb says: "The people of our compound are not helpful, our relatives have no character but we cannot compare them to casual outsiders."[124] This proverb proves to us that experiences have shown to us that it is best to put up with whatever wrong our relatives and neighbours do to us, as they will be more helpful to us in difficult times than people we only know casually. From past experience, people have believed that it is only your relations who will remain loyal to shoulder your difficulties during the trial period.

In African cosmology and ontology the Africans believe that a child who died can still return to the world as many times as he wishes. Thus, a Yoruba proverb used to buttress this case is: "An *Abiku* makes the doctor a liar."[125] The Yoruba believe that when the mother loses a child in infancy it is the same child who returns and dies. Such a child is known as '*Abiku*'. The above proverb is a metaphysical view of the Yoruba which have been supported in many ways by empirical evidence. '*Abiku'* is the name given to a child who is destined to die. It is believed that a mischievous spirit (panpsychic animistic spirit) has taken the place of the child in the mother's womb. When the spirit child is about to be born, he promises the other spirits that he will return to the spirit world soon. It is for this reason that children sometimes die young. The spirit has the power to re-enter the same woman several times, if he wishes. An African Panpsyhic animistic seer or native doctor is thought to have no influence on the '*Abiku*,' hence in spite of the treatment given by him, in spite of numerous medicine and injections, in spite of seeming improvement under the doctor's care, the *Abiku* child

[122] Ibid., p. 152
[123] Owomoyela, Berth, L.O. *Yoruba proverbs* (Ohio, Owomoyela Press, 1973) p. 37
[124] Isaac Delano, *op. cit.,* p.13
[125] Ajibola, S.O., *op. cit.,* p. 50

will eventually die. The doctor, whose treatments may have seemed very effective, will inevitably be made to appear as a fool or a liar. The proverbs might be used by a person who feels that his own efforts are destined to fail because he has no control over certain situation or, it might be used to explain a failure for which a person does not feel responsible.

A proverb concerning the Yoruba's belief in destiny could be seen through the following proverbs; "if you have magic charms and you are not a gossiper the charms will not be effective, for a person's destiny is more powerful than charms, what will be one's status in life cannot be altered by charms."[126] These proverbs came as a form of an advice to someone who is frightened by *juju* or charms, assuring him that if he is honest and straight forward no amount of *juju* can affect him. In African philosophy, people believe in the existence of spirits and the use of charms and amulets but this is not to say that they do not believe in destiny, so that even if someone charms you and you are not destined to die by the charm, nothing will happen to you. The above proverb is similar to the following proverb: "What you find in life is what you choose in heaven."[127] The Yoruba believe that when a person travels from heaven to earth he stops at a certain place, kneels before the person who orders people's destines and chooses his own role on earth. His whole course of life on earth is thus determined before he is born. Thus, he has no one but himself to blame for what he finds in life, for he chose this particular life in heaven. This proverb could be used to reply to someone who is complaining about his lot in life. The proverb has a sort of similarity to the following: "Earth is a market, heaven is home."[128] Underlying this proverb is the belief that people are sent to this world from heaven. They come to earth as to a market, do their business, and return to heaven their home. The proverb serves as a reminder that death is the fate of every man and that a continued existence in heaven lies ahead for the deceased.

The Yoruba believed that no matter how difficult a situation may be those who are destined to survive will survive. This could be supported by this proverb: "Even if the yam meal is made in a leaf, and the sauce is made in the shell of peanut, whoever will be full."[129] This proverb means that no matter how desperate a situation becomes, those in it who are destined to

[126] Berth, Lindforts, *op. cit.,* p. 23
[127] Ibid.
[128] Ibid., p. 55
[129] Collier. Ibid, p. 124

survive will survive. Even if food were to become scarce, there are some people who would be satisfied eating very small portions. Similarly and lastly, the African conception of the "Head" is also important metaphysically. Among all parts of the body, the head is the most important which is mainly followed by the leg. The Yoruba believed that there are two heads, internal head, and the external head. Thus when the Yoruba talk about the head they usually refer to the internal head. The external head only represent the internal head. Whatever a man will become on earth is determined by the internal head. When we talked about choosing destiny before coming to the world, it is the head that man chooses. Whoever chooses good head will be successful in life and the contrary holds for who chooses a bad head. The Yorubas say you could appeal to your head, not to medicine, for medicine helps only in the day of trouble but the head helps everyday.

Thestic animistic communicative prayer

Myths are very important elements of theistic Panpsychic animism. They are stories told to explain the origin of things like God, universe, earth, familyhood, rivers, gods, divinities, etc. They are vehicle for Theistic Panpsychic animistic communicative rationality. They are an expression of the unobservable reality in terms of observable phenomena. They are vehicle for conveying certain facts about man's experiences in his supra sensible world. Carl J. Jong's theory of myths is hereby applied to African arts, ontology and cosmology as the psych of humankind and not the Freudian individual psych and on the basis of human instinct but not on Freudian neurosis. In African arts, one could identify a number of basic archetypes and myths speaking for the communal philosophy of the people. However, the following different definition of myths shows some concurrence with the supernatural assumptions of African aesthetics and theistic panpsychic rationality:

> Myths is fundamental, the dramatic representation of our deepest, institutional life, of a primary awareness of man in the universe, capable of many configurations, upon which all particular opinions and attitudes depend. Myth is to be defined as a complex of stories - some no doubt fact, some fantasy -which, for numerous reasons human beings regard as demonstrators of the inner meaning of the universe and of human life. Myth is the expression of a sense of togetherness - a togetherness not merely on the plane of the intellect, but a togetherness of feeling and of action and of wholeness of living. Myth are by nature, collective and

> communal; they find a tribe or a nation together in that people's common psychological and spiritual realities.[130]

A myth endeavours to give explanatory answers to the questions posed to man in this physical universe in which he finds himself. He attempts to probe and answer question about origins and purpose of man on earth. For example, the Ijaw myth of origin of creation says that in the beginning, *Tamearau* (God) created heaven and earth. Yoruba creation myth says that earth was without form when *Olodumare* (God) decided to create the earth.

He sent *orisha-nla*, the arch-divinity, to create the solid earth.

These myths raise questions about origin and organization of the universe. The explanation offered by each of them is a theistic one; the world resulted from the activity of a divine being. Also questions like why must man sweat before he eats; why women must labour before they give birth to children, and the like are raised. Answers to questions are naturally clothed in stories, which serve as means of communication and handing them down from generation to generation. These myths give us insight into some of the theistic animistic concepts of the African people who evolved them. With regard to the use of myths as man's communication, they tell us a lot about people's worldview, including their religion. There are some myths, which are creeds, or esoteric ritual formulae, which are sometimes learned and recited like prayers. Myths of this nature enjoy a high degree of authenticity and when properly studied with accurate illustrations, it could provide the basis for a scripture in African religion.[131] Besides, some myths actually explain the dramatic break-through of the sacred into the world. For example, the story or how the world came into being is true because the existence of the world is there to prove it.

Africans bear theistic Panpsychic animistic names. It is, therefore, traditional for them to incorporate God's name into their children's name. This is a communication signifying in some cases that the child has been born in answer to prayers, as a result of which the parents wants to thank God for the child. In other cases, it signifies a particular attribute of God, which may be suggested by the circumstances surrounding the child's birth, or it may indicate the parents wish to praise God through the name of their child.[132] In expressing God's wisdom and power, the Barundi (Burundi)

---

[130] Aderibigbe, *op. cit.,* p. 157

[131] Mbiti, J.S. *African Religions and Philosophy* (London, Heinemann Pub. 1996) p. 85-86

[132] Ibid.

name their children *Ntawayankira,* which means "no one can refuse him his way."[133] If it is to express gratitude the *Banyarwanda* (Rwanda) name their children *Ndibo-kuyago,* which also means "I am alive because of him As an indication that God has fought their cause in giving them a child, the Yoruba parents give a name such as '*Olukoya'* (the Lord champions the cause of suffering). When faced with many problems or an experience of attack from evil doers like witches or other social evils especially before or during his antenatal period, when a child is finally delivered, the Yoruba give names such as *Olusegun* (God is victorious) expressing the saving grace of God. And in order to show the parents trust in God, children may be named Ndayisiga (Tanzania) meaning I depend on Him (God)[134] Other names that indicate the concept of God among the Igbos of Nigeria are *Chukwuma* (God is the giver of children), *Chukwuemeka* (God has done well), *Chukwuka* (God is great). Such names are additional evidence, Africans are religious beings living in a religious universe. All these names are means of rational communication with the divine.

Another means of communication is the theistic panpsychic prayer: they pray to God for guidance and blessing in matters of daily life, personal, family or business matters. Africans communicate with God in prayers at anytime in any place. His is their last court of appeal. These prayers are made to God, the deities and the ancestors.[135] Theistic humanistic panpsychic animistic prayers are offered for almost everything, from asking for the gift of children, for health, wealth or rain, good harvest to requesting for success in trade, or hunting, most of these prayers are short and to the point though they are also example of long and formal prayers.[136] Praying is recorded among practically all African peoples through the actual prayers have not often been recorded in written form. Few examples would be considered to illustrate the concepts and contents of African prayers in relation to their beliefs and rational communication with God, gods and ancestors. In an animistic manner, it is common to hear an elderly African man during the early morning hours, asking God to let the day dawn well, to pour upon the people his medicine of health and to drive away the evil forces. For instance, Pygmies pray when there is sickness and before undertaking a journey or going to hunt, asking God to heal the sick, prosper the traveller and give

---

[133] Ibid., p. 67

[134] Nigosian, S.A., *World Religions* (London, G Clark Publishing Co. Ltd, 1974) p. 24

[135] Mbiti, *op. cit.,* p. 61

[136] Ibid., p. 62

game to the hunter. Similarly, a hymn of prayer committing the Yoruba worshippers to the care of God says "father of children" prepare medicine for the children the children have no medicine.[137] This implied that worshippers are entirely dependent upon God who is mightier than other animistic forces like ancestors, gods and divinities. Although most of these prayers are addressed directly to God, most of them come in form of invocation asking God to intervene for a particular purpose. For example an African may ask God, give me rain: Help me oh God: God pity me: These invocations are usually what the individual prays spontaneously and unceremoniously on the spur of the moment. They show that people consider God to be ready to respond to their need and not subject to religious formalities, but most of these supplicators go through the gods and goddesses, ancestors and so on.

Theistic panpsychic social and political system

In the cultural sphere, the communicative rationality of theistic Panpsychic philosophy sustains the moral and spiritual values of the society and its economic, political and social tentacles. Cultural theistic panpsychism is different from the cultural modernity which spurred anomic forces that unleashed hedonistic motives incompatible with the Prational discipline of economic life and undermine the moral fabric of the society. The spiritual and religious nature of theistic panpsychism sustains the faith in oral tradition, authority and conventions of every day traditional African life. The challenge of cultural theistic panpsychism is to reposition Functionalism as methodological counterpoise to the subversive cultural modernity because the society destroyed by cultural modernity must be restored. Cultural modernity is responsible for all those pathological or dysfunctional syndromes, such as hedonism, narcissism, lack of Social 'identity and so on'. The systemic imperatives of an economy and a bureaucratized state infrastructure by the media of money and power have penetrated deeply into the communicative superstructure of the lifeworld, endangering the processes of tradition and cohesion. Cultural modernity is the syndrome of loss of meaning, anomie, personality disorders as well as the dynamics of protest originating in response to the colonizing pressures of the economy and the state vis-à-vis the life world. But for Habermas, it is not cultural modernity that is responsible for all these but societal modernization.

[137] Malinawski, Bronislaw, *Crime and causation in savage society* (Peterson, N.J. Litter field, Adams 1959 P.II

Cultural modernization for him is positively characterized by the increasing differentiation of cultural value spheres (science, morality, art) governed by truth, rightness, authenticity and embodying different rationality structures (cognitive instrumental, moral - practical, aesthetic expressive). If this is what Habermas believes cultural modernity stands for, then it does not only share some values with cultural Theistic panpsychism but is also close to Cultural Functionalism or functionalism as a form of explanation in social sciences and philosophy.

The theory of functionalism as a methodology was developed by Broniski Malinowski. He says that all social processes are causally determined."[138] What this implies is that before any new thing can be incorporated in the cultural system, it must satisfy some human need to justify its existence. Incidentally, Functionalism is a mode of understanding and communication in African thought, although the analytical scheme or framework in African reality is theistic, panpsychic and animistic. Functionalism as a methodology of studying society derives its significance from the fact that it provides an analytical scheme by means of which we can undertake a systematic analysis of any society, or of any social institution based on the role of function to the satisfaction of essential needs of men in that culture.

Malinowski takes the unit of cultural analysis to be the institution. This means, that an analysis of a culture could begin by exhaustively listing the institutions to be found in it - such things as family organization, secret societies, and others which represent the social molecules of say, African societies. A further breakdown provides us with a complete picture of the functioning society guaranteed by a description of the functions and interrelationships in these various institutions within the social system. Hence, Functionalists posit that the existence of any institution depends among other things on a set of values.[139] Such values constitute one way of defining the aims and purposes of which human beings associated with the institutions have come together as well as the basis of change in the society. African society is functionally dominated by a set of values held in network by Theistic humanism and Panpsychic animism which sustains objective natural laws. The hierarchy of forces in African philosophy though theistically panphyschic and animist is conceived and understood as theistic

[138] Ibid.
[139] Ibid.

functionalism which is generated by natural laws. This animistic ontology is the, functional superstructure of communicative rationality, which is the nature of beings that inhabit the world, the structure of the cosmos as conceived in terms of unity and interactive of all beings or forces. Basically, interactive and communicative African traditional ontological order falls into three broad categories, Spirits and forces ,Human beings, Things (Plants and Animals) The interaction of forces, which Placid Temples, describes in his book, *Bantu Philosophy,* applies to conception of the relationship between the beings in nature. The order listed above is in descending hierarchy according to the relative power of spirits. This means that Beings are differentiated in African Ontology according to their vital power or their inherent vital rank. At the head is God who is sovereign over the three worlds posited and those beyond. He posses spirit in its absolute form and have absolute control over all beings. After Him come the deities and ancestors: These are the first fathers and founders of the society. God is not as closely involved in human affairs and natural phenomena as the deities and the ancestral spirits. The local deities and ancestral spirits control natural phenomena while God remains as a kind or superintending power to whom final appeal is made in the event of any injustice. The deity in collaboration with the ancestral spirits controls the moral order. The ancestors constitute the most important chain binding men to God. They occupy an exalted rank in the theistic panpchic animistic ontological order regarded as living dead. This is because they belong to a hierarchy, participating in the divine interactions, and rational communications with all forces including human beings.

The ancestors follow their order of primogeniture. They form a chain through the links of which the elders exercise their authority and influence rationally and communicatively on the living generation. Those living on earth ranks, in fact, after the living dead. The living belong in turn to a hierarchy that is also ordered by their own being in accordance with their primogeniture and vital rank, that is superior and master to other forces that lives on the land. The eldest in an African family or clan is by Divine law the panpsychic animistic authority connecting the ancestors and their descendants, because of his ontological status. It is he who bridges the rational communicative gaps among his people and all inferior forces - animal, plants, etc.

In African monarchical societies, the king, following this panpsychic animistic conception of authority is the father, and the king of the people.

He is the source of all good living; he is as God himself. Any person who is nominated but is not qualified by reason of vital rank and force, cannot be a king or chief among the kingdoms, because he cannot be the rational communicative link binding the living-dead and the living. In theistic panpsychic functionalism, there is an ontological chatter whereby, after the category of human forces comes the other forces, animals, plants and minerals, but the important point here is that within each of these categories, is found a hierarchy based on vital force or power, rank and primogeniture whose material apparatus is culture. And it is based on this that the concept of authority in African political system can be defined and understood.

African monarchical system of government with a strong centralized authority is a systematic, hierarchical and hereditary political system. The king is the traditional paramount authority of some societies. He is the central and supreme authority because in theistic animistic ontological hierarchy of forces, he is nearest to the ancestors. Hence he is the living intermediary between the living ancestors and the living indigenes of the land and more so he is believed to be divinely appointed. The traditional hierarchy of chiefs in African political system is pyramidal with the king or the eldest at the Apex. Next in this canonical gradation are the chiefs or elders whose powers are less than that of kings or the society. Next are the village heads, and last in the line were the clan or hamlet heads.

The hierarchy of forces is the structure of the theistic panpsychc animistic metaphysics, and social order, authority and leadership is the structure of the sociological and behaviouristic pattern of functional theory of society. There is a sense in which the subjective and objective explanation of communicative action and social order or public sphere is justified by functionalism and structuralism.

The functionalists seek for general objective laws which will bind together the largest number of facts discovered not by speculative cognition on introspective data, but by the observation and experiment on behaviour in a defined area. They are concerned with social interactive and communicative actions and the objective results of the actions and not with individual motives. Malinowski's analytical scheme includes the Charter: This defines the system of values (aims and purposes) for which human beings organize and enter into association within the institution. The Personnel: Every human group is organized on the basis of authority. There is some division of function, some pattern of distribution of privileges and duties; The Rules and norms: These are the technically acquired skills, habits and legal standards accepted by members of an institution or which are embedded in the social and natural environment; The Activities: These represent the concrete types of behaviours generated by the rules and provided for by the charter; The Function: This is the integral and objective result of organized group activities. Function is closely related to needs. Needs, in turn, are related to ends or values. The most basic value in all cultures is survival; this includes elements of material culture.[140] For Ernest Nagel, "the functional view of culture insists upon the principle that every custom, material object and others fulfil a vital function within a working whole."[141] Nevertheless, functionalism has been criticized on the fact that there seem to be no place for change in Malinowski's theory of the social system; hence societies he studies in his earliest fieldworks were relatively static as in the case of hierarchy of forces as the functional explanation of authority government and society. In considering this problem of social change the functionalist posited the concepts of evolution and diffusion of cultures as experienced by Africans. New inventions, revolutions, social, intellectual and institutional changes evolve only to satisfy new demands, while elements diffuse from one culture to another to satisfy needs and ensure survival. Another defect of functionalism is that "it is never tired of asserting that it is concerned with institutionalized behaviour and that the units of social analysis were not the acting individuals but the role."[142141] The school did not ask why there should be role of myths in the first place. Again, the school was more interested in establishing what the interrelations of institutions were than why they were interrelated at all. For instance, why there are inter relation of forces, spirits and gods. In other words, it can be said also that functionalists are more interested in consequences than in causes of an institution. These consequences were functions of forces or myths the institutions claim. Finally, the functionalists did not provide a functional theory that was in fact an explanation of social change.

Structuralism as a communicative rationality is one of the non-dialectical methodologies for studying society and interactions social changes. The term 'structure' refers to the constituents of, as distinct from the workings or functions of the object. The structure of societies refers to

---

[140] Punaman, W.G., what is structuralism?" Ryan Alan (Editor) *the philosophy of social explanation* (Oxford regions 1973) pp. 182-202

[141] Nomans, Geoge, "Bringing men Back" in Ryan Alan, The *Philosophy of social explanation* (Oxford regions 1973) p. 51

[142] Ibid.

the constituents of societies. Such constituents of societies, of course, include the groups, relationships, classes, roles, norms and sanctions or even shared concepts and symbols in the society, or family, elders, titled men as it were in African society. The significance of this concept of structuralism as distinct from functionalism is simply that "if a society (like anything else) is to be satisfactorily explained, then the question, what is it made of? will have to be answered. In other words, while functionalism asks the question, what is its function; why it does what? Structuralism asks the question, "what are its constituents or what is it made of?"[143] and justice in theistic panphyschic animistic society is the constituent of the hierarchical order of God, gods, ancestor, elders and so on.

The term social structure is said to draw attention, according to Meyer Forte, one of the notable structuralists, to the interconnection and interdependence within a single system, on all the different classes of social relations found within a given system or society. This system displays a minimum persistence over time and in principle comparable with other similar identifiable systems. Moreover, Ryan Alan also noted that there is a clear distinction between the structure on one side and both history and function on the other. He said that every historical explanation has implicit reference to structure (because of the minimum continuity overtime) likewise every structural explanation has implicit reference to origin and function. Structuralism, according to Radcliff Brown, is to "look at society as a system and to look at the constituents of actual social relations."[144] One major criticisms of structuralism is the fact that it adds nothing new by its method of breaking down structures into their constituent parts. Even though such reductions can constitute major scientific discoveries, they are worth looking for no less in the social than in the physical sciences. However, structural functionalism is an attempt on a large scale to combine the methods of both functionalism and structuralism which is not only extant in African philosophy but also embedded in the practice of tradition. Indeed Theistic Panpsychic rationality is culturally structural and functional thereby qualifying to be described as structural functional Panpsychic communicative animism.

Critically speaking the problems of communicative rationality in theistic panphychic animistic philosophy of culture, that is, African

---

[143] Brown, Radcliff. *Structure and function in primitive society,* London, Cohen and West, 1952 pp 157-159

[144] Steven, Vago, ibid., pp. 84-86

philosophy is inherent in the functional-structural nature or epistemological frame work. The limitations border on the dogmatic and unscientific concepts which are replete in the philosophy of culture such as forces, spirits, gods, etc. Again the vulnerability of culture predisposes all the elements of function and structure to disuse and disservices. Yet Culture cannot be rooted out, rather culture may grow, undergo transformation or it may evolve. However the greatest problems to African rational communicative symbols and actions like oral tradition proverbs, myths and prayers is the impact of acculturation. Acculturation refers to taking on material and non-material attributes from other cultures as a result of prolonged face-to-face contact. According to Steven Vago, acculturation can be the result of war, conquest, military or colonization. Acculturation provides the group with many possible new ways of behaving which might be quite different from those dictated by their own culture, traditional norms, and beliefs. Acculturation brings about greater similarities between two countries. Acculturation plays a role in a variety of activities and behaviours ranging from language use, frequency of sexual partners and condom use among unmarried adult, delinquency , etc.[145] However, African culture appears to have undergone acculturation, in the light of the fact that during the initial contact with Europeans, attempts were made to 'civilize' the African by the teaching of English language, the transmission of rudimentary skill and technologies, the introduction of the Christian faith doctrines and provision for medium-level opportunities to encourage limited mobility, norms, and values, but to a large extent, due to force and pressure for compliances by European colonials. This resulted to socio-economic and cultural transformations in African states but largely in negative sense because of the onslaught of modernity and modernization which destroyed the soul and cultural values of the world in and outside African philosophy.

Contemporary Africa is the result of tremendous ideological and infrastructural changes, all of which have altered the patterns of aesthetic and communicative rationality of Africans, and even the African oral traditions. Access to multiplicity of ideas contributes greatly to the negative and positive definition of rationality form. Access to improved technology made possible the use of foreign production tools and devices, which impact heavily on traditional values. Consequently, there is need to improve and scienticize

[145] William, Shakespeare. *The Complete Works of William Shakespeare* (Oxford, the Shakespeare Head Press, 1999) P. 23

Theistic Panpsychic animism but not to embrace hollow sciences and the god of materialism.

LIFE HEREAFTER POETICS AND METAPHYSICS,THE DREAD OF DEATH *

Death is a legitimate subject of natural philosophy and poetics and further research on it, weather scholarly or non-scholarly is a metaphysical praxis, if not in some cases mysticism. How unimaginable and unjustifiable to do a research on a subject as real and as old as man himself. If it is real and as old as man himself, if it is created alongside men, and with man why is the fuss? There is myth in African antiquity which says that death is as a result of man's sin or disobedience to God. But this story does not tell us how long man lived on earth before death sets in and therefore most likely death following the logic of the myth was synchronic fallout from the drama of creation. This is the most valuable subject of existence. Death steers mankind as an infinity and as a window into nothingness or another incommunicable or 'irrational world'. No one wants to die but we are counselled that this is an inevitable end of man. The fear and anguish that accompany the thinking and reality of death is seen as an evil, a metaphysical one, however. There are evils in the world; physical, moral and metaphysical. The evil in question is a metaphysical one, too deep for understanding, contrary to the physical or cosmological or civil evils like murder, accident, social disorder, etc. Yet the origin, native and modality of death make it a categorical imperative, a necessary end as natural as life itself. There is a saying in African philosophy that when one door closes another opens; when the door of life opens another door that is death opens. The phenomenon and the nuomena of death is an existential and poetic subject matter. In William Shakespeare, the old Talbot in poetic conversation with his servant reflected on the mystery of death in the following line: "where is my other life? My own is gone O, where's young Talbot? Where is valiant John?"[146] Old Talbot is groaning and bemoaning over the death of his son which any father, believes is his other life and with the separation, absolute and irrecoverable one indeed, he bellowed that this own life or part of his life is gone. There is also another sense in which death steers at man in contempt and scorn. Another speech of the old Talbot bespeaks of this nature of

* "Life-Here-After Poetics and Metaphysics" was first published in *KPIM of Death*, (ed) Ukagba U.J (Canadal, Trafford, 2007)

[146] Ibid.

death. "Thou antic death, which laugh'st us here to scorn."[147] It has therefore been argued that death is beyond human experience and inevitable. The Epicureans and stoics argued that the only reasonable attitude towards death is resignation with fear or regret. The existentialists such as Martin Heidegger have argued that living with a conscious awareness that we will die is not only uniquely human but also coming to term with death as an immanent possibility for our own being.

Death is likely to remain an object of dread for man, and most likely no civilization or advancement in the art of understanding and technology may ameliorate the fear that accompanies it. It must be pointed out that the pain in experiencing death is mostly in the death of a friend or relation not in one's death: to withstand death of someone else is the issue because the person dying is himself under going a process. This means that the friend dies, alone, as everyone must, and seemingly the separation is absolute and forever. According to Karl Jaspers, "the death of a friend can be "the deepest wound"[148] in life. In the ancient African and Egyptian history death and burial was accompanied by rituals of farewell amidst wailing and lamentations, all indicating separation from the loved one and journey to the world beyond. Classical tradition has drawn the picture of the 'elderly pass on' surrounded by their families and friends, making their farewell speeches and meeting death instead of being overtaken or snatched by it."[149] However here in Africa, especially and in some other cultures, death comes to people in a sedated and unconscious state. In my *Father's Death* and *Echoes of Hiroshima*[150] I captured the signification and phobia of death and the dread and fear of imminent death in war situations respectively.

Father's Death
Father's death is a sorrowful
Awareness,
It is a meaningful signification,
It is the beginning of a new phase,
For he that lived closest to his father,
For he that appreciate him,

---

[147] Karl, Jaspers, quoted by Gray, Glenn. J. The Problem of Dearth In modern Philosophy" In Paula Rothenberg Struhl and Karste J. Struhl (ed) *Philosophy Now; An Introductory Reader* (New York, Random House, 1972) P. 279

[148] Fietcher, Joseph, "Elective Death" in Paula Rothenberg Struhl and Karsten J. Struhl, ibid., P. 289

[149] Dukor, M., "Father's Death" in *Guest Poet:* The *Post Express on Sunday,* January 20, 2002. p. 16

[150] Dukor M, "Echoes of Horishima," Poetry*: The Guardian, Satorday, February 9, 2002*, P.31

Father's death is an absurd
It reminds us of our foundation,
Backward we look,
But the Father is no more,
The foundation has slipped away,
Forward we look with disconsolation,
Only to see our children's phobia,
Which faith can surmount,
Father look after your children,
Children look after your father,
He is the root form eternity.

Father's transition reopens the windows,
Into infinity and eternity,
It is sweet bitter experience
Which expose our frailty and emptiness
Father's death destroys our Ego,
And reminds us of our mortality,
Much as our love of him,
And the chord between us.
And him sublimated,
As we desire to join him,
On the journey to the unknown,
But serene and beautiful heaven,
Where every thing is defined,
By the speed of light,
In space and Time,
Oh, God help us.

ECHOES OF HIROSHIMA

Boom! Boom! Rent the harmattan air,
Innocent creatures of human republic,
Gazed at the sky and heaven with,
Wonder. Rapt attention and mouth-agape!
Alas! Not explosions of knock-outs of,
Christmas and New Year!
Rumours of war and mutiny of the dragons,
And the re-echoes of Osama bin Laden,
Na bomb o! Na war o! Bomb o!:
God O! God O! Bomb O!

The echoes of horror, Hiroshima and Nagasaki.
Sleeping bombs, stock pile of ammunition,
Agent of terror and darkness,
In the darkest corner of darkness,
Running berserk at the bequest of Lucifer,
Wasting the unsung heroes,
What a barrack time bombs!
As the sky sparkled red,
The ground watered with bombs,
Fire! Fire! Everywhere' she shouted,
A harvest of fire and minefield of bombs,
Evil and horror rained and reigned,
Quote she, "Lord unto thy hand,
I commit my spirit."
"Where are my Children?"
Exodus at the mercy of elements,
Thronging to the canal of death,
It is war and hell on earth,
Mind boggling. Terror, death,
Devastating enemy attack!
Human misery and harvest of death,
Parents, men, women, children,
Scampered for safety and hiding,
But stampeded they were,
To the canal of death,
Grief every where as rescuers fish out,
Corpses from the doom day canal of death,
On the dark, black holy Sunday,

Death as a necessary end

To comprehend death and accept it as a necessary end is one most difficult circumstance of men. We rush to hospital for check up, to care or treat diseases and or to subject the body to cares with a view to elongate life and soul. From a psychiatric point of view, "in our unconscious death is never possible in regard to ourselves."[151]

> It is inconceivable for our unconscious to imagine an actual ending of our own life here on earth and if this life of ours had to end, the

[151] Kublex, Ross, Elizabeth, "On the fear of Death" in Paula RS and KJS, *op. cit.,* P 266

> ending is always attributed to a malicious intervention from the outside by someone else. In simple terms, in our unconscious mind we can only be killed; it is inconceivable to die of a natural cause or of old age. Therefore death in itself is associated with a bad act, a frightening happening, something that in itself calls for retribution and punishment.[152]

The feature of our existence brings with it anxiety and the realization that we must die. In our efforts to cope "with this anxiety we attempt to transform death into a public event; we surround it with trappings, we render it more and more impersonal."[153] On the contrary, existentialism treats the actability of our death as a primary datum of human experience. Martin Heidegger use the term "Being-toward-death"[154] to capture the intimate relation between human existence and death and to prove that death is a permanent possibility: Spinoza similarly surmised that a free man thinks of nothing les than of death and his wisdom is not mediation upon death but upon life."[155] On Death, Karl Jaspers would argue that spiritually, we are all exposed to the yawning abyss, the primal night to which we all return.. For him death is a 'boundary situation."[156] This means that every individual lives at every moment in a situation, one that is constantly changing and never totally grasped or understood.

> Boundary situations are situations involving a limit or an end, and, unlike the ordinary one, they do not charge in essence. These situations which reveal the limits of our being to us, and which are inescapable and constitute of genuine life are experiences of guilt, of suffering, conflict, chance and death.[157]

Therefore, death is a boundary situation into the uncertainty. For Jaspers and for Heidegger each person must regard death as a permanent reality. Nietzsche on his part re-echos Zarathustra's saying "Die at the right time."[158] Following this he argues that a proper life requires a proper death and enjoins one of us to die at the right time and in the right manner. He

---

[152] Gray, Glenn, *op. cit.*, P. 273
[153] Martin, Heidegger, quoted by Glenn, ibid.
[154] Spinoza, ibid.
[155] Jaspers, ibid.
[156] Glenn, ibid.
[157] Zarathustra, quoted by Nietzsche, in Walter Kaufmann. *Existentialism from Dostoevsy to Satre* (New York, A Memdian Book, Now American Library, 1956) 128
[158] Nietzsche, ibid.

says "many die too late, and a few die too early."[159] Every body considers dying important, yet death is no festival as men suffer in anguish to dread it. He advised; "I show you the death that consummates - a spure and a promise to the survivors. He that consummates his life dies his death victoriously, surrounded by those who hope and promise…"[160] In praise of death a victorious and consummated one, he sang:

> My death I praise you, the free death which comes to me because I want it. And when shall I want it? He who has a goal and heir will want death at the right time for his goal and heir. And from reverence for his goal and heir he will hang no more dry wreaths in the sanctuary of life. Verily I do not want to be like the rope makers: they drag out their treads and always walk backwards.[161]

Hence to believe in death is a progressive thinking. Man cannot be born again but must die to face reality, the reality which in African metaphysics is a transition into another world and for Christians; it is precisely movement to heaven or hell. This means that death is a progression but retrogression to the rope maker. To buttress these assertions, I hereby list the following epigramic and poetic statements at Socrates:

> You are mistaken my friend, if you think that a man who is worthy of anything ought to spend his time weighing up the prospects of life and death, he has only one thing to consider in performing any action; that is, whether he is acting rightly or wrongly; like a good man or a bad one.[162]
>
> To be afraid of death is only another form of thinking that one is wise when one is not; it is to think that one knows what one does not know. No one knows with regard to death whether it is not really the greatest evil. And this ignorance, which thinks that it is knows what it does not, must surely be ignorance most culpable.[163]

---

[159] Ibid., pp. 128-129

[160] Ibid, P 129

[161] Plato (Trans) Tredennick H. "Apology" in *The last days of Socrates* (New York, Penguin classics 1982) P.59

[162] Ibid.,p. 60

[163] Ibid., p. 62

> If I am what I claim to be, and you put me to death, you will harm yourself more than me.[164]
>
> Ordinary people seem not realize that those who really apply themselves in the right way to philosophy are directly and of their own accord preparing themselves for dying and death.[165]
>
> You have brought about my death in the belief that through it you will be delivered from submitting your conduct to criticism; but I say that the result will be just the opposite.[166]
>
> Death is one of two things, either it is annihilation, and the dead have no consciences of anything, or, as we are told, it is really a change, a migration of the soul from this place to another.[167]
>
> Now it is time that we were going, I to die and you to live; but which of us has the happier prospect is unknown to any one but God.[168]
>
> Has the boat come in from Delos - the boat which ends my reprise when it arrives?[169]
>
> There is something in store for those who have died and something much better for the good than for wicked.[170]
>
> If a man has trained himself throughout his life to live in a state as close as possible to death, would it be ridiculous for him to be distressed when death comes to him?[171]

Death in its metaphysical nature begs for recognition from its most notorious opponent, the second conjunct, matter. Apart from its notorious metaphysical nature discussion on death could only be meaningful as first an ontological object with much commitment on the part of concerned men and second, in the context of an antithetical world of matter which is an empirical object. However the reality of death again is conceptualized from the prism of its opposition to the concept of matter as its dual opposite. In linguistic and moral terms the duality of death and life (symbolized by matter) is a categorical continuation of the traditional dualistic concept of night and light, good and bad, Man and Woman, etc., all of which command

164 Ibid., p. 107
165 Ibid., p. 73
166 Ibid., p.75
167 Ibid., p. 67
168 Ibid., (crito, 43^A 43l - 44^A) P.80
169 Ibid., p. 106, Phaedo 62E - 64A
170 Ibid., p.113 phaedo 62E - 64A
171 Dukor, M., "Destiny" in *Guest Poet: The Post Express on Sunday,* January, 200 - 2002 P. 16

moral, aesthetics and linguistic ontological discourse in order to give meaning to explicable dimension of the universe and infinity. But death as a continuation of life seem to have diffused the whirlwind of confusion and mystery over the tragedy and pain of death since time immemorial, but some of the materialists, agnostics and sceptic's argument on death as the final end of man continue to challenge the sensitivity of mortal man. At linguistic, poetic and natural levels poets have romanticized death as chiefly an emotional and a language problem.

Spirit and Matter Epistemology

Some poetic, aesthetic and linguistic treatment of death has removed the pains associated with it into the realm of phenomenon hence, an object only good as ingredient of phenomenalism and phenomenology. Yet the tendency to treat Death with such refrain and unseriousness draws man to the abyss of nothingness whereby the whole of life is a dream and death's traditional opposite, matter as merely articles of subjective consciousness. The problem of poetic and aesthetic conception of death brings to the fore the inability and handicap of poet in grappling with the ontology and metaphysics of death. Poets are not always the best ontologists or metaphysicians neither is poetry the philosophy to investigate the reality of death, yet poets opens up the emotion and sensibility, and metaphysics digs into the reality of life and death.

The poets subjectively explain the appearance and emotion entailed in the wailing and lamentations associated with life and death but without the knowledge of grappling with nuomena and reality of life, matter, after life and the universe. Life ends with the world for most poets and the so called humanists. The agnostics are not bothered with anything and the skeptics are in doubts over any reality. For these classes of concerned thinkers, there is no reality except the celebrative, the aesthetics and the phenomena. But there are other natures and attitudes that promote life beyond the earth and that is that death is a transition to another surface of realm of existence. The argument that in the world there is a dualistic conception of reality to everything shows that apart from the reality of night and day, darkness and light, bad and good, there is also the dualistic conception of life and death, spirit and matter, etc.

The concept of spirit is not only the warp and woof of dream, but also is the essence of man's immortality. The being called spirit is the metaphysical symbol of man's existence and connection with the divine and the ultimate justification of its subsistence in the realm of mortality (bodily form) and immortality (divine form).

Spirit in reality is the dualistic opposite to matter. In African philosophy, the spirit is a personal possession; it inhabits the whole personality, emotion and body. The spirit person concentrates more in the head, the heart and the mind. It is the sit of unconsciousness and consciousness. The spirit is older than the physical shell, hence it transcends and immanates the entire being as well as guides and pilots the mortal bodily activities. The spirit is the holy grail of immortality, and is revered as such because it vacates the body when the letter is weak and undergoes the regenerative rapture that throws the spirit itself into the other realm of existence which in African philosophy is called the world of ancestors and the Supreme Being. The meaning of death emanates at the middle of the tension between spirit and matter, the metaphysical categories of being, becoming and unbecoming. But there is a sense in which matter is spirit and spirit matter. It is the sense in which Karl Marx described consciousness as matter in motion and as matter reducible to consciousness vice-versa. Death and life are obvious dualism just as spirit and matter are. Each is a converse situation in the being of beings. The categories of death, life, spirit and matter are both states of potencies and actualities obeying both the spiritual laws of Aristotelian unmoved mover and Plato's ideal forms. Life as spirit is like a river that flows and death is like a channel of re-flow or passage to higher or lower dimensions. And life as matter is like a body that rots and death is like a release of the spirit person to external salvation or damnation. In every existential situation, therefore, man is confronted by the eschatology of life and death, Spirit and matter.

In dreams while asleep, mind which is matter-constituted suffers conversion in which it becomes spirit and zooms into the world of theistic panpsyhic animistic infinity. For the Africans this is the journey of souls and spirits at temporary and permanent rest. Except robotic and unlively persons dream is a means of power revelation, evidence of creativity and connectivity to the highest God, angels, and ancestors. Dream is evidence of the dualistic nature of man, that is, the mind and the body or the spirit and matter. It presupposes the separability of the mind from the body. The spirit in matter and in dream world is like a river flowing to other realms with different names like rivers. The soul of a spirit suffered mortality to arrive at the immortal end or the ultimate principle of epistemological end and metaphysical nature. The rhythms of birth and death could portray a purposive trajectory in African philosophy as I tried to capture in this poem. *Destiny*[172] about my father's death.

DESTINY
A spirit was born into the world
Of influenza and World War I,
And left the world,
Of a devastating terrorist attack,
And global anti-terrorism Coalition,
It takes a great spirit,
To meet a world
        Of scourge and war
And transit from a world,
Of terrorism and imminent war.
Children of God,
Fight not one another,
Peace, indeed, is a mission.

The wisdom of ancient understands not only of the things of this world but also of the other worlds within or outside the objective physical realities. Socrates says this of the ancients. "They also have sanctuaries and temples which are truly inhabited by gods; and oracles and prophecies and visions and all other kinds of communion with the gods occur there face to face. They see the sun and moon and stars as they really are; and the rest of their happiness is after the same manner."[173] The ancients understand the modalities of existence, their necessities and possibilities in life and therefore, Socrates says, "But those who are judged to live a life of surpassing holiness-those are they who are released and set free from confinement in these regions of the earth, and passing upward to their abode, make their dwelling upon the earth's surface. And of these such as have purified themselves sufficiently by philosophy live thereafter altogether without bodies, and reach habitations even more beautiful, which it is not easy to portray-nor is there time to do so now."[174] Socrates enjoins man to leave nothing undone before death to be able to attain some measure of goodness and wisdom; for the prize is glorious and the hope great. For this reason the ancients had sanctuaries and temples to satisfy the demands that the possibilities and

[172] Plato, Phaedo, ibid., p. 174
[173] Ibid., 178
[174] Ibid., p.174

necessities of subjective spiritual life entails. They also have understanding not only of the spirit but also matter and constitution of the earth. The nature of the earth is about matter and consciousness inherent in it. Socrates narrates the mystical and objective descriptions of earth as follows:

> Such is the nature of the earth as a whole and of the things that are upon it. In the earth itself, all over its surface, there are many hollow regions, some deeper and more widely spread than that in which we live, others deeper than our region but with a smaller expanse, some both shallower than ours and broader. All these are joined together underground by many connecting channels, some narrower, some wider, though which, from one basin to another, there flows a great volume of water, monstrous unceasing subterranean river or waters both hot and cold; and of fire too, great rivers in Sicily that flow mud before the lava comes, and the lava stream itself. By these the several regions are filled in turn as the flood reaches them...All this movement to and fro is caused by an oscillation inside the earth, and this oscillation is brought about by natural mean,
>
> ...One of the cavities in the earth is not only larger than the rest, but pierces right through from one side to the other.[175]

It is of this that Homer speaks when he says, Far, far away, where lies earth's deepest chasm.[176] In spirit and matter epistemology and metaphysics there are many possibilities and necessities. Either it is annihilation and the dead have no consciousness of anything; or it is really a change: a migration of the soul from this place to another. Now if there is no consciousness but only a dreamless sleep, death must be a marvellous gain. Socrates supposed that if anyone were told to pick out the night on which he slept so soundly as not even to dream, and then to compare it with all the other nights and days of his life, and then were told to say, after due consideration, how many better and happier days and nights than this he had spent in the course of his life.[177] We most likely, would find these days and nights easy to count in comparison with the rest. "If death is like this, then, I call it gain because the whole of time, if you look at it in this way, can be regarded as no more than one single night. If on the other hand death is a removal from here to some

---

[175] Ibid., 174 - 175

[176] Homer, (Illiad Viii. 14) quoted by Socrates, ibid., P.175

[177] Apology, *op. cit.*, P. 75

other place, and if what we are told is true, that all the dead are there, what greater blessing could there be than this, gentlemen?"[178]

Personal Identity and Life-here after

God it is said, is the answer to the question „why does anything exist at all? God is a necessary being because existence is perfection. So the god-idea provides a final answer, because God existed from all eternity, uncaused. Matter/energy existed from all eternity, with supernatural ideas to account for it from the time that human beings first became capable of abstract thought, to look for an explanation of existence. There are only two possibilities, either something existing or nothing existed - and the plain fact is there is no prior contact of non-existence. The mindboggling vastness of the universe (in relation to human size), its timescale, and its incomprehensible complexity, all add to the wonder of it-though the complexity is possible just because of the vastness and the timescale. The science of cosmology, especially, is at present in a stage of rapid development, and we are tentatively piecing together the cosmic jigsaw puzzle. Recent discoveries favour the 'Big bang' theory for the origin of our universe. But that does not mean it came out of nothing. More likely, as one theory describes, the universe "oscillates - expanding and collapsing alternately, without any beginning, without any end."[179] According to supporters of this theory, the universe is likely to go on expanding for billions of years, but eventually it may begin to slow down. This means we can expect the whole process to go into reverse. Everything in the universe will then rush together, faster and faster, to form the densest possible mass once more. Mythological and anthropological explanation of the world does not support this theory. This theory does not support life here after. God is an anthropological being which necessitates a theological explanation of life and death or spirit and matter. It is probable that there is eternity of ever-changing matter and energy (as Democritus suggested nearly five hundred years before the Christian era). There is also the alternative theory that matter suddenly came into existence at some point in time, before which there was nothing - or nothing except an all-powerful spirit with a sudden creative urge. However, taking a scientific view of the universe may destroy our sense of awe and wonder, which is spiritual, subjective and creative.

---

[178] Smooker, Barbara. *Humanism* (Ibadan, Gadfly publisher 2006) P. 39
[179] Ibid.,p. 38

We have, as a means of finding a solution to the problem of death argued that in the realm of possibilities and necessities that the categories of spirit and matter are epistemological insights to the phenomenon of life and death. In the widest possible sense, death which is generally regarded as an evil is essential to life. Without death there could be no birth, no younger generation coming along, and certainly no change or promotion. Death is not injury, but rather a privilege. But to the humanist, death implies, as Epicurus said, the end of life. To most people, however, it is a transition to a better life. Indeed, it is fair to say that the doctrine of a life hereafter is the one ingredient that makes religion so popular. This is what Bernard Shaw said about it: "Now the man who has come to believe that there is no such thing as death, the change so called being merely the transition to an exquisitely happy and utterly careless life, has not overcome the fear of death at all: on the contrary, it has overcome him so completely that he refuses to die on any terms whatever."[180] But the world is so wonderful that it must have been designed by a Supreme being who must also have designed the afterlife This world is said to be so temporary that there must be another perfect one ready to put it right Since life on earth is so unjust, there must be another life to redress the balance, a perfect world, a necessary world of perfect things beyond the contentions of possibilities. Anyway, why are most people so desirous of an afterlife? They generally think of it as life in a perfect world. The chief theological argument for an afterlife is that the existence of an omnipotent God of love demands it. But however, humanists have asked why God cannot or will not prevent evil from triumphing here, why assume He can or will manage things better elsewhere? Yet, personal survival after death raises the whole question of personal identity.

I think that the whole controversy surrounding personal identity borders on the distinction between the scientific mind or self or I and the spiritual mind or self or the I, Some argue that the self emerges as experience accrues and it is constructed as the organism actively engages the eternal world i.e. the self develops. In other words the ego is an after-the-fact construction, not a before-the-fact condition for the possibility of experience. The ego or the self, as an after - the fact construction has a pedigree in the doctrine of empiricism where proponents and adherent hold dearly and cognitively on the experience as the only true source of knowledge. To that effect we recall John Locke's primary and secondary

[180] James, William, *The Principle of Psychology, 2 vol. 5.*(New York, Dover, 1990) pp. 332-334

qualities as progenies of our sensible world, Freudian stipulation of the mental life in term of *id, ego* and *super ego* as only a function of experience and Kantian faculty of understanding as the category responsible for our cognition of the empirical world. Investigating personal identity with this empirical frame work would only terminate this sort of inquiry before the fringes of the immortal self, ego or the soul.

Accordingly the subjective self is, as 'I' or 'me', the social and empirical entity which also as knower is on empirical self, phenominal self and not the nuominal or transcendal self. In African philosophy, in Igbo metaphysics each of us is an agent with an identity. There is a sanctuary within the citadel of our personal and community life, the sanctuary of the divine manifold in the social I and Me, of the past, the present and the future collectively represented by the community or African theistic panpychic animism. In the empirical or physicalist doctrine, the spiritual self belongs to the empirical self which is said to be entire collection of ones states of consciousness, ones psychic faculties and dispositions taken collectively. On the contrary, in Igbo metaphysics the life of demarcation between the spiritual self and the empirical self is thin, but the later belongs to the former. All state of consciousness, psychic faculties, dispositions, the capacities of sensation and will, the capacity to desire and the experience of emotion are all the other side or the mirror of our spiritual capacities which are legislators and governors of the social, empirical life and collectively represent our personal identities. The empirical self is an evidence for postulating a real self, an antecedent 'I', a transcendental ego. In African philosophy, therefore, the active spiritual self interact or is co-joined with the identity- constitutive aspects of the material and social life.

On the contrary, James in the tradition of John Locke argues that there is no such thing as a person or a proper part of a person, her ego, self, or mind's 'I' that is exactly the same overtime. "The sense of our own personal identity is exactly like any one of our other perceptions of sameness among phenomena. It is a conclusion grounded on the resemblance in a fundamental respect."[181] According to him the present thought in the stream of consciousness stands as the representative of an entire past stream with which it cannot be identified. This is because "the passing states of consciousness, which should preserve in their succession an identical knowledge of its past, wander from their duty, letting large portions drop

[181] Ibid.

from out of their Ken, and representing other portions wrong. James says that the identity which we recognize as we survey the long progression can only be the relative identity of a slow shifting in which there is always some common ingredients maintained; the commonest element of all, the most uniform, is the possession of some common memories. Therefore "the identity found by the I in its Me is only a loosely constructed thing, an identity 'on the whole."[182] He says that because the 'I' appropriate the contents of an ever changing stream and because it meets that stream with models of 'Me' of complex self whose parts are undergoing constant revision, the 'I' itself is continuously enriched and renewed because the system is dynamic. Therefore, "no part of the system resembles the soul, the ego, the self, or the I of traditional metaphysics; there is no mind's I that stands behind all experience as the condition of its possibility.[183] But Omen Flanagan offers an argument which is supportive of the theistic animistic super structure of African philosophy thus; "my present state of consciousness is continuous with the past. The past determines the felt quality of the present, and many parts of my life are recoverable as my memories. Past conscious thoughts make themselves felt in the process of approximation in the fringe, in the penumbra."[184] In African philosophy the concept of the higher other self means the spiritual self that determines and manifest in ones personality. It is the divine spark in the conscious stream of the theistic panpsychic animistic universe where the monads, selves, beings, inanimate and animate objects are aggregates. A possible interpretation of this or an extrapolation from this is that the overself is the real self, a transcendental ego or a mind's I that accompanies all experience. This is against all interpretations and theories that explain away the conscious in a mechanistic and physicallist analogies such as that the self is the centre of narrative gravity; the higher order self is one of the many models contained in the brain; that the mind must have a single control device contained in a box, whose job is conscious control.

The fuse about death and transition to the hereafter life is caused more by not only the distinction between spirit (or soul) and matter but also by what should constitute consciousness and personal identity. The concept of spirit is mystical and that is why scientists and philosophers seek a better

---

[182] Ibid.

[183] Owen, Flanagan, *Consciousness Reconsidered* (London, A Bradford Book, the MIT Press, Cambridge Massachusetts, 1998) p. 187

[184] David, Home, "Personal Identity" in Paula R.S. and K.J.S. *op. cit* P. 95

explanation of 'person' in what constitutes personal identity. Rene Descartes thinking substance 'I' would have been a truce in the whole controversy as serving not only the spiritual *Ego* but also the substance of personal identity. On the contrary David Hume questions the epistemic validity of 'I' and argues that there is no single entity of which we are conscious that we can call a self. The empiricist and positivists generally would argue that Death is a transition to no where, but a total annihilation. David Hume's position proceeds from the empiricist premise that every true idea must be derived from experience, from some concrete impressions. He says that upon reflection he cannot find any distinct impression that can be labelled a 'self' What we call the self is no single thing but merely "a bundle or collection of different perceptions, which succeed each other with an unconceivable rapidity, and are in a perpetual flux and movement."[185] The concept of self is scientifically and technically taken further as a process or a psychological matter which however does not coordinate with the belief in life after death in African and oriental philosophy. One belief which could be understood in Cartesian or African terms is thus expressed: "Whatever happens between now and any feature time, either I shall still exist, or I shall not. Any future experience will either be my experience, or it will not."[186] To exist is a subjective reality whether it is a bundle of perception or not. What is the personal identity in the successive perceptions? And why do we have uninterrupted and invariable existence through the whole course of our lives? Why any future experience will either be my experience or it will not is because "we have a distinct idea of an object that remains invariable and uninterrupted through a supposed variation of time"[187] and this idea we call personal identity in the physical and spiritual sense in African philosophy. This concept of identity in African philosophy does not require further scientific or technical explanation but a metaphysical cognition and it accordingly inheres from the concept of spirit and soul.

Personal survival is possible after death, contingent however, upon the state of the soul which determines the survival of the spirit person from matter, the earth form of the soul. Similarly the cat*ego*ries of mortality and immortality of the soul or spirit is conditionally earth bound, that is, ability to escape from spirit matter to pure spirit. According to Socrates,

---

[185] Parfit, Derek, "Personal identity" in Jonathan Clover (e) *The Philosophy of Mind. Oxford Readings* (oxford OUP, 1985) P. 142

[186] Hume, *op. cit.,* p. 98

[187] Plato, Phaedo, ibid., p. 170

> if the soul is immortal, it demands our care not only for that part of time which we call life, but for all time; and indeed it would seem now that it will be extremely dangerous to neglect it. If death were a release from everything, it would be boom for the wicked, because by dying they would be released not only from the body but also from their own wickedness together with the soul; but as it is, since the soul is clearly immortal, it can have no escape or security from evil except by becoming as good and wise as it possibly can. For it takes nothing with it to next world except its education and training; and these, we are told, are of supreme importance in helping or harming the newly dead at the very beginning of his journey there.[188]

Epistemology of Spirit-person

According to Socrates when any man dies, his own guardian spirit, which was given charge over him in his life, tries to bring him to a certain place where all must assemble, and from which, after submitting their several cases to judgment, they must set out for the next world, under the guidance of one who has the office of escorting souls from this world to the other. They undergo the necessary experiences and remained as long as is required. Another guide brings them back again after many vast periods of time. He says the wise and disciplined soul follows its guide and is not ignorant of its surroundings, but the soul which is deeply attached to the body hovers round it and the visible world for a long time, and it is only after much resistance and suffering that it is at last forcibly led away by its appointed guardian spirit. The soul which is impure through having done some impure deed, either by setting its hand to lawless bloodshed is shunned and avoided by all; none will company with it or guide it, and it wanders alone in utter desolation until certain times have passed, whereupon it is borne away of necessity to its proper habitation. But every soul that has lived throughout its life in purity and soberness enjoys divine company and guidance, and each inhabits the place which is proper to it. And when the newly dead reach the place to which each is conducted by his guardian spirit, first they submit to judgment:

> both those who have live holily, and those who have not. Those who are judged to have lived a neutral life set out for Acheron, and embarking in those vessels which await them, are conveyed to the lake. There they dwell, and undergo purification absolve by

[188] Ibid., pp. 170 - 171

> punishment from any sins that they have committed, and rewarded for their good deeds, according to each man's deserts. Those who on account of the greatness of their sins are judged to be incurable, as having committed many gross acts of sacrilege wicked and lawless murders or any other such crimes - these are huled by their appropriate destiny into Tartarus, from whence they emerge no more. Others who are judged to have been guilty of sins which, though great, are curable; if, for example they have offered violence to father or mother in a fit of passion, but spent the rest of their lives in penitence, or if they have committed manslaughter after the same fashion these too must be cast into Tartarus; but when this has been done and they have remained there for a year, the surge casts them out-the manslaughters down Cocytus and the offenders against their parents down Pyriphlegethon. And when as they are swept along, they come past the Acherusian Lake, they cry aloud and call upon those whom they have killed or misused, and calling, beg and entreat for leave to pass from the stream into the lake, and be received by them. If they prevail they come out and there is an end of their distress; but if not, they are swept away once more into Tartarus and from there back into the rivers, and find no release from their sufferings until they prevail upon those whom they have wronged; for this is the punishment which their judge has appointed for them.[189]

This is the destination of the spirit-person to life hereafter, according to Socrates. For Socrates the separation from matter to another spirit matter world is the destiny of souls. However for Lobsang Rampa the soul or the spirit separates from the body and ascends to greater reality[190] leaving behind empty shell of the body.

Greater Reality
'Oh Spirit about to depart,
For Reality the Greater,
The True Life beyond this,
Your time of release has come.
Stertorous breathing ratty raggedy,
His chest heaved and fell,
Suddenly he gave a short, sharp gasp,
Almost a cough,

[189] Rampa, Lobsang, The *Thirteenth candle* (London, Gorgi Books, 1979) P.26 190 *Ibid.*, p. 28
[190] Ibid., p. 28

And his body arched upwards,
Until it was supported by the,
Back of his head and his heals,
A rigid flesh and bone.
Then all of a sudden the body jerked,
Upwards an inch, two inch,
from the ground, Then it collapsed,
Sagged like a half-empty sack of wheat,
Thrown carelessly aside.
A last despairing wheeze of air,
Escaped from the lungs,
The body twitched and still,
Then came gurgling of fluids,
The rumbling of organs,
And the settling of joints.

As the body of a dead man lay inert upon the floor, there comes the gurgling of fluids ceasing their flow and finding their own levels. There comes too the rumbling and groaning of organs giving up life, for a body does not die instantly, but in stages, organ by organ. First is the death of the higher centres of the brain and then, in orderly procession, other organs, finally deprived of the direction of the brain, cease to function, cease to produce those secretions or pass on the substance which is necessary for the continuation of that complex mechanism referred to as body.[191] The life force withdraws at the death of the body and floats into its next journey.

JOURNEY BEYOND
As the life force withdraws,
Leaves the confines of the body,
And assembles outside,
Congregating in an amorphous mass, Just above body.
Hovers by magnetic attraction.
There is yet some life,
There is yet some flow of life particles.
Departing their former host,
As more and more organs line,
Up their life force,
The tenuous form float above the flesh-body,

---

[191] Ibid., p. 29

Comes more and more to resemble it.
At last,
When the resemblance is complete,
The magnetic attraction ceases and ,
The 'spirit body' floats off on its next journey.

Now the spirit is complete and held to the dead body by only the most fragile of threads. It floated, as it is confused and terrified. Being born to life on earth was a traumatic experience, which meant dying to another form of existence. Dying or death means that the spirit body is being born again on another world, on the spirit world.[192] Now the form hovered, floated higher and sank lower, floated, and waited the instruction of the telepathic Lama, one whose whole life was devoted to helping those who were leaving earth. In ancient Buddhist tradition the lama guides the dead to the world beyond according to Rampa:

> We are but puppets of the One who is Higher, put down on earth that He may experience the things of earth. Your life from the cradle to the grave has been enmeshed in superstition and false fears. Know that many of your beliefs are without foundation. Know that many of the devils you fear will hunt you out of your own making. We sense but dimly our immortal birthright, our eternal associations, and sensing so dimly we imagine, we fear, and we rationalize.[193]

I see devil
The spirit form ceased and watched,
The silent cloud figure before him,
And saw the gradual awakening,
The quickening into awareness,
Sensed the panic, the uncertainty,
Felt a measure of the dreadful shock,
Torn from his familiar places and things.
Sensed, and understood.
The spirit-form dipped and swayed,
The spirit-form pulsed and wavered,
Ripples undulated throughout its length,
Then, like the first faint cheep,

---

[192] Ibid., p. 30
[193] Ibid., p. 34

Of a bird newly hatched from the egg,
Came the wall of a frightened soul,
The spirit-form whimpered with terror,
And said, telepathically,
But I see devils,
I see gibbering monsters
Poke their taloned hands in my direction
They will devour me
I see the features of those
Whom I wronged in life.

There is a silver cord, that collection of lines of electric force linking you here with your soul, that cord of bluish light which connects the physical body to the spirit body. In the spirit realm it shimmers puling with light and life. It was like the umbilical cord which connects the mother and the new-born child, the child whose physical body cannot exist for a moment if the Silver Cord is severed:[194]

Silver Cord of Life
An old mandarin Seng was,
His aged eyes peered short-sightedly,
Through,
The window of his room,
He could dimly discern the beautiful,
Gardens,
With the strutting peacocks.
Softly to his failing ears came
The song of birds,
Returning to the trees as the,
Day grew old.
Seng lay back, relaxed,
Upon his cushions,
Within himself he could feel,
The rustling fingers of Death
Loosing his bonds with life,
Slowly Old Seng sank back,
Upon his cushions,
A harsh rattling breath hissing,

[194] Ibid., p. 36

Through his teeth.
The sunlight faded, and,
The title lamps in the room were lighted
But old Send had gone, gone,
With the last dying rays of the sun'
"Old Seng lay slumped upon, His cushion.
His body sounds creaking,
And wheezing,
Into silence,
No blood through arteries and veins
No body fluids gurgle within.
The body of Old Seng was dead,
Finished with of no more use,
A light blue haze,
Form around the body of Old Seng,
Life over the body floating,
Horizontally above,
Attached by the thinning Silver cord.
The Silver Cord,
Thinned themselves,
And parted,
The Soul which had been Old,
Seng floated off,
Drifted like a cloud of incense smoke,
Vanished effortlessly through the walls,
The Soul drifted on through realms,
Through dimensions.
At last it reached wondrous parkland,
Dotted with immense buildings
At one of which he stopped,
Here the Soul that had been Old Seng
Made his way across a gleaming floor.

A soul according to Rampa, in its own surroundings, is a solid as was upon this world. The soul in the world of the souls can be confined by walls, and walk upon a floor. The soul there has different abilities and talents from those we know upon the Earth.[195]

[195] Ibid., p. 37

SELF JUDGEMENT

This Soul wandered on,
And at last entered a small cubicle,
Setting down,
He gazed at the wall before him,
Suddenly the wall appeared to vanish and,
In its palace he saw scenes,
The scenes of his life.
He saw,
The Akashic Record,
The Record of all that has ever happened,
And which can be seen readily
By those who are trained
It is also seen by everyone who passes
From the Earth life,
To the life beyond,
The Record of successes and failures
Man sees his past and judges himself.
No sterner judge than Man himself.
The Soul that had been Old Seng
Saw, and sorrowed for his many faults,
And then he rose and left the cubicle,
Going speedily to a larger room,
Where men and women,
Of the Soul World awaited him.
Silently, smiling compassion,
And understanding,
They awaited his approach,
His request to be guided,
Sitting in their company,
He told them of his faults,
Of the things he had attempted to do,
Meant to do, and failed,
Seeing his past and his mistakes,
He now approached these Advisors,
In order to receive their suggestions.
The Soul sat with the Advisors
Said the qualities which he had to grow
His Soul before he could evolve further,
First would be helped to find conditions

Essential for his further progress

LIFE BEYOND

The Soul that had been Old Seng,
But a Soul ready for rest,
He returns to the Land Beyond.
He rested and recuperated,
Studying the lessons of past lives,
Preparing for the life to come,
Here in this life beyond death,
Articles and substances
Were as solid to his touch
As they had been on Earth.
He rested until the time and
Conditions were pre-arranged,
At some pre-determined time,
The Soul in Waiting was called,
And was led forth into the World,
Of mankind.

BACK TO EARTH LIFE

They stopped, invisible to,
The eyes of those in the flesh,
Watching the parents-to-be,
Looking at the house,
Assessing the probabilities this house,
Would afford, the desired facilities for leaning,
The lessons which had to be learned,
Satisfied, they withdrew.
Months later the Mother-to-Be
Felt a sudden quickening inside her
As the Soul entered and
The Baby came to life.
The Baby was born,
To the World of Man.
The Soul that had once activated,
The body of old Seng,
Now struggled anew,
With the reluctant nerves,
And brain of the child Lee Wong,

In humble circumstances in a fishing
Village of China
Once again the high vibrations of a Soul
Were converted to the lower octave
Vibrations of a flesh body

According to Rampa a man or woman has a certain allotted span upon the Earth. If one ends his or her life before that time, them he or she has to return almost immediately. Thus we have the spectacle of a baby born to live perhaps a few months only. That may be the soul of suicide returning to take over the body and so live out the time which should have been lived before. "Suicide is never justified; it is a grave offence against oneself, against one over self."[196]

Speculations on life Here after

Death in African theistic panpsychic animistic metaphysical universe is a transmigration kind of transition to the world beyond but within or superimposed world. Life, therefore, is a continuous process from this world to the world within or beyond. The idea of life after death is inferred from the idea of life here on earth with virtually all that were experienced and observed in present world order are believed to be the same with what is to be seen or experienced in the future world order. Hence the panpsychic animistic ontology which acts as a force that binds the community and society together are believed to continue to be at work in the after life world order. Man in panpsychic animistic universe in African metaphysics is undergirded and circumscribed by panpsychic forces, as it were, he is convertible or transmigratable into any of the forms of panpsychic forces, spirits and powers which are also symbolic of man, animals, snakes, lions, bulls, leopards, cattle, lizards, birds, etc. Death as a transmigration could mean a man dying to enter the animals or big trees like Iroko as the animating spirit. In African theistic panpsychic animism there are animals or trees that are held sacred and untouchables; they have human but animistic spirits as a result of transmigration from earthly life to life after death.

Again death as transition does not only imply transmigration in the sense above, it may imply transition to heavenly worldly order in the sense of Christian category or concept of heaven. In this case death is a transition to

---

[196] Dukor, M., "The Glimpse" in *Guest Poet: The Post Express on Sunday,* January, 20, 2002 p.16

heaven superimposed to this worldly earth. The idea of the category or concept of Hell is not clear but is close to what Mbiti calls 'Hades' in African traditional philosophy and the category of heaven is close to the order of bliss inhabited by elevated and sanctified persons and spirit beings. In the theistic pansychic animistic ontology and metaphysics, which is the true African philosophy encompassing all that is unknown, known yet, to be known the concept of heaven and hell are distinctive in culture and philosophy but universal in category and ontology. In African philosophy, the heavenly or the hellish world which is a consequence of the African State of environment is at the command and mercy of almighty God, who is also the superintended overseer of the heavenly or the hellish state of the European, the Asian, etc., whose environment, perfect, near perfect or imperfect is a superimposition of their heavenly or hellish abodes in life after death. The point is that heaven and hell are universal categories but wear the gab of race, culture, environment, belief, development and civilization. What one sees in the African heavenly state represents the state of African development and different from the European heavenly state. Similarly an European hellish state in life after death represents the hellish state of the European present environment and state of development but not same as the African hell in life after death which is theistic panpsychic animistic hell. Therefore, as a proof of the unique nature of culture and philosophy of culture, it all means that the state of development in the West awaits those Westerners who are qualified to go to their heaven or hell to the exclusion of Africans and Asians who are bound to their respective heavens or hells. As far as African metaphysics is concerned, the heavenly or the hellish otherworld is superimposed in this world such that immediately after transition ,less transmigration, the truly worthy sprint person navigates over amidst pain and anguish to join his ancestors in particular necessary stations of life there. In the *Glimps*[197] and The Other World[198] the poetic metaphysical reality of death is expressed more concisely.

THE GLIMPSE
It was down,
Asleep I went,
The vision lifted,

[197] Dukor, M., "The other world," ibid P.16
[198] Swedenbog, Emanuel, *Heaven and Hell* (New York Swedenborg foundation Inc. 1982) P. 549

A different night sleep,
And enchanted flight,
Are not yet,
Encountered, not yet,
Imagined,
The window of eternity,
Opened,
Grey silhouettes brushing the early,
Sky, joy consumed and sorrow,
Lived to its limits,
The setting and flower images,
Are familiar,
A tremendous night air,
As I navigate the boundary,
Between life here and,
Hereafter,
This is death, dance and
Revelation,
Death of beloved old man,
I praised, I was free,
And astonished,
Of what would follow this gift of rope,
And tender sunshine,
I floated and swim,
The rivers and the canvas,
Of eternity,
The land of ancestors and angels,
And God,
And behold! My beloved old man,
Disembarked from the automobile unto,
Eternity.
I was astonished,
And floated along,
As he walked away like a soldier,
In triumphant gallantry,
As the heavenly city,
Opens,
Persons are at work,
Unqualified, beautiful serene,
Natural air of candour and aesthetics,

Of lined up duplexes and mansions,
In the desert of harmattan grasses,
In the eternity and,
Under the shadow,
Of grey air and red sunshine,
Peaceful, quiet eternal,
Universe.
The curtain veiled and the heaven,
Closed,
I jetted uncontrollably,
Sinking back to my,
Automobile,
Bloody beast ,
Goodbye Daddy.
Hope to reunite with you
Again,

THE OTHER WORLD
In this bright hour,
Death looms,
And transition around the,
Corner,
Near the doorstep,
The sun collapses under bed sheet,
Where beloved Daddy lay,
Like a holy,
And helpless,
Child.
The fountain bleeds,
Mercury,
In the basement,
His image rises,
Like a medallion,
Like an obscura,
Reminding him of lilies,
In rainy season and gestures of true love,
He walked out of his prison paradise,
Greet all sailors with steady embrace,
'Hurray!!! Say the sailors,
With triumph, he walked into the city,

In communion with the first and final,
Origin,
In the new aboard-home,
Overlooking us,
Candour and aesthetics,
Of line-up mansions,
In the desert of eternity,
And peaceful and external,
Universe.

The Process of transition or dying, leaving the shell and scale of physical matter here into the ribbon of spirit, into the spirit matter of the other world or life-after death is a universal meta physical reality, a universal in metaphysics, in African philosophy, Indian philosophy, Chinese philosophy and western philosophy save that salvation in life after differs as much as salvation in this life. Salvation at death means dying into nobility or heaven but unsalvational death means dying into poverty of spirit and soul or transmigration into totemic world of sacred animals and pythons or lower spirit forms and elementals in the waters, rivers, forests, groves, mountains, deserts and valleys. This is universal reality in all metaphysics. To quote Emmanuel Swedenborg:

> After death, immediately on their arrival in the world of spirits peoples are precisely classified by the Lord. Even people are promptly attached to the Jewish community where, as to their ruling love they were during their life in the world, and good people are promptly attached to the heavenly community where, as to their love and charity and faith, they were during their life in the world.[199]

The world is a spirit and the universe a macro spirit under the control and guidance of the ultimate, God. Man is one of the many spirit forms and persons among rivers, waters panpsychic and pantheistically incarnated forces and objects that make up the universe. The spirit man has the capacity of immanence and transcendence in self-realization or in unification with divine universal being. Man could also descend to the lowest forms of life in incarnations of spirit elementals or animal totems, birds, trees waters, etc. Therefore at death, a spirit person could ascend to a higher being or descend to lower spirit things. To quote Swedenborg again,

---

[199] Ibid.,

"The world of spirits look like a valley among mountains and cliffs, with deep and rises here and there. The doors and gates to heavenly communities are not visible except to people who have become ready for heaven. Other people do not find them. For a given community there is a single way that divides into several as it climbs. The gates and doors to the hells are not visible except to people who are about to enter; for these people they are opened.[200] In Africa philosophy death is not annihilation of life; it is a migration to life beyond. African philosophy of death agrees, if not the original thought, with a lot of Western and Christian thinkers on good life as a preparatory disposition to a better life here after. It is African to say, as Socrates said in *Crito* that the *really important thing is not to live, but to live well,* and in *Apology*, that *the gift of prophecy comes most readily to men at the point of death.*

---

200 Ibid.

Chapter 3

Cosmopolitan African Philosophy

GLOBALIZATION AND AFRICAN IDENTITY*

This has been a historical erosion of African identity and authenticity through the processes of colonialism, neo-colonialism and imperialism. Globalization is skeptically viewed as another phase of political and economic neocolonialism. Enculturation and acculturation are out of the question because they are supposedly tentacles of imperialism. But Globalization ideally is the philosophy of a cosmopolitan city that benefits all races; no centre and periphery nations, where every race match up and down without fear or favour in the Global express ways and village; where multiculturalism, plurality and diversity diffuse the problems of racism, ethnicity and gender. Globalization in the sense of real and even development is predicated on intercultural philosophy.

Definition of conceptual terms

It is rather scientific to recognize these otherwise technical terms, 'Globalization' and 'African identity' by offering them as universally as possible working definitions and assumptions without which the objective of this thesis which is to locate Africa necessarily and sufficiently in the global village will not be achieved. We shall adopt that globalization is a process by which a network of cultural, political and economic advantages and interests of the different peoples of the world work naturalistically for their mutual benefits. It is expected that in this regime of social change, the identities of different races and people of the world, if they exist, would merge, clash or conflict to the disaster of global peace and unity, irrespective of the contributions of science and technology to the advancement of the standard of life generally on the planet. As mankind look up to the social change called globalization to embrace, there are, however, many years and

---

*"Globalization and African Identity" was first published in *Essence, Interdisciplinary – International Journal of Philosophy,* No. 5, 2008.

apprehensions, some of the foremost which are ethnic and race identities, self-preservation, racial pride and survival, political and economic sovereignty, self-determination and cultural and religious freedom.

Against the above questions impinging on the mind and personality of prospective participants in the drama of communications, cultural and scientific exchanges involved in globalization, choices have to be made and freewill exercised. The natural problem races, nations and peoples would have with globalization is definitely going to border on the metaphysical problems of free will, cause and effect or determinism, all collectively or severally encroaching upon the uncompromising virtues of liberty in the "reactive attitudinal aesthetics of love, respect, gratitude, resentment, indignation and hatred..."[1] mentioned in the path-breaking essay of Peter Strawson called the 'reactive attitudes'. There is again the question of moral control and responsibility in the global village; would persons or races in the cosmopolitan market have the freewill and liberty of self control and moral responsibility for every bit of their reflexes and movement? The moral and social predicament of the African identity in the global configuration is best illustrated by Joel Femberg metaphor of unlocked and locked switches and open opinion. He says,

> we can think of life as a kind of maze of railroad tracks connected and disjoined, here and there by switches. Wherever there is an unlocked switch which can be pulled one way or the other, there is an open opinion, wherever the switch is locked in one position the opinion is „closed'. As we clung along over various tracks in the maze, other persons are busily locking and unlocking, opening and closing switches, thereby enlarging and restricting our various possibilities of movement...[2]

This metaphor is somehow and somewhat implicated in the international politics of globalization. It is imperative to observe a fundamental condition for a global and free interplay of the forces of cultures and religions which is that there be no switches at all, not to talk of the switches being locked and that the global era be characterized by open

---

[1]Fischer, M. J., "The metaphysics of freewill," in *Aristotelian Society Series*, vol. 14. (Blackwell, U.S.A., 2004) p.2

[2] Feinberg, Joel. "The interest in liberty on the scales," quoted by Fischer, ibid p.4.

opinion, but if mechanistic view of the world were correct, determinism would have no room for personal choice, hence freewill will be a delusion.

The identity question, apart from the associated problems of freewill and choices, is a big problem itself, because as human nature, its predictions can or cannot be about its substance and hope. Prediction is much more possible in the inorganic, but less in the organic and, in particular, human thought and action. In considering the organic, the maternal sphere of human actions and behaviours, no two objects are even quite the same in character let alone in time and space, so classification of behavioural phenomena is itself subjective and unpredictable. This can be especially prejudicial with respect to the classification of humans according to religion, race or gender which is based on the fictional assumption that similarity equals 'sameness'. Determinism has its limits just as mathematics which is the quantitative language of science, has been shown to have limits to its logical validity. At a sub-atomic level, the deterministic relationship between 'cause' and 'effect' breaks down completely and the laws of probability comes in to help qualify the uncertainty of forecasting by replacing relationships between variables with relationships between probabilities distribution of variables."[3] Similarly, the science of probability is also quantitative and, therefore, is still fictional tool too. Determinist model seem therefore, a construct of human mind to buttress freewill, choices, identity and personal predilections, so when determinism is used to represent the real world-which seems to be fundamentally indeterminate in its character it can be very misleading"[4] especially in explaining issues about the developed and underdeveloped. Can mathematics thread where science has failed, that is, in the area of race differentiation and inequality, since it is the quantitative language of science? The answer is equivocal, not categorical. Mathematics according to Stewalt "was born of our relentless search for order in the universe, even though it has perhaps no ultimate order and is, therefore, only an invention of our own minds."[5] Therefore it might be quite erroneous to assume it can tell us absolute truths about the world.

---

[3] Godel, quoted Faupal, John. "The Freewill myth and its consequences." in Essence Interdisciplinary -International Journal of Philosophy, No. 5, 2008, pp. 1-15

[4] Ibid.

[5] Stewalt, quoted by Faupal, John. "The free will myth and its consequences"." in *Essence, Interdisciplinary International Journal of Philosophy*, No. 5, 2008, pp. 1-15

Identity, Freedom and Determinism

Any moment we cogitate on the possible beginnings with regard to identity, colour and race, we tend to cognitively sink into the abyss of the unknowable world as far as cause and effect is concerned. This is perhaps, why John Faupal, in his paper, 'Freewill, Myth and its Consequences' argues that "underterminacy seems to be intrinsic to the evolution of life itself. After all, an amazing diversity of spaces that have evolved over countless generations from their humblest beginnings indicates that any 'cause' must have an underterminate number of possible effects."[6]

In other words, 'causes' have their ripples effects which are again subject to chance variation in the Darwin sense of diversity of species and identities, and perhaps, struggle for the survival of the fittest. There is the tendency to reduce all colours, races and identities to one being, oneness of humanity, while carefully avoiding *reduction absurdum*. In so doing, there are still possibilities of chance and determinate episode in choices, opportunities and evolution. Faupal says, "nature does not but 'choose' to change over time, it does so by chance variation about parental norms so that those variations themselves become new norms from which, again, chance variation occurs in the next generation. And whether any of these variations survive or not depends largely on their compatibility to the environment in which they find themselves again by chance..."[7] Globalization phenomenon could be an evolutionary chance or determined process of reducing diversity to unity or oneness of being in the global village. The notion of 'being' here is the philosophic notion that denotes "something that is existing and the totality of really existing things the sustaining reality."[8] In the global arena, the problem should not be diversity but how the different existents or people can be reconciled in one by interaction, mutual understanding and compromises in the cosmopolitan city with one common necessity and equal freedom for self-determination and growth, thus in the sense of which 'freedom is the realization of necessity.' Hence, "thoughts, effects and actions of people emanate from natural (divine) necessity. If we do not know nor realize it we are not free but if we realize and know it our actions and thoughts will be free. Freedom is the realization of the necessity, the following of the necessity, it means going

---

[6] Faupal, John, *op. cit.*

[7] Ibid.

[8] See Solodukho, N.M., *Philosophy of Nonbeing*, Tupoler Kazan State Technical University Press, 2002, p. 138

the way of necessity."[9] Isn't evolution an intrinsic process of freedom, trial and error-elimination just as scientific progress has been? as Karl Popper would have asked? One can surmise that the series of cause and chance events that produced plurality and diversity are by the modern norm of science pulling every bit of them together again- the black, the mixed black, the white and the mixed white, by the same process of trial and error-elimination implicated in the globalization process.

Attribution of white and black is not only a moral problem but also a hereditary complication with morally laden overtones; whereby we put ourselves before or after others out of freewill and moral choices that discriminate among species of one humanity. Therefore, the question of identity was born out of the crisis of existence, moral burden and choices. It is possible choices are consciously made on the bases of colour, identity, race because they are products of heredity and accumulated experience. This questions the authenticity of 'free and independent will' to make or declare such moral choices or pronouncements. Exactly how and when man consciously came to make moral jugdements on the bases of identity black and white has created a problem of socio-anthropological and neurological nature that, for Faupal, finds an answer in the history of man, ten thousand years ago or thereabout, when such beliefs were unreasonably absent in human thoughts. The palaeolithic man or the hunter-gathers seem to have behaved simply according to tradition, rather than adhering to any consciously constructed codes of morality. "Therefore, all feelings we now have about human behaviour that imply an ethos of morality with its associated connotations of reward or punishment do not seem to have existed in the minds of palaeolithic man."[10] All the accidents of history with regard to individuals, nations and African identity in the evolutionary ripples might have been the functions of first cause, free will and chance. Developed or underdeveloped, backward and forward were all predicate of lack of free-will, will, reason or chance in the struggle for the survival of the fittest. John Faupal, in his paper made some remarks that painted a picture of the moral anthropological, neurological and methodological problems to be tackled by globalization before the veil cast over mankind by race, colour and identity questions could be wiped away. He says, ever since the birth of the city-state

---

[9] See Kazhimurat, Abishev, "Freedom as a human's being", A paper presented to the World Congress of Philosophy, Istanbul WCP 2003.

[10] Fuapal. John, *op. cit.*

we have become conditioned to believe we were capable of exercising free will in our choice of social conduct and should therefore be rewarded or punished accordingly, yet, we still seem no nearer to achieving better standards of harmony and peace with each other than are any of the other species of flora and fauna. The evolutionary process of trial and error-elimination by which all nature has evolved seems to apply equally to that of all human thought and action and hence to our own destiny."[11] Freewill in international relations and mutual co-existence of mankind therefore, seems to be non-existence directly, because civilization and progress of mankind is a natural process and secondly in the interlocking *Egos* of races and nations some wills of nations and races will superimpose on the will of others.

Globalization as cultural imperialism

It is against the above background that globalization is seen as a natural outcome that negated the fictional or created boundaries and identities among human race. Globalization is "a light or ray beaming from one end to a galaxy of uninformed, unmoved worlds. Yet it is a philosophy of a village of nations and homosapiens starting from somewhere but no where because it is a philosophy of change for an interconnected network of a people in the universe."[12] I see globalization as an innate cognitive instructive process of man which the ancient African partook. Hence, the first phase of globalization is the ancient phase when man had the natural impulse and prompting to communicate economically and culturally within his imaginable and known world or universe. Drawing from the actions of Gbusaizu Dukor, high chief and priest, an ancient African elder with intellectual sagacity, this phase is called the animistic globalization.[13] In addition to the animistic phase are the phases of empires and slavery, colonialism, Western technology and the current globalization process characterized by social and economic integration of people of the world through information, communication and science. Apart from the African version, Anshi Martin and Jando Francisca in their paper, *Preserving African Identity in the Global Process,* traced the phenomenon back to the month of May of the year 34 B.C.E. when a Macedonian war Lord, Alexander the great (336-323), with his great array of soldiers and military generals, initiated a

---

[11] Ibid.

[12] Dukor, M., "Globalization and Social Change in Africa" *Essence*, Interdisciplinary - International Journal of Philosophy, No. 5, 2008 pp16-48

[13] Ibid.

ground programme of unification of the Macedonians and Persians in one kingdom to make them one people and the dissemination of Greek language, culture and way of life among all peoples of the earth, moved in part by the Ray-Hellenic ideal, which he inherited from, his teacher, Aristotle, according to which Greek culture was superior to all others, and influenced by vastly more mundane motives."[14] These two scholars share the view that there is need for a conscious and aggressive rediscovery and integration of the African identity in the current global process with African contributions to science and technology, the main plank and axis of globalization. Chris Tagbo Ugwu argues that African identity in this era of globalizations and in all the previous phases suffered a serious eclipse because of the imposition of Western religious beliefs and practices to the decapitation of the African religious beliefs and practices.[15] For them the preservation of African identity means restoration and repropagation of African religious beliefs on God, gods, ancestors, in short, animistic practices (or theistic panpsychic animism) as against its inferior and devalued spectacle created by the European because the religion is naturally and supernaturally equipped with survival instincts amenable to globalization.

In globalization, the identity of minority ethnic groups among nations is as important as the identify question of races among races. Zaato Mathew Knor identified the two sided nature of the phenomenon which are respectively pro and against the minority identities in Nigeria and perhaps worldwide. "Globalization is seen "as a magic word to pull Africa out of the doldrums of underdevelopment and other related problems. On the other hand, it is criticized for being neo-imperialist and neo-colonialist."[16] In a globalized world, ethnic identity is mostly one unique element that is usually under threat. "All ethnic groups, be it so called majority or minority, easily identify their ethnicity by their cultural values which are sacrosanct to them. In other words, ethnic groups identities find meaning in their cultural forms, social situation, history and kinship system that make up their social intercourses. As a result, it is only through the cultural variables of the different ethnic groups that their identities become manifest for an empirical

---

[14] Wang, A.M., and Jando, Francisca, "Reserving Africa identity in the Global process," in Essence interdisciplinary -International Journal of Philosophy, No. 5, 2008, pp.48-61

[15] Tagbo, C. Ugwu, "The Eclipse of Africa identity: Religion on lens of the camera". in *Essence* interdisciplinary international journal of philosophy, No. 5, 2008 pp62-73

[16] Knor, Zaato, M.," Identity of minority ethnic groups in Nigeria in the face of Globalization," in *Essence*, interdisciplinary -international journal of philosophy, No. 5, 2008, pp.74-94.

observation."[17] Views like this have taken the position of preservation of culture as the hallmark of peoples' identities, yet in the global culture of science hence identity of minority ethnic groups in Nigeria, just like their counterparts in other nations, are therefore threatened by two evils, namely, internal colonialism and imperialism and other form called globalization resulting from external forces of change. The minority languages/cultures or groups so threatened by this double tragedy are according to Knor Oron, Ibibio, Eket, Urhobo, Esan, Ukwale, Ijaw, Kana, Abua, Itsekiri, Ibibio, Calabar, etc., Zaato Knor is of the opinion that the minority ethnic groups in Nigeria or elsewhere must be made sacrosanct even in the globalized world by a deliberate government policy towards the preservation of minority ethnic cultures through the education and empowerment of their languages as well as sensitivity to ethnic cultural identity respect and dignity. Benedict Michael revisits the challenges posed by information technologies on African cultural identities. He argues that "from the ethicizing perspective, African identity appears as the emphatic politicized condition for participation in intercontinental processes of communication, knowledge, production, co-operation, intervention. From the development perspective, "African specificity used to be underplayed in favour of universalism in science, economics, and in societal and constitutional matters. These two simultaneous movements led each to a different appreciation of such cultural programming as structures everyday life, political organization, and forms of production, world views and religious practices."[18] He argues that computer technology will not favour the growth of African philosophy and culture because the digital system in general including the language proposition, syntax and semantic of computer technology are the mindset of Western culture imposed on another culture. It is viewed as another form of Europeanization of Africa through European mental construct, reminiscent of the philosophical theories in the time of mercantilism, imperialism and colonialism when "the 'African' was constructed in Western thought as the other par excellence, another to whom such philosophical insights in the human conditions, and such human rights as derived from such insights, scarcely applied."[19] In similar tone Bamgbose J Adele, argues that it was in

---

[17] Ibid.

[18] Benedict, Michael, "The Influence of Information Communication Technologies on African Philosophy and Culture," Essence interdisciplinary -international journal of philosophy, No. 5, 2008, pp.95-109.

[19] Ibid.

the process of developing African communities that Africans were forced to deviate substantially from their indigenous governing systems of government."[20] According to him the imposition of foreign culture destroyed some symbols of culture. For instance, in pre-colonial societies in Africa, certain symbols of culture were reserved for those managers of institutions whose responsibilities was to guard the tradition of these societies. The checks and balances that were inherent in the indigenous rulership in Africa, the children's moonlight play and respect that the young ones give to the elders have all been subdued by colonialism and imperialism.

On the other hand, when people are receptive of change or Western civilization, it is termed a form of globalization in a negative sense. In other words a receptive or dynamic or porous culture that assimilates easily the Western type is portrayed in the negative sense. Nnedum O.A. and Ezeokana O. J. criticized the emerging African culture from this negative perspective. They say that the psychological influence of globalization on the cultural life of the Africans especially the Igbo people of Nigerian is an epitome of humanitarian crisis that results to the destruction of cultures and existence of African people. Among the Igbo people of Nigeria this culture is viewed "as *odinani* on the one hand and *omenana* on the other hand. Culture viewed as *odinana* has rational practicality"[21] in the normative customs and mores. According to them the substantial knowledge and traditional experience of the Igbo people are conveyed through the medium of communication, language or expressed in idioms, metaphors, proverbs and so on.

In literature, philosophy and values, the current disposition among scholars is to globalize African values and metaphysics. There is the need to globalize African theistic panpsychic animistic rationality or what Onoba calls cultural imagery or mythical consciousness in Wole Soyinka's and Christopher Okigbo poems. Okigbo's poems are no less mythical or animistic than that of Soyinka despite the former gross disposition to Western pattern of poetry. Both goddish and theistic animistic transcendentalism runs through their poems informing their respective

---

[20] Bamgbose, J., Adele. "Globalization as An Impediment to African Culture." *Essence*, interdisciplinary -international journal of philosophy, No. 5, 2008,pp. 110-124

[21] Nnedum, O.A. and EzeUkana. O.J. "Globalization and Cultural Expectation in Igbo Cultural Area of Nigeria." Essence interdisciplinary -*International Journal of Philosophy*, No. 5, 2008, pp.1125-143.

pretentions to originality. Examples of this abound in Soynika's *Idanre* and Okigbo's *Labryinths.* The goal, advertently or inadvertently, of this in African literature is a commitment to the preservation of African identity as a contribution to the global pull. Soyinka is notably more astitute in this agenda as exemplified in his outburst in a threatened aircraft: aboard a plane, that ran into turbulence throwing the passengers into panic; each passenger cried out to God, fanatically shouting 'Jesus' and 'Allah' respectively, but Soyinka sought safety in *Ogun*, the Yoruba god of iron, saying, *omoogun ni nu, ogun o ni pa omo e* (I am *Ogun's* son ogun can't kill his own son).[22] However, some aspect of African culture which has been considered by eminent feminists as not worth globalizing is women subjugation. African culture is largely blamed for being responsible for the plight of women in Africa. J. N. Okoye observes that women in Igbo society of Nigeria must be "regarded as personalities and accorded the rights and respect, freedom and responsibility that go with dignity without any unjustifiable discrimination."[23] If anything has drawn the anger and dagger of women in this global flux, it is the African concept of widowhood which according to Okoye, is a state in which excruciating hardship influenced by tradition and culture is assigned to women whose husbands are diead. In most part of Nigeria, the thought of widowhood sends shivers down the spine of any woman. "Associated with widowhood are characteristics like physical and emotional depression, tension, anxiety, state of uncertainty, shock, insecurity of the future, mental distortion and financial difficulty."[24] Champions of women liberation in Nigeria have a predisposition or knack for a globalized African lady free from the cultural shackles in which African women are presently circumscribed in. Hence, globalization is an instrumental and existential phenomenon that will necessarily help in the liberation of African woman but less of African identity; a globalized African lady would be free from Africanist or theistic animistic cultural shackles. Nigeria's value system with regards to "the place of a woman is dominated by the interest and outlook of the socio-economic dominant class which determines the values

---

[22] Oriole, S.A., "Unraveling Meaning from the obscure..." *Essence* Interdisciplinary -International Journal of Philosophy, No. 5, 2008, pp. 144-160

[23] Okoye S.N., "Customary Practice against Widows in Nigeria. The Igbo Experience," *Essence* Interdisciplinary International Journal of Philosophy, No. 5, 2008, pp161-172

[24] Ibid.

of the society as a whole.[25] This class is no other than the male folks who usually tries to represent and sell its own values as the values of the entire society making the women folk believe that Nigerian value system is an organic community of interests shared by everybody, rich and poor alike. In controlling the means through which these values are communicated the members of the group ensure that those values which become widespread in Nigerian society are those which suit them best.[26] What is being pointed here is a particular aspect of African culture that is not dignifying and need to be dehydrated and replaced with a more edifying culture.

Globalisation as intercultural Philosophy

From the discussions and opinions x-rayed so far, for Globalization to become a cosmopolitan world 'philosophy', it must be predicated on interrelation of cultures or what some have called intercultural philosophy. Cultures develop in ethnic and national locations but at the same time interrelate with one another. This is why globalization "involves the problem of the universal and its relation to the particular, different and local."[27] It is a trend towards homogenization as against emphasis on individuality. Within cultural identities, there are some values which are shared by people, thus maintaining them locally and socially. In contrast to the relativist negation of universality, the protagonists of globalization argue for both particular and universal, focusing on their interrelation. Roland Robertson addresses the epistemological problem of combining both uniqueness and coherences. He shows that diversity, multiculturality and polyethnicity do no exclude forms of cultural unity.[28] It seems that most protagonists of national or ethnic culture and identity like Frantz Fanon agree with Roland Robertson on the "increasing global dramatization of ethnicitywithin-humankind."[29] Today, the recognition of diversity in gender, race, ethnicity and plurality of cultures is expressed in the idea of multiculturalism."[30] On the other hand, "the higher level of relations to others and their cultures implies an impartial view, accepting pluralism as a norm of life and recognizing others as equals, and a reciprocal

---

[25] Okediadi, N., "Nigerian Value System; the place of the woman," Essence *Interdisciplinary - International Journal* of *Philosophy*, No. 5, 2008 pp173-182

[26] Ibid.

[27] See Edward, Demechonok. "Intercultural philosophy" A paper presented at the XXI World Congress of Philosophy, Istanbul 2003.

[28] See Robertson, *Social Theory and Global Culture*, (London, Suge 1992) p.104

[29] Ibid.

[30] Edward, Demenchonak, *op. cit.*

understanding, rapprochements, and collaboration."[31] This has been described as interculturality, a term variously understood as "a mental and moral category, an attitude towards others, or a 'spirit' which approves the values of pluralism, diversity and difference."[32] It has been used to characterize culture philosophy, theology, politics, and pedagogy. Intercultural philosophy reflects on the impact of the cultural framework on philosophy, exploring the "fundamental differences of cultural coinages in the forms of thinking itself."[33] It brings to the forefront the problem of the interrelation between cultural specific and the universal in philosophy. However for some philosophers, the notion 'intercultural' seems incompatible with philosophy as a universal knowledge. However, a philosophy accepting intercultural dialogue as a context of its reflection enters inevitably into the process of large-scale transformation, which requires it to reconstruct its history, its methods and forms of articulation. The transformation creates conditions so that a philosophy is able to reach a universality prizing from shared communications between different cultural universes."[34] It can be forcefully argued, therefore, that the ideal of globalization as a universally accepted ideology and culture must be one erected on the pillars of multiculturalism, plurality and diversity. Epistemologically, it is a process and end product that would reconcile uniqueness and coherence, particular and universal into a unified whole or universe of mutual respect and dignity. In this postulated universe, diversity is recognized in gender, race and ethnicity and others will be recognized in a reciprocal understanding, rapprochements and collaboration.

Again Intercultural Philosophy would absolve the conflicts between the sacred and the secular in the postcolonial Africa and the world at large. The modern-day conflictual episode of the sacred and the secular is an accidental diversion from the evolution of the spirit leading to satanic incarnations in the form of the secular gods of human rule, instrumental rationality, technological rationality, monotheistic reason, etc., which are by and large representative manifestations of the dragon and the beasts which, in turn,

---

[31] Ibid.

[32] Mall, Ram, Adhar. Intercuktural Philosophy., "Lariham, MD: Rowman and Littlefield, 2000."

[33] Wimmer, Frantz, "Introduction to intercultural philosophy" Topoi, An Interbational Review of Philosophy, 17(1), 1998, pp.1-3.

[34] See Fornet-Betancourt, Raul. Transformation intercultural de' la filosofia. Ejerciciois teoricos prac hcos de filosofice intercultural desde latinoamerica en el contexto de la globalization. Bibbao: Declee, 2001

with their manifestations and influences constitute the contrary spirit to the Most High God. Evolutionary diversion of the spirit of the Most High God was caused by the enlightenment philosophy of the classical modernity because of the exaltation of reason above the preter-natural explanadum of the cosmic intelligence. The crisis of modernity with its spread in the economic stasis of developed and under developed nations and the conflict of the sacred and the secular in the societies of the world today is an epitome of the evolutionary end of reason and the re-triumph of the spirit. This 'spirit' is still in tack in African philosophy as the fundamental explanans of man and the physical world, explaining the conflict of the sacred and the secular originated in the West, and the enculturation and acculturations of Africa continent by Europe. The sacred and the secular existed in African philosophy not as separate categories in perpetual conflict but as two in one epistemological category. In Western philosophy the traditional problem of mind and body is as old as the problem of the sacred and the secular much as the origin of the later is traceable to the wider implication of the former. In African philosophy the oneness of the categories of mind and body is as old as the oneness of the sacred and the secular, hence, the absence of the conflict of these categories in African traditional societies; there is no traditional problem of mind and body, or the spiritual and the physical. The world is a spiritual arena. In African philosophy, the spiritual or the spirit is both the primary and second-order category that explains everything in the universe; therefore both the mind and body are one spiritual entity explaining why there is no distinction between the sacred and the secular and the absolute absence of the conflict between the two in the pre-colonial Africa. In African metaphysics, the body is a logical construct from the spiritual essence in the sense of platonic form and their physical correspondents or categories. There is no conflict, no disarray and no assymetrism between these two worlds; any conflict of any kind results to turning the table tumbling in the spiritual realm into space and time. That is why to understand, appreciate and honour God, the Almighty creator; Theistic Humanism is humanism unqualified with any kind of adjective or predicate like scientific humanism. 'Scientific humanism' presupposes secular humanism, very much the progeny of enlightenment and modernity in Western philosophy but veridically absent in the huge spiritual library of Africanity and logic of African philosophy. The theistic humanism addresses the core of African philosophy in African society totally bereft of the conflictual episodes of the phenomena, the secular and the sacred in the world of modernity, technology and reason without infinite soul-spirit. It can be argued that there cannot be humanism without theism, stream of consciousness, pantheism and animism. The question of, or the debate on, the conflictual or complementariness of faith and reason acquired its legitimacy from the age of instrumental reason in Western civilization, philosophy and history. Colonial experience transferred this philosophical burden to the African mind by virtue of the advancement in Western technology and imperialism which altered, diluted enculturalized and destabilized the continuum and asymmetry between faith and reason in African theistic panpsychic humanistic world view including its metaphysics, epistemology, politics, ethic and philosophy of history. The progress and decline in the various phases of Western civilizations denote the limitations of reason in accounting for human conditions at all times. Firstly reason, as agent of logic, can arrive at truth with certainty but cannot achieve absolute certainty except in conjunction with the absolute symbols of faith under the necessary and sufficient condition of the faith-cultural universe without which there would be conflict. The armour and torchlight of reason which is technological progress has as its ideological partners, the notions of liberty, equality and fraternity whose disfucntionality or their inability to be carried forward in the face of world economic political turmoil and economic crisis, has brought to an abrupt end the machinery of reasons and rationality. This is a situation where communalistic reason backed by faith is not allowed to synthesize the liberty, equality and fraternity of theistic humanistic universe as is the case in African culture. It has been argued that reason as a governor of society can secure freedom only by overriding the demands of equality, and if it attempts to secure equality it is obliged to strangulate freedom. The highest reason could achieve in the order of fraternity is temporary comradeship and pragmatic or utilitarian cooperation. Scientific and ethical experiences show that reason cannot arrive at any final truth because it cannot get to the root of things. It deals with the finite, the separate, the limited aggregate and has no measure for all and the infinite. Reason is the cause of things in general which cannot be exhausted by the finite mind. It is also an inquiry into what we know with certainty, with our cognitive capability. The epistemological limitations of human mind, therefore, have necessitated an inquiry beyond practical reason of science into the pure reason of rational faith in the nuomena called the supernatural. This is where most of us disagreed with Immanuel Kant on the impossibility of metaphysical knowledge. The Africna philosophical experience on the interplay of reason and faith is characteristically opposed to the naked instrumental reason, scientific reason, egostic reason, racist ego, evolutionary ego, modern civilization and cultural racism. In African philosophy, rational inquiry can go beyond science in form of pure reason to trace the root and objective subjective truth of things in the transcendental apperception of unity. Pure reason in the African theistic panpsychic humanistic calculus operates in the realm of the transcendental with their variables such as cultural symbolism, pantheistic faith, anthropomorphism and polymonotheism.

FEMINISM IN THEISTIC HUMANISM: THE QUESTION OF GENDER DISCOURSE IN AFRICAN PHILOSOPHY*

An inquiry into the ontology of critical gender consciousness in Africa Philosophy is long over due. 'Hitherto discourses on gender problems lost focus because of the tendency to leave out the gaps in culture created by colonial experience, modernity's assaults and unAfricaness in ontology and essence. It is argued here that the fulcrum for a legitimate feminist doctrine is Theistic Humanism, the philosophy of African philosophy that exposes the epistemological and metaphysical basis of the rightful and ethical place of women in the society without injury, injustice and abuse on womanhood. Theistic Humanism as an ontology and cosmology abhors class struggle between husbands and wives, sons and daughters, etc. Class struggle between men and women degenerated from the oneness of being ontology and Gender community where husbands and wives were happily married with different complementary social roles for the preservation of society.

Feminism and theistic humanistic superstructure

The question of feminism and gender discourses consequent upon historically perceived discriminations against women, though it has found cultural and critical normative relevance and positions in modernity, post modernism and history of Western civilizations, is hereby being analysed and discussed with the African metaphysical paradigm. This contribution to Gender discourse in Africa is an opening of another horizon but deeper substratum of the metaphysical, cultural and social ontology of feminism that justifies, validates and sustains womanhood in every social context in

---

* Feminism in Theistic Humanism: the question of gender discourse in African philosophy" was first published in *Philosophy Study, Vol. 3, No. 11,* 2013, USA and in Proceedings of the XXII World Congress of Philosophy, 2008, 28: 63-75

the society. In African society, the entire gamut of social relations is an effect of historical (diachronic) structural patterns originating from ontic infinity through a living immanence to future transcendental infinity, an apocalytic salvation. Justice therefore, is structured and sustained as a normative deontology that respects and distributes natural inclinations of creation and gifts of God on the platform of Theistic Humanism, (God and love of man). The question of gender discourse in African philosophy, in Theistic Humanism,[35] is the ontological place of women in the coherence and correspondence theory of justice and the gamut of social and ontological network of relations, values, politics and economics in African society. Feminism in Theistic Humanism is by this cognitive paradigm the question of women gender value in African Philosophy. Problems in the pre-colonial feminist gender social milieu in Africa are multifaceted and varied from place to place. There are female gender mutilations, relegation of women to the social, economic, political and cultural backyards, unavailability of equal opportunities extendable to the women, lack of women education. It should be taken note that these supposedly negative indices are fall out or neglected elements of Theistic pampsychic[36] social structure and norms, yet within the same structure were justifications that were inferred from the rock bottom of African culture and pre colonial experience. What African philosophy could offer to the global market is an explanation of that social order based on Theistic panpsychic humanistic philosophy. On the other hand the postcolonial and contemporary developments and modernist dispositions in Africa have brought with them additional problems to feminism. Such problems as women abuse with clubs and kanes, excessive rate of divorce, marital litigations, women slavery to foreign countries, rape, sexual harassment, the class struggle between men and women were added dimension in the plight of women in Africa.

The problem of gender discrimination either does not exist in African social structure or culture or is not understood properly as ‘post colonial

---

[35] Theistic Humanism is the philosophy of African philosophy encapsulating and unifying African cosmological and ontological views about the black man’s conceptions of God, nature and man as a trilogical teleology. It is the belief that man is the centre of the universe in appreciation of nature, the God’s gift to humanity. Theistic Humanism or African Humanism (ethnocentrically called) is, therefore, a non-atheistic Humanism that is predicated on the belief that God created man and has interest in his affairs always. For detail see Dukor Maduabuchi, Theistic Humanism.

[36] Panpsychism is often misconstrued as atheistic in western philosophy; so also is crimism. But panpsychism which I consider to be synonymous in content with pantheism and animism are truly authentic African philosophy concepts explaining the divine nature of the universe, its substances objects and modes with ultimate allegiance and unity in God.

social and ontological aberration.' This is the reason for current investigations into gender related concepts historically and contextually in Black Africa today. Be that as it is, a deeper philosophical investigation beyond the political, sociological, anthropological and cultural approaches that gloss over the existential import of every status, desert and relational calculus that underline the creative and justiceable relations between man and women and consequent interest actions and abuses, has become necessary. Despite the ontologies and cultural justifications for the existing or existed social gender order in Africa philosophy, there are two opposing and conflicting social gender problems in the colonial and post colonial African society; namely, the question of unequal ontological and social status between man and woman and secondly the extant abuses of women in the same black society, a social problem that, though had been subliminal, grew like a cancer with colonialism, christianity and modernity. To worsen this existing problem in Africa is the wave of gender disseminations against women in addition to the already existing problem in a gender separated society. Therefore, a successful social engineering aimed at redressing or reforming the contemporary African society will, of necessity, critically reconcile African culture and philosophy with the colonial, post colonial and globalized African.

Gender philosophy is the solution to gender problems and African gender problem requires African philosophy, *theistic Humanism* which is uniquely neutral. To get to the root of the problem it is necessary to approach it with sympathy and empathy by identifying and participating aesthetically, emotionally and spiritually with the people, or to state the obvious, in the context of what can be called African gender philosophy. African gender philosophy, for the avoidance of doubt and to be wholesomely contemporary and effective is a critical gender consciousness in contemporary Africa philosophy. Gender philosopy is a systematic and universal discipline of effective thinking about man and the universe yet it has to "derive much from all kinds of experiences", be it Western, African, Asian, so far as they are amenable to rational interpretation. This is because values and moralities, like feminism, so far as it is human, should be based upon universal positive self-validity. African gender philosophy or critical consciousness should be a set of propositions inferred from first, African personality and second, human nature in general. The primacy of African personality in gender critical study is not an ethnic approach lacking in universal self validity but a cultural product and outfit in a world of cultures and philosophies. On the other hand human nature in response to gender consciousness is predicated on a universal and generic concept of man in general and the reference framework is either African, Western or Asian personalities. This is because cultural personality is a generic product of human nature in general. When some philosophers of the empirical turn of philosophy distinguish human nature as objective, universal and abstract standard from particular cultural nature, they wrongly bifurcate the essence of man in the generic sense and philosophy as a unified common enterprise with common goal, but bearing different cultural sign posts. Again the over flogged separation of the abstract logical nature of philosophy from the transcendental supernatural philosophy in addressing the problem of mankind is ideological and contrary to the neutral status of philosophy and philosophy as the practice of wisdom or the exercise of the truth which is amenable to all human experiences, abstract, physical or supernatural. Therefore African gender consciousness and study as a philosophical enterprise is to exert values that recognize the women dignity, self-respect and self-determination in objective and self-evident manners.

Human nature is as mystical as the human cultural personality because the ultimate explanation, beyond the physical, is the metaphysical always captured by the 'I' or the '*Ego*' components of human cultural personality. Philosophy analytically and intuitively captures in a wholistic manner the human personality as a product of nature or God as well as a by product of culture. Philosophy knows no barrier in its methodology; neutrality is the torchlight of an authentic and result oriented philosophical enterprise. It recognises the physical and metaphysical components of man while the positivists and some empiricist failed to cognize the place of metaphysical in objective and physical explanations of things. Hence the empiricist and positivist comprehension of feminist ideology is largely empirical and non supernatural, while the African and the rationalist understanding of feminism is based on God's creation that created woman's nature in man's nature.

The metaphysical foundation of feminist discourse in pre-colonial African philosophy is therefore, that man and woman are two separate species in one, in the generic sense but physically endowed with different sexualities. Ontological differences that engender ontological and metaphysical inequalities are by creation non-existence, yet some of the ontological endowments have yielded to separate and different physical endowments and assignments on earth. The justification of this platform or paradigm for feminist discourse in Africa is again based on the unity of consciousness or the holistic personality of the African. In the concept of African conscious or holistic personality there is no ontological or metaphysical bifurcation of mind and body or soul and spirit, they are one spiritual entity. Interactionism could be the best technical explanation of the relationship between the mind and body; neither parallelism nor occasionalism. The interaction between the mind and body is not physical but spiritual, metaphysical and ontological. This is therefore the onotological justification for the theistic humanistic paradigm of feminist discourse in African philosophy.

Gender Discourse in Africa Epistemology

Gender discourse in Africa and in African philosophy should be based on a theistic charter that defines the system of values for which human beings interact and enter into association within the society. Every sex group is organized on the basis of some division of functions, pattern of distribution of privileges and duties. All technical skills, habits and legal standards acquired and accepted by different sex groups and which are embedded in the social and natural theistic environmental relationships are therefore concrete types of behaviours that are generated by ontological and metaphysical norms and rules provided by the theistic humanistic paradigm and charter. This theistic, perhaps, panpsychic humanistic feminist paradigm is functionally related to needs and these in turn related to ends or values of justice, freedom, equity and fairness. In African feminist paradigm and discourse survival is mutually and not exclusively distributed. These propositions form the epistemological basis of human relationships in general and in the special sense man and woman relationship. The metaphysical or epistemological foundation of African gender Philososophy is derived from the theistic panpsychic animistic African world view which Christopher Ukhun aptly couched in the following words: “in precolonial Africa, there was reverence for mother earth… the spiritualization of the relationship between humans and mother earth gave rise or brought about respect for non-humans[37] and by implications suggestive of the monistic modal explanation of oneness of being or African theistic animistic existentialism. African theistic existentialism is an expository and

---

[37] Ukhun, C., “The Problem of Ecofeminism in Africa: The oppression of Rural Men and women” in Ukhun C, *Critical Gender, Discourse in Africa* (Nigeria, Hope Publications, 2002) P.83.

hermeneutical turn in the epistemology which does not quest to defend the indefensible or engage in reforms, otherwise constructive or deconstructive, but excavate sublimmal enduring truths. This is basically ontological and should be tackled as such. Hence going by the aforementioned theistic animistic charter, we confront some of the controversial questions in the gender discourse in Africa.

The proposition that women are viewed or conceptualized as 'weaker' vehicle is an ontological 'obfuscation' of the role of the 'being' called women in the ontic galaxy of mutually inclusive, equal, interdependent existents. This realm of theistic divine animistic kingdom of ends as an order of mutually self respecting beings with dignity and natural justice where duties, responsibilities and roles are ontologically created for the sake of harmony and peace among the citizens of the earthly plane in this epistemological regime presuppose that "cultures make it the woman's duty to keep home,"[38] but this is a question beyond culture and in African case it is rooted in the continental epistemology. But from this same epistemological worldview, it is hardly a justified proposition that women are conditioned by any other thing other than the theistic animistic equality to be "dependent on men for their happiness and fulfillment in life."[39] Women are neither simply vessels nor irresponsible. Because of their ontologically and existentially assigned roles in their husbands' homes, it is a true proposition that "those who are married are respectable women"[40] in the society. The question of land inheritance" in favour of men is because land, as a mode or cardinal animistic theistic being is patriarchal in nature and conception.

Clitoridectomy or critically and derogatively speaking, „women's genital mutilation' is a controversial cultural issue whose justification is heavily embedded in the theistic animistic ontology and with the cosmic purpose of preparing the woman for her assigned role in domestic and public life (spiritual and political). It is because of specifically creative role of women that a number of actions, instrumental and analogical, emerged contrary to ontology of being. One is the prevention of women's promiscuity, an action based more on the need to equip women with the spiritual capacity for destined roles than because they are "more

[38] Nwankwor, Nkechi, *Gender Equality in Nigerian Politics* (Nigeria, Lagos, Deutche publishers, 1996) P 61

[39] Ibid.

[40] Ibid.

promiscuous or have less sexual inhibitions than men."[41] Propensity for sexual pervasion and moral deficiency happened to be one of those ontological and cultural reasons for the practice of clitoridectomy. The present trend of women vulnerability to trafficking in female sex and money all over the globe justified the reality and progostination of African theistic panpsychic animistic principle on women and men. It is in the same sense and for the same reason that women who naturally often fell into menstrual trance are assigned to perform spiritual worship and leadership.

Examining gender and class equality in African epistemology will yield glue picture of the truth about it in the context of animistic and hylozoic paradigm which is one of the ontological concepts of theistic panpsychic humanism. African Animism is the panpsychic conception that forces pervade the universe and objects of nature have panpsychic powers surrounding them. This idea, by implications, means that matter, which some scientists ordinarily treat as lifeless, has a psychic life which unites it with nature and the ultimate God. The radicals in the West have defended gender and class equality on the basis of animistic and hylozoic paradigm. The same principle is applicable in African philosophy where animistic forces in their numerical diversity ontologically represent democratic culture and equality of classes. Since in African philosophy, the spiritual or ontological world is superior to the physical world, the ontological equality is the bench mark for asserting the equality of men to women; hence difference that exist among men and women in the physical earth subsist as division of responsibilities to accord with man and woman's nature which are really not inequality. We can use the historical material to uncover some element of the African philosophy or theistic panpsychic animistic gender and class equality especially within the context of early interests in hermenticism and magic as well as the interests of the Renaissance Scientists and Philosophers like Galileo, Newton, Boyle and some contemporary scientists and philosophers like Albert Eastern in Mechanistic philosophy. Curiously enough, it seems that mechanism and Hermeticism indeed serve the ends of gender and class equality, that is, both from scientist point of view and African epistemology or theistic panpasychic animistic paradigm.

The passivity of matter argument certainly is not amenable to gender and class equality. It has been argued that Boyle's theological belief (rejection

---

[41] Ukhum, "On the moral Basis of clitoridectony in Africa," in Ukhum C., *Critical Gender Discourse in African* (Nigeria, Hope Publication 2002) P. 47 Rose-Mary Sergeant.

of animism and hylozoism) "were compatible with his ontological belief that matter, as it exist in the world after the initial creation, is causally active."[42] Hence that the passivity of matter is a fundamental principle of Bolye's mechanical philosophy or mechanism in general is suspicious. Yet the popular view or conclusion is that matter is causally active, hermeneutically, meaning that it is animistic having some force or power; the plurality which justifies democratic culture as well as gender and class equality in animistic ontology and social animism of African philosophy, save apparent differences resulting from culture. Therefore gender and class equality which is hermeneustically, thereby interpreted into the theistic panpsychism of African philosophy is also hermeneutically interpreted into the mechanistic philosophy of the scientific West by the activity of matter.

In order words the question of gender and class equality or inequality is an intrusion into the human nature, say in African philosophy, to say the least. Mechanistic and hermetic ontology presupposes gender equality by virtue of their psychic attribute and this abhors class struggles among husbands, wives, sons, daughters, yet, there are nature of ontological and natural distributions of functions, rights and privileges. Alternatively put, "The struggle for equal rights of the sexes is going to prove more difficult than decolonization because, in essence, it is a struggle between husband and wife, brother and sister, father and mother."[43] There are already class struggles between man and woman; this negates the philosophy of the African people where there is unity of purposes, attributes and functions of men and women; it is a negation of personhood, manhood, womanhood and Godhood in African philosophy of theistic panpsychic humanism. Hence the class struggle between men and women in African today is the outcome of a process of ontological degeneration or acculturation. This ontological retardation leading to the emergence of a class struggle could be represented in the following Venn diagrams, which I call '*Gender stress ontology Venn diagram.*'

---

42 Sex, Rose-Mary, Sergeant. "Review: Constructing Boyle's Gender Politics By Elibabeth Rotter" in *Meta Science*, Vol. 12, No.1 March 2003.

43 Rose, lyne, Hellew, Lung'Aho, "Ideology for the Liberation of women of Kenga," in Ukhum C. *Critical Gender Discourse in Africa* (Nigeria, Hope Publications 2002) p. 93.

Gender Stress Ontology Venn diagram

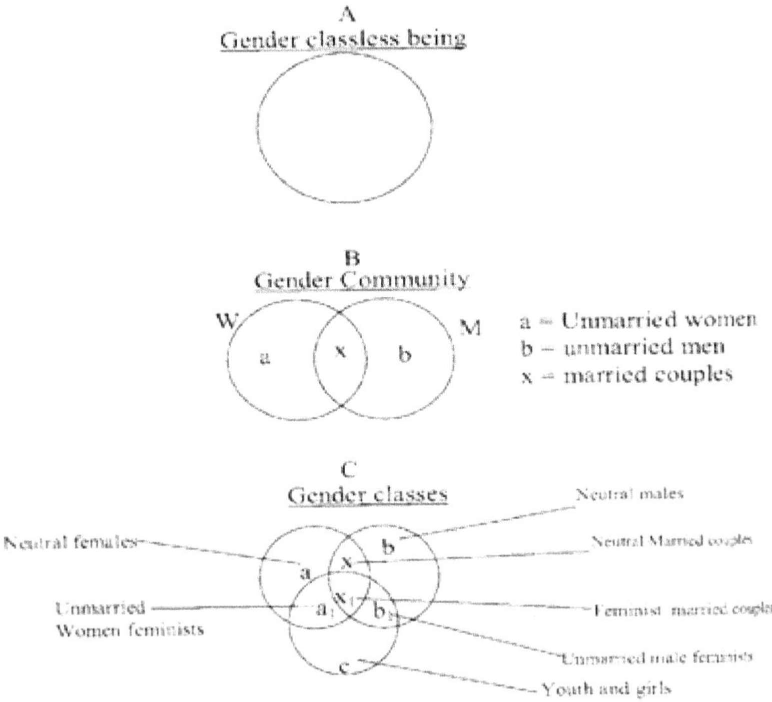

The above vein diagrams represent different faces of gender consciousness stresses in Africa spanning from gender classless ontological regime through gender community of balanced psychic and material order to gender class struggle. This is aptly the result of accelerated influence of acculturation and enculturation. The first stage A, is the state of being without male and female' differentiation. It is the innocent pristine state of man without the ontological significations or male and female differentiation and to show the oneness of human specie or humanity in African theistic panpsychic universe. On the other hand, B is the African gender community on earthly existence where men and women differentiation is for proposes of interaction, mutual and healthy procreations. The marriage between man and woman signifies unity and for the purpose of multiplying, elongating and preserving genealogical spirits and beings where the youths await for and look forward to entry into the society of X, the conjugal society of fathers and mother, and the community yet unborn. Finally C is a fallout of colonial experience where in the regime of acute male and women autonomies, without African ontological and existential responsibilities and wearing the mentality and bespectacle of the Western modernity's ontology, there emerged the class struggle between man and woman called women liberation within and outside marriages, in the social life of youths, in the schools and in the private sector and public life.

What African philosophy can therefore offer to the global market in gender discourse is Feminism in Theistic panpsychic humanism located within the universe of gender community, a classless social order devoid of class struggle with sufficient and necessary opportunities for women for the realization of their aspirations and goals in life. The problem of gender discourse in Africa is a language and semantic one in feminism which I think is the study of women's nature and women problems in special and peculiar circumstances different from women liberation which totally negates the female ontological existential commitments and which amount to confusions and class war. Feminist studies in Africa should rather concentrate on the examination of the denial of opportunities to women, lack of woman education, women slavery. The problems associated with widowhood and so on and so forth,[44] but certainly less of concentration on men's equality to women.

GLOBALIZATION AND AFRICAN DEVELOPMENT*

It is argued that a concept of Development that respects cultures, individualities and authenticities of races must be the answer to the inherent contradictions in Globalization the current worldorder. Despite the truce offered by the doctrine of postmodernism into the Western oriented public discourse on themes and motiffs of culture and development, such discourse still centres on economics, scientific and technological developments of Western prototypes. The nudging and prompting of culture and authenticity of African culture must co-exist with that of other races in the Global orbit. Hence any concept of development that negates the African prototype or the Asian is automatically out of the global process. In every culture and in particular African culture, there are scientific elements. Therefore, a culture

---

[44] For detail of the discussion on the appropriate gender studies see Dukor Maduabuchi, "How not to Empower women" in Dukor M (ed) *Philosophy and Politics. Discourse on values and power in Africa* (Lagos, Malt house Press ltd 2003).

* "Globalization and African Development" was first published in *Essence, Interdisciplinary International Journal of Philosophy, No. 4, 2007.*

of scientific, technological and economic development must be cultivated and propagated from within Africa in the global age.

Globalization and Authenticity

Existentialists of all shades from Martin Heiddager, Kierkegaard to Sartre were gospel preachers of 'authenticity'. Curiously enough, over time, over the ages, this message from thinkers of radical and humanist orientation has remained relevant to the world's motley of distinctive cultures. But the interpretation of cultural repose of authenticity is undermined by the existentialist gospel of authenticity as reality and freedom. More often than not, culture, well maintained, dies hard and is always static. Where then lies the reality of freedom of existentialism? Existentialist doctrine says men must choose the principles by which they live because existence precedes essence that is, men make their essences as they go along and do not live out a predetermined essence or blueprint.[45] For Frantz Fanon, every generation of a people must out of relative obscurity discover its mission, fulfil it or betray it.[46] If men live their essences and if on other breadth men discover their essences which one is the African predicament? Today, in this age of post modernism, public discourse still centres on economics, scientific and technological developments of Western prototypes. But the nudging of culture and authenticity of the African has the need to co-exist with the Western propelled jet-age. Hence, there seems to be somewhat a contradiction in the concepts of development and authenticity that negates the African prototype.

Across the length and breadth of Asian and African communities there is that conscious and inexorable desire by the people to preserve their aboriginal cultures, retain their identity and live the authentic life. The authentic question is not only a cultural question but also a development question. If that is case, we have to review the relations between the triad problem of authenticity, culture and development. If according to the existentialists, men are free and live or act out their essences as they go along in their life Odysseys, what then is the relevance of all the cultures and traditions we celebrate when we are reminded by a contrary culture of Western science and development that culture and tradition are negative and static? Cultures particularly in doubt are the carnivals, feasts masquerades

---

45 See "Existentialism" in A.R. Lacey, *A Dictionary of Philosophy* (Routledge and Kegan Paul, London) pp. 63-64.

46 See Frantz, Fanon, *The Wretch of the Earth.*

and jamborees that only show the primitive mentality of pre-civil society of the Africans. This line of reasoning is with due apology to the concept of culture as the bedrock of scientific and technological development.

Is there any way we can establish that existentialism is cynical of cultures that re-enact, remember and refuse to die? Here is a further existentialist world-view. "Men are conscious of their contrast between themselves and things, of their eventual deaths, and of their power to choose and become what they are not."[47]

This leads to the notion of 'not-being', or 'nothing' which the existentialist treat as a thing of condition in its own rights.

According to the existentialists, sometimes this 'nothing', and sometimes the contingency of things in general, provoke an emotion or condition of *despair, angst, and angoisse*. If men have power to choose and become what they are not then they should discard their cultures which 'add nothing new.' They should look forward to what they are not in terms of new cultures in the process of 'becoming'. Heraclitus, a presocratic philosopher of note, pre-dated the existentialists in this line of thought in his impermanence theory of 'flux'.[48] Hence this notion of 'not being', nothingness', 'flux', 'becoming' as condition in its own right would regard cultural carnival as a transitory and temporally phenomenon that would not have been of any significance since it would be a state of 'nothingness'. It all means that the essence of all things, including the festivals and cultures we celebrate are so contingent to be 'nothingness'. So why the dances, drumming, masquerades, dressing, songs, and habits of the ancients which are today being re-enacted with pageantry and pomp? For the existentialists, they are all states of 'unbecoming'.

In the context of existentialism, therefore, national culture and authenticity inherent in it are all 'nothingness'. It also renders 'nothingness' the Frantz Fanon contention that 'each generation must, out of relative obscurity discover its mission, fulfil it, or betray.' In underdeveloped countries the resistance to the erosion of national culture by colonialism would existentially be of no use. Indeed, the highly volatile issue this discourse on existentialism has generated is that there is nothing like preservation of African culture. It also means that theories like Negritutude,

---

[47] A.R. Racey, ibid.

[48] See Rex, Warner, *The Greek Philosophers* (New York, A mentor Boak from American library, 1958) pp 25-29

Africanism, and a host of other theories that have a tendency to re-echo African past are nothing but non-existent things since they are neither nothingness' nor 'becoming'. If a true explanation of the world and authenticity is existentialism; then all the talks about European, African and Asian cultures would be empty. Hence, authentic life does not reside in the nudgings of culture and the re-enacting of the past. It goes to show that the concepts like cultural matrix, nostalgia and narcissism would be nothing but concepts of dread, despair, anguish, angst and *angoisse*. As existentialists, we should, please, forget the past and face the future with creativity and freedom.

The Nonpartisanship of Globalisation

One prime benefit of globalization is its envisaged general value to mankind as a whole, hence the debate on its universal suffrage has been hinged on whether it is actually a non-partisan development locomotive, nonracial and non ideological. The debate partly stems from its cultural implications which tend to obfuscate the real agenda of the phenomenon and project; what scholars and concerned persons have diagnosed as the imperialist and neo-colonial agenda on the part of the West. However, Ikechukwu, Nwakaeze Ogugua and Oduah I.C., argue that "the receding of geography, the shrinking of space-time for contacts, etc., weaves a delicate web-like nature of our interdependence and shared vulnerability, although the global seems localized and the local globalized. This scenario x-rays the present image of our current world order. This process moves at an unprecedented and immeasurable speed, it is no doubt inevitable and irreversible."[49] They identised the analytic approach to globalization which sees the individual and the market as the heart of the leap into modernity, Secondly as a process that results from the internal mechanism of growth in capitalism, thirdly as monopoly that goes beyond the regulations of nation which is identified by cybernetic materiality. They also articulated the economic, the political, the information and cultural kinds of globalizations, most of which according to scholars are neo-colonialist, imperialist and enculturalist. Yet, those authors recognized the unavoidable question of the philosophical and universal foundation of globalization in materialism which is that matter is the primal element justifying universalism and equality; monism which is that there is

---

[49] Ogugua, I. M. and Oduah, I.C., "Globalization and Development," in *Essence Interdisciplinary - International Journal of Philosophy*, No. 4, 2007, pp.1-25.

one and only one feature of the universe; Darwinism anchored on the principle of the survival of the fittest and self preservation; naturalism which presupposes a monistic and universal conceptions of phenomenon and reality and consumerism which as an emphasis on pleasure and material justifies the non spiritual goal of globalization. Yet globalization has emasculated cultures of the peripheral bringing about development to the west while spreading alienation and poverty through IMF, World Bank, etc.

In talking about development, one must bear in mind that the concept is a holistic concept which manifest the cultural, the political, the social and the scientific, even the scientific is embedded in the cultural substratum of the social and the political, hence all are interwoven. It is within this context that attention is hereby drawn to the question of corruption and unethical practices in the public sphere as an integral problem of development in general. Jimmy O. Chijioke argues that "the problems of good governance, transparency and accountability are increasingly receiving both natural and international attention. This is so because the solution to these problems is a condition precedent to tracking and reporting the related problems of corruption and unethical practices, especially in the public service, at both national and international level or at global level.[50] The recognition of the negative international import of corruption and unethical practices in the public life has valued globalization as a mechanism and instrument for a universe fight against the evil. "World wide international cooperation is required to fight the monster. With the globalization of the economy and internationalization of crime, international cooperation among governments and institutions has become more urgent in the fight against corruptionand other forms of unethical practices both in the public and private sectors.[51] While looking at globalization from the optimist contention that will bring real development and accountability in public offices, it is important to look also at the pessimist's contention that it has not brought real development in terms of social and economic empowerment to some people. This is the view expressed by Henry Ekyor. He argues that globalization has increased interconnectivity, communication, transactions and trades among various nations. Many nations have benefited more from these new developments than others. The greatest beneficiaries are multinational corporations from

---

[50] Chijioke, J., "Evolving Global mechanism for Tracking and Reporting Corrupt and Unethical Practices". Essence interdisciplinary -*International Journal of Philosophy*, No. 4, 2007, pp.25-50

[51] Ibid.

the developed world who have penetrated every nook and corners of this earth with their products and activities. Most of them have discarded the basic international rules governing their operations. Their intention is to maximize their profits. The activities of the multinational companies in the Niger Delta have devastated the area..."[52] He chronicled the underdevelopment globalization has brought upon the Niger Delta region of Nigeria as follows: oil spillage in the area; gas flaring; high rate of unemployment; health hazards and the fear of extermination; the diffusion of culture; the pollution of the Ijaw culture; the mode of dressing and the adoption of English names; prostitution; the profit motives of multinational corporations; increase in violence and cultural imperialism.[53] Against this background the cause of development and not underdevelopment as a result of globalization should be pursued by reversing the later in concrete, official and pragmatic ways.

While it is necessary for the benefits of globalization to flow from the centre to the periphery in terms of the instruments for the fight against corruption, there are however certain things of cultural nature that has been flowing and will continue to flow from the periphery to the centre. In the area of Arts and Aesthetics in general, it is hard to deny that Africa has an indestructible reservoir of which she contributed to the world civilization by way of globalizing African Arts and Sculpture, which at any rate, is theistic Panpsychic animistic. It has been argued that "African art was part of globalized visual culture, long before globalization was formed."[54] C.E. Nwanna argues that

> the systematic collection and preservation of African art started with the African contact with the Europeans, this trend of collection and documentation of African art has continued till today... Although there has been the movement of goods (including art works) from sub-saharan Africa to Europe through the trans-Saharan trade before the 10th century A.D., the globalization of African arts started with the systematic collection of African arts by the Europeans around the 14th century A.D.[55]

---

[52] Ekyor, Henry, "The Dynamics of Globalization on culture: A case study of Niger Delta in Nigeria," Essence interdisciplinary -*International Journal of Philosophy*, No. 4, 2007, pp. 51-66.
[53] Ibid.
[54] Nwana, C.E., "The Politics of Globalization in Relation to Rituality," Essence interdisciplinary - *International Journal of Philosophy*, No. 4, 2007, pp. 67-75
[55] Ibid.

This process of inadvertent globalization of Arts has been described by scholars as cultural imperialism. "As the European imperialists scramble for Africa territories in search of agriculture, minerals and strategic naval ports, they also looted African arts and carried them to Europe."[56] Today, modern African arts are being globalized as they became manifest in the mid-twentieth century with art works created by African artists who had attended European art schools or art workshop that were Western influenced. Therefore, in this era of globalization African visual art will remain one of the greatest contributions of the Africans to scientific knowledge. Beyond visual arts, and the contributions of Professors Chinua Achebe and Wole Soyinka in literature, drama and poetry, the African Artistory has a lot to showcase in the global village. For example, here are Obiora Ude*chukwu* artistic themes; 'Under Younger Eyes: Re-reading the Works of Obiora Udechukwu , Palm Wine Tapper, 1964, Still Life with Bicycle 1964, Still Life with Rainboot 1964, Shoes 1967, Mother and Child 1964, Still Life with Spray 1964, Boy Reading 1964, Study of an Orange Branch 1968...Others are Iri Aha (war dance) 1985, Watermaid 1976, Music Ensemble 1981, Self Portrait 1970, Nne Ochie 1969, Yacht 1977, Mai Ruwa 1980, Dreams of a Cattle Boy 1985, Girl at the Mirror 1985, River Queen 1985, etc."[57] In like manner the contribution of African literature, drama, poetry and visual art to Globalization is the philosophy of theistic panpsychic animinsim. In arts and sculptures it is the same, there is a lot the Africans can contribute to the global village from its tradition and culture. Religion, though a universal phenomenon has many things in it unique to every culture and tradition. The uniqueness of culture in the area of religious priesthood is, therefore, worthy of recognition not only but individuals but also by the world ecumenical bodies, Christianity and Islam. This is the sense in which Uche Chizaramargues that African priests "Offer explanations to the problems of meaning of life and other mysteries associated with human existence."[58] He however, observed that one of the problems or difficulties in globalizing African priesthood is related to the spread of Christianity, Western civilization and changing conditions that make deities loose their priests and worshippers. They are sinking into the limbo of oblivion and inattention and

---

[56] Ibid.

[57] Okey, Nwafor, "Under Younger Eyes: Rereading the works of Obiora Undechukwu" *Essence* interdisciplinary international journal of philosophy, No. 4, 200, pp. 76-90.

[58] Uche, Chizaram, "Globalizing African Religious Priesthood," *Essence* Interdisciplinary - International Journal of Philosophy, No. 4, 2007 pp91--101

a genuinely priestly line may clash with an entirely Christian family.[59] According to him, it cannot be denied that African traditional religions priests do play very important role such as propitiation, appeasement, expiation, worship, service and enforcement of sanctions on people, institutions and relationships in Africa, hence they observe global recognition.

Globalization versus Culture

Against all critical views on globalization as it concerns Africa some scholars believe that African or any people's culture and development cannot afford to be sacrificed on the imperialist and neocolonialist alter of globalization. Africans risk losing their cultural heritage in the face of globalization: not because their culture is obsolete or inferior, but because people have been so taken in by what is Western. This sort of cultural imperialism, which seeks to enslave the African mind has left in its wake a cultureless or culturally disoriented people."[60] Recalling the need to globalize African artistic culture, Kipngeno argues that the phenomenon of globalization "threatens to completely engulf and totally make obsolete the African world-view. The newly acquired and now almost entrenched tastes among Africans in clothing, language, food and other social activities is a testimony of how ingrained the Western culture is in our society..."[61] It has been recognized and pointed out by scholars that the process of colonization of Africa is a process of acculturation and enculturation of their unique attributes while the process of decolonization is the process of restoration of the African cultural virtues and goldmines.

It must be pointed out that the issue of globalization and development borders on culture and real development. The basics or the driving forces are the science and the information technology; unless the Africans appreciate the powers of these forces, they will remain below the lader if a people have something to offer to the global pull, it must be via the information system and whatever hardwares or fabrications a people will contribute must be scienticised or scientific. That is why scientification of African culture is an imperative criterion for Africa in the global village. Yet, an African development in science or scientification of her cultures in

[59] Ibid.

[60] Ugwueye, L.E., "The place of Globalization in Africa," *Essence*, Interdisciplinary -International Journal of Philosophy, No. 4, 2007, pp.102-111.

[61] Kipngene, quoted by Ugwueye, ibid.

general will demand a philosophical and empirical study. The objective connection in African cosmology and ontology is the bedrock of an African scientific methodology. The nature of African culture presupposes objective and subjective realities which are indispensable in an African scientific or ethical world view.

One cannot sufficiently talk of African contributions to science and ethics separately since the two must go together in order to assess the limits and limitations of technologies in any society or what could otherwise be called the relativism of technology.

> Relativism has been defined as an idealist theory of subjectivity and conventionality of human knowledge and cognition. Relativism is opposed to objective knowledge, accepting that knowledge does not reflect the objective world. In contemporary philosophy, relativism manifests itself in the negation of objective historical laws and its uses as a means of struggle against materialist philosophy...[62]

In the twenty-first century, postmodernism not only postulates that knowledge is non-political, or that it is not restricted to any particular race or world view but also welcomes a genuine and true knowledge from any culture, subjective, objective or relative in nature. Relativism, in short, is the plank of postmodernism as a counterpoise to the polarized 'I' and the 'other' in economics, politics and science. It is on this breadth that Fayemi Ademola reinforced the principle of postmodernism with respect to the relative nature of, rationality and scientific methodology using Yoruba proverbs as illustrative examples. Western science is not the only standard of rationality. African Theistic Panpsychic animistic reality is also one of the standards of rationality. These proverbs underscore the African scientific culture and knowledge. According to Fayemi, there are scientific elements in traditional Yoruba proverbs such as a *Bi irin ba kan irin, ikan asite fun kun* (when two men iron rods clash, one will bend for the other) and *Lala to roke, ile lon bo* (whatever goes up must come down).[63] He says that the above proverbs show that scientific knowledge is both latent and demonstratable in African Yoruba culture. Other proverbs demonstrate the powers of reason, laws of

[62] Eberiye, S.S., "Ontological influence in ethical Relativism," *Essence,* Interdisciplinary - International Journal of Philosophy, No. 4, 2007, pp132-140

[63] Fayemu, Ademola, Kazeem, "Proverbism and the Question of Rationality in Traditional African Culture," *Essence* Interdisciplinary -International Journal of Philosophy, No. 4, 2007. pp.141-153

nature, ethics, and forms of rationality such as logic and pragmatism of African culture.

World order and African Emanicipation

However, everything seems to be to the disfavour of the Africans when compared with the Western nations, especially the industrialized countries. Talk of economic development, Africa is backward, talk of political organization and governance, contemporary Africa is handicapped and compare the technological knowledge, vision and skill between Europe and Africa, the former is many miles ahead of the latter. Deplorably, even among the developing nations, Africa wears an unrepentant symbol and beg for identification and appeal for pity. India, Pakistan, Indonesia, Malaysia, Taiwan, China and other Asian countries are gradually isolating Africa, and claiming they no longer belong to the pitiable circumstances in which African is still sunk. Hence, Africa, the infamous black continent but ironically the cradle of civilization, is a land of poverty, hunger, refugees, coup d'etats, wars, economic stagnation and poor governance. Political and economic fortunes or downturn of the developed world of America and Europe cast shadows on the state of economy and politics in Africa. India, a developing country, a member of south-south solidarity of which Africa is also a member, boasts of nuclear prowess and demystifies her long time weakness in her weapon of mass destruction potentials. South Asian countries, until recently, established an economic model which many African countries never hesitated to understudy and copy. It looks as there has been an economic, political and technological albatross hanging over African development.

African renaissance is therefore, her emancipation from whatever are the causes and effects of her underdevelopment and lack of freedom.

The first condition for black renaissance is the knowledge of the fact that there is the African problem of economic backwardness, political instability, technological inertia and total dependence on, and unfreedom from the West. The problem is the knowledge that Africans lack the political will and freedom to determine their destiny in the scheme of things in the comity of nations. Development aids to Africa and the various concerns of the United Nations to Africa are indications of the weakness of Africa to develop on her own.

Again, if African people must emancipate from their present deplorable condition of underdevelopment, the developed world and imperial powers must untie the knot of underdevelopment bequeathed to the continent as a colonial legacy. This singular seed of underdevelopment has always been in form of European and US neo-colonial policies on Africa which have tended to impoverish the Africans and worsen their conditions. It is in recognition of, for instance, the retrogressive impact of debt burden on Africans, that the process of debt relief for the poorest African countries was conceptualized. It is observed that African countries pay as much as three times the amount borrowed from IMF, Paris Club, World Bank in the servicing of the loans and their interests. The conditions of the donor countries' loans make the essence of the loans counterproductive to the African nations' policies and development. It should be acknowledged that the method and mode of donor countries aid to Africa creates a condition of over dependence of Africa on advanced nations which in turn distorts their objective and confident analysis, judgements and assertions over matters of their existence, identity and authenticity. There is no doubt that reshaping the current world order would engage the much-needed African renaissance.

Scientific inquiry as the basis of Development

As in African philosophy and recently in a problem generated or inherent in Western philosophy, there is the question of the fundamental constituent of matter which is reduced to the unobservable or "entities such as electrons, positions, neutrons, quarks, various fields, energy, force, potential..."[64] These are recognized as cognitive empirical concepts in African philosophy and recently, as being pointed by Ramiro and others as playing crucial role in the theories of modern physics like the Theory of special relativity. The unobservable entities, as concepts in theistic panpsychic animistic African epistemology, as a reconciliation of contradictory theories in Western science and as the inner of the innermost rock bottom of sustainable metaphysics of science is the way to be offered by African philosophy to modern physics in a post-modernist and global village. This regime of science therefore, cannot but reduce matter entirely to the unobservable quantum of relative motions and field which renders measuring rods weak and causality relative because of the indispensability of a four-dimensional frame of explanation in quantum mechanics and special theory of relatively. African philosophy or theistic panpsychic animistic knowlege acknowledges the universe as a field

---

[64] Saurabh, Sanatani, see metaphysics of unobservables in metaphysic in *Journal of Indian council of Philosophical Research* vol. XVIII, No.3, July-Sept. 2001 p. 191

of microphysics or subatomic physics. Hence it is anti-realist because it is of the view that "the structure of the world is ultimately not independent of the structure of our theories of the world."[65] On the other hand the realist holds that theoretical terms of a scientific theory refer to entities which actually exist and whose substance is independent of such a theory.

The epistemological basis of the Theory of relativity has recently been undergoing a close examination from the side of philosophy.

In this connection the opinion has been expressed that the theory of relativity has thrown overboard the concept of causality. We take the view that it is perfectly satisfactory from the standpoint of the theory of knowledge that is to say, relative motion is the cause of the contractions, in the theory of relativity.[66] Hence, the fourdimensional frame of the theory of relativity also has an epistemological origin. The Lorentz transformation within this four-fundamental frame is correctly the dictionary of the metric from inertial systems, and defines a new epistemological situation to the relationship on the effects of verifiability to the frame articles of relativistic metric in the spacetime connection.[67] Transformations are *a posteriori* sentences in the spacetime metric, because they show the sense of metric stationary in the spacetime relationship. These predicates refer to the transcendental and universal opportunity. The main point here is the fusion of time and space to four-dimensional space-time, as formulated by Minkowski.

Epistemologically, time and space are fused into a relativistic unity. This fusion of time with the space leads to the concept of space-time in the theory of special relativity. This concept, however, leads to important role of simplifications. Many cases of this can be found in physics, especially where relativistic effects enter the game. In quantum field theory, e.g., integrations are in general performed on the four-dimensional space-time. Also space and time coordinates are not treated completely and necessarily identical, however the difference is not easily noticeable.[68] Consciousness at one time can reach only one three-dimensional plane of this four-dimensional space time. This plane, however, is an arbitrary point of reference: arbitrary in the

---

[65] Ibid.

[66] Cf., P.C.W., Davis. *Space and Time in the Modern Universe*, University Press Cambridge 1977. 29-56.

[67] Ramiro, De Meneses, "The Way of Special Relativity: From Metricto Philosophical Foundations," in *Essence* Interdisciplinary -International Journal of Philosophy, No. 5, 2008pp.154-163

[68] Ibid.

same way as a certain point in space."[69] Again with the same four-dimensional frame of analysis the relation of events at different times is in principle not different from the relation of events at the same time in a different place. This is usually taken to imply that there is symmetry between past and present just as well as left and right are symmetrical to each other. From a metaphysical and relativity perspective, the four-dimensional reality and the micro world are equivalents. What is achieved in special theory of relativity of Albert Einstein and what will be achieved in African Theistic panpsychic animistic frame is a four-dimensional or transcendental apperception of reality of the unity or fusion of space and time, past and present and the relation of events at the same time. Hence since all measurements and observations take place in the macroworld with macroscopic instruments, the transition across the boundary between classical physics (macroworld) and quantum physics (microworlds) is made possible by Theistic panpsychic animistic apperception of reality or by the relativity theory, relativity of motions and consciousness or divisibility of matter or its four-dimensionality.

The special theory of relativity is an adaptation of physical principles to Maxwell-Lorentz electrodynamics. From earlier physics it takes the assumption that Euclidean geometry is valid for the laws governing the situation of rigid bodies, the inertia frame and laws of Nature is assumed to be valid for the whole of physics as special relativity principle. The Maxwell-Lorentz electrodynamics takes the postulate of invariance of the velocity of light in a vacuum according to the light principle. The laws of transformation for space-coordinates and time for the transition from one inertia frame to another, the Lorentz transformations as they are termed, are unequivocally established by the hypotheses concealed in the assumption that they are free from contradiction. Their immediate physical significance lies in the effect of the motion relative to the used inertia frame on the form of rigid bodies. According to the special relativity principle the laws of Nature must be covariant relative to Lorentz transformations: the theory thus provides a criterion for general laws of nature. It leads in particular to a modification of the Newtonian print motion law in which the velocity of light in a vacuum is considered the limiting velocity, and it also leads to the realization that energy and inertia mass are of like nature."[70] The philosophy

[69] Ibid.
[70] Saurabh, Sanatani, *op. cit.*, p. 193.

of microphysics is the bridge between the observable and the unobservable in the Einstein's Relativity theory and Maxwell-Lorentz electrodynamics. It is perhaps because of the philosophy of microphysics or the Theistic panpsychic animistic philosophy that made Einsten render his theory independent of any special assumption of the constitution of matter. The insight into the microworlds has made it possible to understand matter as a concept of divisible atom whose nucleus is "thousands of times smaller from the atom itself, and yet contained most of the atom's mass, similar to a miniature solar system."[71] It has been shown that matter not only composed of void, but is/was mostly void. In African philosophy there is no doubt cast over the reality of the existence of subatomic entities, otherwise, called forces or spirits.

Scientific discovery is mentally exacting task and unless dreams and mystical visions are given an outlet to see the light of the day, scientific discovery will remain elusive. Without sensation of the light from the cave mankind would have remained mental dwarfs. Solipsism is an attribute of a god rather than a social being. A closed society without alternatives is at best solipsistic while an open system is the beacon of intellectual freedom and the vehicle for scientific development. Intellectual freedom is not freedom to steal, to dupe, to destroy or to infringe others' rights. It is freedom to think and reason and possibly make a contribution. The dialect of thoughts which cannot be without freedom of the mind is an attitude and deposition that lead to innovation and progress.

Blacks are under the burden of intellectual bondage. The ancient African societies cannot be said to have suffered the yoke of this bondage. There were sages, wise men (men of ideas) and professionals like medicine men who exercise intellectual freedom, accommodate criticism and give room for alternatives, but regrettably within the wider ambit of small world of tradition. The market-place dialects and debate, an arena of synthesis of ideas and growth of wisdom recorded in the Greek Socratic tradition equally subsisted in the ancient African societies complemented by the institution of village (communal) square, a forum for discussing the burden of human frailty and limitations, settling of disputes and celebration of humanity - a somewhat cartharsis against all unwanted burden and problems in the society. From this intellectual and conceptual latitude, progress was

---

[71] Cf. A., Chinerowicz, *Theories relativists de la gravitation et del l' electron agneticiame, masson et cie, editeurs* (Paris, 1955), 3-26. Cf. J.G. Taylor, *Special relativity* (Clarendon, Oxford, 1975), 1-12.

anticipated. It was the motive and objective of anticolonialism. But political freedom from the colonialist and modernity instead paradoxically plunged the black's society into a labyrinth of intellectual bondage self-narcissism and solipsism. It was a decay and contradiction that calls for internal struggle against the enemies of progress within.

Since the dawn of political freedom from colonial rule African societies have been disorganized. The assimilated Western civilizations impinge negatively on the society and the aboriginal and native civilization are either adulterated or completely disregarded. African world presents a glaring and absurd example of a world where there are intellectual bondage and dishonesty; where individuals are conceptually and circumstantially coerced into states of intellectual solitude, scientific solipsism and cavelike type of existence. The redemption of black Africa could require a radical departure from the values of a closed system to an intellectual engagement of global import and relevance, where there would be alternatives enhanced and nurtured by intellectual honesty and freedom. The miasma of blockade of intellectual freedom and development is only artificial and sub-cultural. There are scientific ideas sitting in the minds of the youths but which were refused outlet because of the cult of elders who do not believe in the dexterity of the youths. The syndrome of elders in social economic and social life in Africa, for instance, has done more harm than good in the development of the youths particularly in their intellectual freedom from which the greater tomorrow in science and technology can be assured. The unorthodoxy of elders' cult lies in it constituting a kind of a fetter or a succuba on the initiative and talents of the youths.

In the epic novel by Chinua Achebe, *Things Fall Apart*, the Igbo elders monitor the youths' developments to know what each and every one of them will become and will not hesitate to honour a youth that distinguishes himself. The hero, Okonkwo, among others was discovered on the basis of this philosophy; Okonkwo himself never hesitated to openly expressed reservation over his first son (Nwoye) sluggish and lackluster development. African universe is open for exploration and inquiry to both the elders and the youths. In history, most touch-bearers of scientific, literal and artistic discoveries were not the elders. Yet the case with most African states today is bizarre. The vision of scientific and technologically developed Africa is not necessarily hinged on eldership. Elders constitute a hindrance to the emancipation and discovery (or recognition) of scientific-minded but less privileged youths through their selective feudal and class hypotheses.

If there is a place where intellectual freedom is needed most to foster scientific initiatives and discoveries, it is in the research institutes, polytechnics and universities. Ironically these are the places where you have intellectuals subdued by the cynical and myopic elders. The present abysmal level of scientific research in our universities is partly traceable to the abandonment of the African respect for initiative, and deficit in intellectual honesty and autonomy. There are only few professors who can appreciate the work of his junior in most of African universities; neither would some authorities make available research facilities to the promising researcher with great potential. Most professors who very much cherish the elders' cult would never like to see a junior fellow having the right or ability to make a scientific discovery. Hence University autonomy would be hollow and meaningless without real academic or intellectual freedom. The greatest emphasis in Africa in global village should be on intellectual freedom and honesty among university lecturers and researchers without which many vision about Black Africa would be meaningless. Most senior fellows hide under the canopy of supervisors to suppress or discourage the initiatives of youths that are yet to come to public glare. Granted that these human factors against human resources development do not have their roots in pre-historic African traditions and cultures, a culture of scientific technological and economic development must be cultivated and propagated from within Africa in the global age.

PHILOSOHY AND AFRICAN SALVATION: AFRICA AND SECULAR CHALLENGE*

African people are indeed, more than ever, in need of apocalyptic and dramatic emancipation from the shell of Dark Age and pathology of traditionalism into a rationally and scientifically defined metaphysical world view for the sake of the salvation of the race and her individuals. For the moment what there is as African philosophy is an inherent and primitively absurd body of varying and contradictory, if not parallel thoughts that work against themselves and the humanity in Africa. It is up to the Africans to take their destiny in their hands, and to work value into nature and into their labour. "After primal man had discovered that it lay in his own hands, literally to improve his lot on earth by working, cannot have been a matter of

* "Philosohy and African Salvation" was first published in *American International Journal of Social Science,* Vol. 3, No. 3, May, 2014.

indifference to him whether another man worked with or against him..."[72] Africans must be capable of living in a competitive world. The focus of this paper, therefore, is on the metaphysical and existential questions of being and nonbeing, becoming and unbecoming, essence and existence, all bordering tangentially on the African salvation as a man or human specie and as a spirit of soul. This paper proceeds with the assumption of the interplay of freewill and determinism in human activities and in particular Africa's attempt to emancipate technically. Hence, there is an implicit acknowledgement of Sigmund Freud's notion of determinism and the notion of free will as necessary categories for Africa's development. Against the background of African religious and metaphysical world view, there is need to advocate what Jurgen Habermas characterized as "the change in the form of religious consciousness that can be understood as a response to the chanllanges of modernity, where as the secular arwarenes of living in a post-secular society gains a sophisticated articulation in post-metaphysical mindiset."[73] This kind of response to modality will adapt where Habermas calls "clearing process"[74] that would combine effectively *in apriori* synthetic way the metaphysical worldview of the African and the secular challenge to their humanity.

Theistic panpsychic animism versus Theistic monotheism

The African is faced with two choices for her salvation; to leave the shell of panpsychic animism and enter into the kingdom of Theistic monotheism or to remain in the kingdom of theistic panpsychic animism and find her salvation therein. The kingdom of monotheism is the kingdom of the universal mighty God and His order as symbolized by Jesus Christ. The constructive attribute of this order is its universal, all embracing characteristics that unify all races, that transcend myopic understanding and comprehension of things and values, that explores and creates nature that mirrors and expresses the mind of God in nature and beings and which transcends panpsychic animistic levels of being and becoming into the universal vicissitudes and apperception of unity of the cosmos as created and creating process. Theistic monotheism is the metaphysics and science of

---

[72] Freud, Sigmund, Civilisations and its Discontents (Trans) James Strachey (London: W.W. Norton and Company, 1961), p.46.

[73] See Jurgen Habermas." Religion in the Public Sphere", Lecture presented at the Holeberg Prize seminar, 29 November 2005. P. 5.

[74] Habermas, J., *op. cit.,* p. 5.

creative process in the physical and social sciences. It is perfection in motion caused by the perfect Being and set in motion by Him who is omnipresent, omnipotent and omniscience. Theistic monotheism is a principle, theology and development; hence it is the motif force behind Egyptian mystery school, Roman Empire, Greek philosophy, the Renaissance and the Enlightenment. These periods not only represent the historical progress of mankind but also the integral realization of divine being and integral liberation in integral yoga of Sri Aurobindo. It is a state of realization and liberation in which the individual being attains unbroken contact in all parts with the divine and by which the divine nature is acquired by the transformation of the lower being. Transformations, for Sri Aurobindo means:

> "*some change of the nature* - I do not mean for instance, sainthood or ethical perfection or logic siddhis (like the Tantrics) or a transcendental (cinmaga) body. I use transformation in a special sense, a change of consciousness, radical and complete and of a certain specific kind which is so concerned as to bring about a striving and assured step forward in the spiritual evolution of the being of greater and higher kind and of a larger sweep and completeness than what took place when a mentalised being first appeared in a vital and material animal world. If anything short of that takes place or at least if a real beginning made on that basis, a fundamental progress towards this fulfillment then my objective is not accomplished. A partial realization, something mixed and inconclusive, does not meet the demand I make on life...[75]

Theistic monotheism and its power over consciousness and nature is the essence which Sri Aurobindo is pursuing and its link between the supernatural and the physical nature is undoubtable in any ramification. There is no incipient bifurcation or tangential opposition between the two worlds, for as Rene Descartes and school of interactionism must have pointed out; there is a relation which subsists not because one has overwhelming influence on the other but because none can subsist without the other. Yet, the fact that the conscious is the creative platform or the motif of the creative process a superior duty is therein assigned therewith to maintain the ontological balance in life of the Spinoza's monistic universe. It

[75] Joshi, Kirest, (ed.), *Philosophy of Supermind and Contemporary Crisis: A Compilation of Passages from Sri Aurobindo's Writings*, India Council of Philosophical Research, New Delhi, 2003.

is a matter of both theoretical and practical interest to note here that the "supermind" in Sri Aurobindo and Neitchiez as well as the super '*Ego*' or 'I' which informed the enlightenment conquer of nature and subsequent European colonization of Africa is fallout of theistic monotheistic monologue. The idea is that supramental transformation must of necessity precede natural transformation. Dualism is one characteristic that pervades being and the universe which is a form of being, a necessarily dualistic source confirmed by philosophers ranging from Plato to Descartes. The mind and body necessity (no problem) exist in everything, in the supermind of scientists and naturalists, the humanists as well as in nature, between the mind of the creator and the physical universe. African salvation is predicated not only on the realization as Sigmund Freud pontificated regarding neurosis and dreams, but also on the need to confront nature boldly as the west has done, to depersonalize African mind from empty concentrations and the accompanying aesthetics and poetics of tradition, folklores, proverbs all of which in linguistic paradigm is a narcissistic glorification of the past without still the super mind, the abstract power, force, purity to control and conquer nature, in short using the mind to confront nature, using an aspect of the dualism to overcome the other aspect as the west had historically and ontologically did. It will require the employment of special self-observing and critical agency in the *Ego*, i.e., the *Ego* ideal, the censor, conscience and even beyond the two principles of mental functioning, i.e., narcissism and instincts and their vicissitudes[76] for positive exploitation of nature and emancipation from mental slavery to technological breakthrough and civilization.

In Africa, happiness in life is predominantly sought in the enjoyment of beauty wherever beauty presents itself to our senses and our judgment, the beauty of human forms and gestures, of natural objects and landscapes and of artistic and even scientific creations. However, according to Freud, "aesthetic attitudes to the goal of life offer little protection against the threat of suffering, but it can compensate for a great deal."[77] Yet the African just like the European has her umbilical cord attached to nature, the more reason for the exploration of nature's space for better life and scientific breakthrough. Yet, this umbilical cord is between man or a mind driving

---

[76] Freud, Sigmund, *Beyond the Pleasure Principle* (Trans) James Strachey (New York, W.W. Norton and Company Inc., 1961), p. xviii - xx.

[77] Freud, *Civilisations and its Discontents*, *op. cit*, p.29

body (not a robot) and nature. The mind qua European mind is what has confronted nature to yield the vast world of scientific and technological breakthroughs. The mind is European mind, for the avoidance of doubt. The African needs this (mind) to confront and conquer nature. The ontological tie between this mind and nature is an ontological relationship which is being understood in abstract and dualistic terms. And in deciphering these categories a lot of meta-linguistic platforms and paradigms are set in motion either as the religious, the mystical, traditions and customs of races and societies or aesthetics and poetic visages for periscoping nature. Here again I assert that the African should de-emphasise attaching themselves to secondary qualities as in the celebration of the religious and aesthetic categories but rather should confront the primary qualities of space, taste, feeling, touch, odour, in the Lockean senses, etc., with a view to understanding and tapping nature. Yet, this is a task that could only be accomplished with appropriate logical predication of mind as a quality and essence of the aesthetic and the religious, as a dualistic component of the body or nature the universe and above all, a superior entity, a conquering entity and a steerig pilot of nature in a preter-natural world.

There are three sources from which our suffering comes, according to Freud - "the superior power of nature, the feebleness of our own bodies and the inadequacy of the regulations, which adjust the mutual relationships of human beings in the family, the state and society."[78] Africans must in this era of globalisation submit to the challenge to confront nature and exploit it for their benefits. There is a complex syndrome and fallacy in the defeatist approach of the African in relation to the European in terms of using the yardstick of the West in paradigmatic study of the African condition, example, a situation of African X as a challenge of European X, African Y as a challenge of European Y or rather more sequentially as African religion versus Christianity, African history versus European history and so on. The Africans could be salvaged not merely by imitating the methodologies of the West or adopting their paradigms, they could more effectively do that by existential assertions in all spheres of life. Yet, there is a sense in which assertions could legitimately, logically and ontologically be made in linguistic and ideological fulcrums simply because the aesthetics and the ideological are the forms of consciousness, the mind, which must be cultivated and

[78] Ibid., p.33

pitted against physical nature and for physical nature values. Recapturing the Hegelian in the sense in which history is a universal, unified and progressive one means that the West leads in shaping and directing the world history with the African and her culture fallen by the wayside or under utilized.

An advance in converting African theistic panpsychic superstructure into a scientific are could be achieved by what Habermas calls learning process of the secular and religious kingdoms albeit, with special emphasis here in transforming the dogmatic ethos of theistic panpsychic science into a deep science of African orign that could challenge the cultural modernity in all its ramifications. The African mind and adaptability to nature's process would, I think, depends to some extent on a post-metaphysical mind-set that "represents the secular counterpart to a religious consciences that has become self-reflective."[79] It is a process that draws "a stick line between faith and knowledge. But it rejects a narrow scientific conception of reason and the exclusion of religious doctrines from the genealogy too would not require total seclusion of the religious in the African reason."[80] A little bit of analysis is needed here. The post-metaphysical consciousness an context because a lot of structures upon which theistic panpsychic animistic elements are configured like myths, gods, spirits, etc., would be undermined. A post-metaphysical analysis of these elements should be sought to re-confirm their objective significance to science and nature. According to Habermas, post-metaphysical thought "refrains form passing ontological statements on the constitution of the whole of beings,"[81] yet there are aspects of beings that are ontologically entailed like the theistic pampsychic animistic science. Even natural science stands on ontological framework. There is a sense in which science could be said to have begun from ontology. Rather post-metaphysical thought should be a special kind of ontological constitution that demystifies mysticism and dogmas.

Primordial nature in the creative process examined

How will the African be at the pinnacle of world history? It could achieve this by self-exaltation over and above that of the West accompanied by the utilization of the mind greatest potentialities in tapping physical nature's potentials and values. There is no doubt that the world history as of now is European history simply because of their scientific prowess and that means

[79] Ibid., p. 12.
[80] Ibid., p. 12.
[81] Ibid.

that African is part of the world history which European history is spearheading. The question is what will be the role of Africa in this history? Is its role that of the servant or the slave? For Africa to escape from this historical and ontological absurdity, perhaps, it must fight its way by playing the European initial and historical game of *Ego* exaltation, narcissistic, monological, monotheistics and ideological dance of imperialism and intimidation. This, however, is a different ball game, which must go on with experimenting and conquering nature, and forging ahead with scientific progress.

Africa must have a radical break with the past and all its inhibitions in the subconscious as a means of destroying the deterministic impulses and elements that hinder development, for as Freud has remarked, historical experiences and group or personal actions and behaviorisms such as slip of tongue, faulty actions and dreams are determined by hidden causes in persons' mind,[82] which are more often than not a replay of past actions or activities. This might seem to be a denial of freewill in African freedom; yet, it must be acknowledged that freewill must confront the deterministics in African destiny in order to radically break away from the shadow of the primitive era to the phase of globalism and technology. According to Sigmund Freud, "nothing which a person does or says is really haphazard or accidental; everything can in principle be traced to causes which are somehow in the person's mind."[83] In other words, historical experiences are also matters or subjects of sub consciousness in dialectical and apperceptive continuum. This manifests in the conscious, preconscious and unconscious or the id, the *Ego* and the super*Ego*. The id contains all the instinctual drives, the *Ego* deals with the real world outside the person, mediating between it and the id and the super *Egos* contains the science, the social norms acquired in childhood.[84] The super *Ego* reconciles the conflicting demands of id, superego and external reality. The African *Ego* in question here is the determination to ideologically, monologically and scientifically confront nature and its objects for technological development. *Ego*, therefore, is the force behind every human achievement so much as it is same for races, nations and societies.

---

[82] Freud, "Psychoanalysis" in *Seven Theories of Human Nature* (ed.) Leslie Stevenson (Oxford: Oxford University Press, 1973), p.75.
[83] Ibid.
[84] Ibid., p.8

African salvation requires pursuits that tend to unite African with humanity, things that stand for exploration of nature and advancement of science. This must precede the aesthetics, the religious, the poetics and the politics that belongs largely to the secondary agenda of African salvation, which is the ideological and monological narcissism. In discovering this truth about Western civilisation and the question of African salvation, spirituality is central and also the bridge between the scientific and the aesthetics in authentic and progressive human advancement. It is the common and constant factor and denominator in the transitions from antiquity, through religion, philosophy to science. Sri Aurobindo captures this challenge very bluntly as follows:

> the strongest of these favourable forces is the constant drawing close of knots of international life, the manipulation of points of contact and threads of communication and an increasingly community in thought, in science and in knowledge. Science especially has been a great force in its direction, for science is a thing common to all men in its conclusions, open to all in its methods, available to all in its results: it is international in its nature and science also has created that closer contact of every part of the world with every other part, of which some sort of internationalism which is the idea of humanity as a single race of beings with a common life and a common general interest is the handwork of science, unifying element of human race in the era of globalisation and the touch bearer of Hegelian history.[85]

The African must unite with the global family on the same and equal leverage in order to globalise and scientize. Falling by the wayside or remaining in the lowest part of the evolutionary ladder is out of the question. We are hereby reminded by Reinach[86] that the ability to gaze at the sun without being dazzled belongs only to the eagle, which, as a dweller in the highest region or the air, was brought into especially intimate relation with the heavens, with the sun and with lightening. We learn from the same source that the eagle puts his young to a test before recognizing them as his legitimate offspring. Unless they can succeed in looking into the sun without blinking, they are cast out from the eerie. It is important to say that what is

---

[85] Joshi, Kirest, *op. cit.*, p.39

[86] Reinach, Cultes. Mythes et Religions, 1908 quoted in Freud, *Three Case Histories* (New York: Collier Books, 1963), p.1 84

ascribed to animals is nothing more than a hallowed custom among men. The procedure gone through by the eagle with his young is an ordeal a test of lineage, such as is reported of the most various races of antiquity. In this global era, therefore, the African would be required for the sake of joining other races in the scientific global race, to gaze, at the sun without blinking to draw down the culture of technology and science.

Science and Theistic panpsychic humansim

Africans should embrace the need to globalise along with others. This need is again predicated on science by Africans and for Africans in the Hegelian boat of universal world history. But again this has less to do with empty celebrations of culture and traditions which are only meaningful in the realm of aesthetics, analytics and poetics. I call this estate of aesthetics and celebration the residual culture which only celebrates the progressive culture of science and nature's prowess. Science and nature prowess is apriori the means and ends of knowledge which aposteriori is the progressive value for the unity of humanity. Accordingly Sri Aurobindo asserts that "the growth of knowledge is interesting the people in each other's art, culture, religions, ideas and is breaking down at many points the prejudice, arrogance and exclusiveness of the old nationalistic sentiments."[87] There is no gain saying the fact that natural pride is often foisted on the ambers of national culture, art and religion but not before the scientific attributes must have been achieved as the fulcrum of survival and happiness. The African question is nonetheless predicated on putting the cat before the horse as entailed in the ideological importance of African religion, African history and African this or that, or the lot of religion which is the heart of Africa. It is not the celebrations inherent in it that matters but the spirituality which calls for an estachalogical renewal of African personality and being in the direction of theistic panpsychic humanism, a metaphysical and empirical superstructure from which a veritable unique science of African origin could emerge. "Religion is beginning to realize a little dimly and ineffectively as yet, that spirituality is after all its own chief business and true aim and that it is also the common element and the common bond of all religions."[88] Africans have to awaken from their spiritual slumber, from the diminished humanity to enlightened specie of being by not only embracing and emphasizing God

---

[87] Joshi, Kirest, *op. cit.,* p.39
[88] Franz, Fanon, *The Wretched of the Earth,* Penguin, 1961

into the Africa panpsychic and pantheistic universe and theistic humanity but also by apocalyptic political, economic and political liberation. Franz Fanon rightly remarked that every people must out of relative obscurity discover itself or miss it. This entails spiritual and material emancipation from the doldrums of spiritual and political dwarfism. This poem below is a warning to individuals, nations and races who retard individuals, families, communities and nations by their negative actions and wake up spiritually in protection and defence of their members and neighbours.[89]

SUN RISE AND SUN SET
Sun rise sun set in gloom.
Sun rise sun set in bliss.

Think not that forever,
You will be the same,
For the spring and summer,
Take their respective tolls,
Your wickedness in the morn,
Dares you in the wake of even, In old age.
Time is but a duration
That bequeath man interlude,
Of recompense and contrition,
As time ticks
We behold
The realities of our omission
And commissions.

From,
Early morn dwell on truth,
Eat the food daily,
Not when it is late,
When you cannot make around,
When there are grey hairs and lack luster

The omnipresent and omniscient eye,
Watch from universal presence:
Man is like a mustard seed,
Everyone shall grow,
In the midst of others in

[89] Dukor, M., Guest Poet.

Equality and justice.

Not wisdoms
Giving only your progenies;
Others are yourself.
Forever remembered is
He who others call father
Honour of universal love
Fatherhood, Give only your progenies not
So that many would call you father.
The sun rises and set
So is life,
No condition is permanent
Spring and summer come and go
Behind left the beneficence of
Nature's magnanimity

Know,
That a blind man
Knows not that a cattle that
Does not have tail
God drives flies away for her,
A wise hunter when he sees a
Prey dancing in the forest
He is vigilant
That a powerful being
Is playing music for her,

Steal show not,
Where you did not sow reap not,
Advantages take not,
Eat your cake and have it not,
The stone rejected
Can it be your corner piece?
As you make your bed so
You will lie on it.

He who climbs to the top
And removes the ladder
Lives a life of dishonour and
It accompanies him into old age.

The unjust wicked man
In his old Suffer the inequity he had
Brought to many.
Lucky
Is he who suffer consistency and justice
For she would accompany him
To the grave.

On this throne,
He kick and hack,
The poor and the less priviledged
Yet he know not,
The son of who!
The son of man or God?
So he know not
The affliction that knock
The door in time
Sun rise and sun set in gloom
Sun rise and sun set in bliss

Theistic panpsychic perfection and Secular adventures

We must recapture the base and understand the secular in the universal vision of humanity. The liberal conception of politics in the separation of the state and the church had been practised in the land of African for near three decades since the departure of colonial rules, thereby leaving behind a body politics with reference to rule of gods and ancestors. The consequence of this is also in the weak nature of states and political instability in African as demonstrated in the above poem on the condition of Nigeria state. The dislocation of the state from within the religions and metaphysical world of the African is therefore part of the problem. The argument here is a post-independent African with post-secular and post-metaphysical world views synthetically combined in post modern reason which is the epistemic reason for the justification of a state which depends on religions slegitimation and liberal conception of democratic citizenship. In this context liberal ethos of law and politics and the religious obligation and demands would influence each other in a consangious atmosphere where the learning process by which alone religious thinking and secular thinking can achieve those self-reflective attitudes on which the democratic ethos hinges.[90] From the point of views of contemporary history, African political instability characterized by break-down of rule of law, civil strife, fermine, wars hunger poverty, etc., is not something whose solution demands alone the interloculation of liberal political ideology but rather a unity of an authentic African personality with but salient challenges of modernity culminating in the post-modern reason and accommodation. These are the challenges the African would face in reaching out for a metaphysical and epistemic solution to her problems. At the same time a post-metaphysical thought in the cultural post modernity, as in African salvation, would reject "a kind of scientism that reduces our knowledge to what is at each time represented by the state of the art in natural science."[91] In the spirit of post-modernity metaphysical thought process should reflect on the metaphysical world hermitage of both Western and African philosophies and discovers the internal relationship among world philosophical hermitages in the period which Karl Jaspers calls the 'Axial age'.[92] What I have construed as theistic panpschic animism of African philosophy could also be applicable to Western and easterm philosophies. While we may agree with Habermas that post-metaphysical thought insists on that difference between certainties of faith and validity claim that can be publicly redeems or criticsed, we disagree that the thought process can remain "agnostic"[93] where God, gods and spirits remain variables in the scientific culture of theistic panpsychic animism. In laying a formidable post metaphysical and post-secular superstructure of the scientific theistic panpsychic animism of the global relevance a unity of complemntality of cultural need to be posited and evolved instead of polarization of ideas. Hence while self-reflection is introduced into the religious consciousness of theistic panpsychic animism "there is a similar step towards the self reflective overcoming of a secularist stubbornes."[94]

African land is a panpsychic and animistic world that is prone to the kingdoms - the kingdom of god and the kingdom of Satan. Of course God and Satan are mutually necessary but exclusive concepts, i.e., the existence of the other entail the other. The reason for the existence of God is the existence of Satan and Satan exists because there is God whom he entered into

---

[90] Habermas, J. *op. cit.*, p. 25
[91] Ibid, p. 12
[92] Ibid, p. 12
[93] Ibid, p. 13
[94] Ibid, p. 13

competition with. The paradox of African theistic panpsychic animistic ontology and worldview is that the Almighty God that it owes its ultimate obedience is not appropriated both in its nature, dispositions and perfections. There is imperialist acculturation of the panpsychic and animistic subterranean world by the forces of Satan and demons to the exclusion of the place of God and his perfections. The sharp contrast between the European land and African land in terms of rule of law politics and development is the appropriation of perfections in the former and the malignant imperfections in the later. Similarly, the absence of the culture of demons and devils in advanced countries and the predominance of Satan and its attacks on individuals and societies in Africa is because of the order of perfection in European society and the absence of the same in African society and governance. The symbolic nature of perfection is light and where there is no light there is darkness, there is no perfection, and therefore no light but darkness in Africa world, the reason for the dominance and inhabitation of demons and devils. The departure and fleeing of demons does not solely depend on prayer but largely on working out a system of perfection in the polity and in the traditional society. Demons exist and they are realities but their existence is predicated on the existence of imperfections on the part of man and the imperfections in Africa have accordingly constituted the board and feeding of demons and devils.

Demons, imperfections exist, walk tall shoulder higher because the Africans, though rightly worshipped and adore gods, refused to surrender everything to and worship of the most high God, the universal and scientific God. The African has refused to acknowledge the perfection in existence and that God exist therein, hence, the metaphysics and the ontology of African predicament presuppose perfections and the lack of rule of law in African land. God loves perfection, order and holiness. Satan, Lucifer is symbolic of all imperfections, disorders, corruptions, lawlessness, underdevelopments, backwardness, primitivism, dwarfism, wickedness, racism, ethnicism, political instability, wars, rumours of wars, etc. The poem is a graphic picture of society formed from the mind of Lucifer, the colonialist.

THE KINGDOM OF ENDS

Here is - the ends
The celebration - indeed carnival,
The domain of the leperous,
Racist humanity,

And the height and epitome,
Of the diminished humanity
That justifies the means
In the edge of the Atlantic,
The tropical, semi-desert
And desert lands.

Man is reduced to lesser beings,
By the master and civilizer of
The natives, Columbus with his Brother, James.
Alas, they say, this is the kingdom,
Cattle, sheep and goat,
And rat, rabbits, crocodiles,
Among the kingdoms
Of elephants, donkey, buffaloes
Lions, antelopes and monkeys
In the state of nature.

At one end of the field,
Columbus and James assemble
The cattle, the sheep and the goat
The rats, the rabbits and the crocodiles
And baptize them with names,
For rearing and business.

They acquire
The field, the forest and the Inmates,
And their commonwealth,
They are the superior race
From the old world across the Atlantic
To a new world.

Mr. James, the missionary and civilizer
Reared his pets to his own
Natures contradiction therein
The cattle inherit political power
The goat commerce and education
The sheep the economy
The goat rebelled and his education
Dance to the sheep

The cattle, the ambitious and true to nature,
An inmate of the forest,
Is selfish and power drunk,
Wears the toga, born-to-rule,
His religion as faith and ideology.
He eyes the resource and hates the infidels
From the desert to the edge of Atlantic.

The goat courageous and true to nature,
An inmate of the forest,
A gold-digger and Egoistic,
A republican and rebel homosapien
Who craves relentlessly for
Survival and fittest
Into the homes of other inmates
The sheep sly and true to nature,
An inmate of the forest
A bird of all weathers, suspicious of
Of cattle and goat families
Who noses for the good in the
Commonwealth in extroverted
Narcissism and cheap blackmail.
The rats, rabbits and crocodiles,
The crying inmates true to nature,
An inmate of the forest
The famished owners of the commonwealth,
The inmates of the colonized corner
The domain of the leprous
Racist humanity

The chess-political game,
Board were carved by the civilizer,
Instead of being free to choose,
The inmates of the jungle
Distinct politically and demographically.
The cattle is the king,
The sheep is the queen,
The goat the bishop,
And the rats, the rabbits and the crocodile, the pawns

Now contradictions set in,
A new playing field created,
No more king, queen, bishop
And the pawns
And no more chessboard,
But a football field
In the level playing field,
Even the rat, the rabbit and,
The crocodile throw their weight
About in the bid to be king,
The cattle want to be king
The sheep wants to be king
And the goat wants to be king

The inmates must leave
This state of nature
For prosperity and unity
Columbus and James must leave
Each and every
Inmate to live independent life
Outside a commonwealth.
Neither Bakassi war nor
Survival of the fittest
Can be better than
Social contract to depart or unit.

Christ and African salvation

Lucifer is the head of demons and devils that perfect all these imperfections and disorders. African universe and mind is subjected by the Lucifer to help him achieve his purpose on earth after he had been refused dominance or chased away by the developed worlds. However, the categories of African mind are adequate and sufficient in the Kantian sense to grapple with development but yet subjected and underdeveloped by agents of Lucifer who cripple leaderships, development, economy, politics and visions. These agents of Lucifer include man, gods and some traditional institutions, which subsist only at the mercies of the gods and demons of localism, nativism and backwardness. Africa must not be alone in the struggle for survival, emancipation and development; there is need for a union with other races in the spirit of globalization. "Just as a planet revolves around a central body as well as rotating on its own axis, so the human individual takes part in the course of development of mankind at the same time as he pursues his own path in life."[95] African's salvation will require a radical retirement of traditional institutions in subordinations to the almighty God, preferably through Jesus Christ and the subjection of local, environmental, village, community gods and ancestors in favour of the scientific and universal God. They have to go back to history to rediscover themselves in the old and new testament as God chosen people, for understanding, according to God's precepts and testimonies to see like God, feel like God, walk in His righteousness, scientific and universal like Him, and above all, perfect and developed in His likeness and not blind, dumb, short, dwarfish, imperfect, visionless, paralysed and unintelligent like gods and goddesses who pay no homage to the Almighty God. Psalm 135:15-18, says "the idols of the heathen speak not; eyes, ears, but they hear not; neither is there any breath in their mouth. They that make them are like unto them; so is everyone that trusted in the work of men's imagination and powers of spoken words cast in images and objectified, they speak not, see not, hear not and breathless,[96] hence, the African that make them is like unto them. Again Psalm 33:12 tells us that "Blessed is the nation whose God is the Lord; and the people whom He had chosen for His own inheritance,"[97] African race is not blessed because she is yet to go beyond her gods for the universal almighty God who consequently is yet to choose her for His inheritance on earth.

EPISTEMOLOGY OF OUTER SPACE*

This is an inquiry and prolegomenia into the nature and reality in the outer space, the solar system namely the stars, sun moon, mars, venus, vista, jupiter, the existence of astriods, unidentified flying objects and blackholes. It is an investigation into the existence and sustainability of the laws of thought: the law of identify, excluded middle and non-contradiction in the galaxies for the sake of man and his future habitation in outer space. This paper is of the view that a cognitive science otherwise called naturalized epistemology is the torch light to unraveling the mysteries of the outer world. Accordingly, African philosophy has special contributions to make, if

---

95 Freud, Sigmund. Civilisations and Its Discontents, *op. cit.*, p.88.
96 Holy Bible, *Psalms*
97 Ibid.
* "Epistemology of Outer Space" was first published in *Essence, Interdisciplinary – International Journal of Philosophy,* Vol. 6, No. 1. 2009.

rigorous self-reflection is undertaken by it, on the theistic panpsychic epistemology of the space.

The logic of the Age of space exploration

Needless presuming that the action of a rethink is an empty, vacous project because it is a positive action that focused on and promotes globalism. It is positive 'freedom from' to positive 'freedom to' in the collaborative efforts to push back the horizon of knowledge and civilizations as instruments or pencil in the hand of an intelligent being. Hence, a rethinking of philosophy and logic in the age of space exploration is an attempt to erect a bridge between philosophy and logic in the age of space exploration and that of the world of outer space while critically analyzing the relevant normative and ontic standards, paradigms and logic in order to apply human reasoning on ontology, ethics, existence, ecology, economics, politics and possibly gender question. One is short of saying that existentialism either as a school of thought or an ontological scientific paradigm is in question here. How do we explore philosophically man's existence from this space to the outer space. This, of course, fundamentally requires the tools and laws of logic for exploration into the world of stars, black holes, asteroids, mars, vista, Jupiter, as well as the moon and the sun. The contribution of African philosophy to the study of the external world, viz: the earth, space and time, the solar system, the planets and the galaxies is doubtlessly traceable to or rooted in its commonality with the Spinoza's monism, Leibniz monadism, Einstein's General relativity, the philosophical foundations which are hereby readdressed as a form of naturalized epistemology. The problem of inhabiting other planets, exploring the space and galaxies is squarely the problem of our knowledge of the external world which is stated as one of how a self with private mental states can come to have knowledge of the external world of not only tables, molecules, light rays, retinas, air waves, prime numbers, infinite clauses, joy and sorrow, good and evil but also the planets, galaxies, asteroids, spaces and time. However, the focus of this inquiry is the external world of the outer space of the planets, the galaxies, etc.

The structure of knowledge and rational thought in theistic panpsychic sense will help to unravel the science of the external world. For Kant, knowledge results from the joint operation of two faculties namely, the faculty of sense perception [sensibility] and the faculty of thought [understanding]: through the sensibility objects are given to us: through the understanding they are thought. Therefore knowledge is a cooperative affair between the knower and the thing we know, and our minds always bring certain ways of thinking to things, and this always affects our understanding of them as the red-glass affects a person's vision, Kant again argues that activity of the mind is to unify our experience. It achieves this unity first by imposing on our various experiences in the "sensible manifold" certain forms of intuition; space and time. We unavoidably perceive and intuite things as being in space and time. But space and time are not ideas derived form the specific configuration of the stars, moon, sun, venue, Jupiter, mass etc. they are encountered immediately in intuition and are at the same time *apriori* senses through which we always see objects of experience that is sense perception [sense intuitions] take place on the presupposition of space and time. *There can be no sense perception except in space and time; these are the frameworks within which it takes place. Space and time are therefore apriori forms of sense perception, or in other words, the apriori necessary condition of sense perception. The human mind is structured in such a way that no object can appear to us [and therefore no sense perception can take place] except in space and time.*[98]

In addition to space and time, which deals particularly with the way we sense things, there are certain categories of thought which deal more specifically with the way mind unifies our experience. The mind achieves this unifying act by making various kinds of judgments as we engage in the act of interpreting the world of sense and the external world. The many type of experience is judged by us through certain fixed forms of concepts, such as quantity, quality, relation, and modality; when we assert quantity, we mean one or many, when we make a judgment of quality, we make either a positive or a negative statement. When we make a judgment of relation, we think of cause and effect on the one hand, or of the relation of subject and predicate on the other; and when we make a judgment of modality, we mean that something is either possible or impossible. All these ways of thinking are what constitute the act of physical and scientific synthesis through which the mind strives to make a consistent single universe out of the manifold of sense impression of the world. However Kant would refuse to see this single universe as a theistic panpsychic monism or totality.

Theistic panpsychic mind makes it possible for us to have a unified grasp of self and experience. Far Kant, it is the mind that transforms the raw

---

[98] Olen, J., *Persons and Their World: An Introduction to Philosophy*, (New York: Random House. Inc. 1983), P. 286.

data given to our senses into a coherent and related set of elements. But this leads Kant to say that the unity of our experience must imply a unity of the self, for unless there was a unity between the several operations of the mind, there could be no knowledge of experience. To have such knowledge involves, in various sequences, sensation, imagination, memory, as well as the powers of intuitive synthesis. Thus, it must be in the same self that one senses an object, remembers its characteristic, and imposes upon it the forms of space and time and the category of cause and effect. All these activities must occur in some single subject, otherwise, there could be no knowledge, for if one subject had only sensations, another only memory, and so on, the sensible manifold could never be unified.

For Kant, it is the transcendental unity of the „self" that accomplishes the unifying activity. He uses the word transcendental to indicate that we do not experience the self directly even though such a unity, or self, is implied by our actual experience. Thus, the idea of this self is *apriori* a necessary and panpsychic condition for having a unified knowledge world of nature. In the act of unifying all the elements of experience, we are conscious of our own unity, so that our consciousness of a unified world of experience and our own self-consciousness occur simultaneously. Our self-consciousness, however, is affected by the same faculties, theistic panpsychic powers that affect our perception of external objects. I bring to the knowledge, of myself the same apparatus and, therefore, impose upon myself as an object of knowledge the same lenses through which I see everything says Kant. Just as I do not know things as they are apart from the perspective from which I see them, so also I do not know the nature of this transcendental unity of apperception except as I am aware of the knowledge. I have the unity of the field of experience, says Kant.

Theistic panpsychic epistemology is based on the assumption that human knowledge is accessible to the thing-in-themselves, nominal or the inner most of the outer space. Hence, I disagree with Kant that human knowledge is forever limited in its scope. For Kant, this limitation takes two forms. In the first place, knowledge is limited to the world of experience. Secondly, our knowledge is limited by the manner in which our faculties of perceptions and thinking organize the raw data of experience. He distinguished between phenomenal reality, or the world as we experience it, and nominal reality which is a thing in-itself. We can obviously never have an experience of a no sensuous perception. All objects we know are sensed objects. Still, we know that the existence of our world of experience is not produced by the mind. The mind, rather, imposes its manifold of experience, which is derived from the world of thing-in-themselves. This means that there is a reality external to us that exist independently of us but that we can know it only as it appears to us and is organized by us. For Kant the concept of a thing-in-itself does not, then, increases our knowledge but reminds us of the limits of knowledge. Yet it paradoxically reminds us of the limitless capacity of our mind.

The logic of African space science

We agree with Kant on the ideas of three regulative ideas that lead us beyond sense experiences but about which we cannot be indifferent because of our certain tendency to try to unify all our experience. These are the ideas of the self, the cosmos and God; they are transcendental because they correspond to no object in our experience. They are produced by intuition and pure reason alone. They are however, prompted by experience in the sense that we think of those ideas in our attempts to achieve a coherent unity of all our experience. Kant says that,

> the first idea is the 'I' itself viewed simply as thinking nature or soul... endeavoring to represent all determinations as existing in a single subject, all power, so far as possible as derived from a single fundamental power, all change as belonging to the states of one and the same permanent being, and all appearances in space as completely different from the actions of thought.[99]

In theistic panpsychic naturalized epistemology there is hardly any difference between intuition and Kantian pure reason. We don't agree with Kant that the cognitive capacity of mind cannot go beyond experience. Pure reason tries to unify the various psychological activities, we are aware of into a unity and it does this by formulating the concept of the self. Similarly, pure reason tries to create a unity of the many events in experience by forming the concept of the world so that:

> The second regulative idea of merely speculative reason is the concept of the world in general...the absolute totality of the series of conditions...an idea which can never be completely realized in the empirical employment of reason, but which yet serves as a rule that

---

[99] Audi, R. *The Cambridge Dictionary of Philosophy* (Cambridge: Cambridge University Press 1999), p 771

> prescribes how we ought to proceed in dealing with such series...The cosmological ideas are nothing but simply regulative principles, and are very far from posting...an actual totality of such series.[100]

For Kant the third idea of pure reasons, which contains a merely relative supposition of a being, that is the sole and sufficient cause of all cosmological series is the idea of God which like all speculative ideas, seems only to formulate the command of reason, that all connection in the world be viewed in accordance with the principles of a systematic unity as if all such connection had its source in one single all-embracing being as the supreme and sufficient cause.[101] Kant's use of these regulative ideas epitomizes his way of mediating between dogmatic rationalism and skeptical empiricism. According to him, the ideas of the self, the cosmos, and God cannot give us any theoretical knowledge of realities corresponding to these ideas. The function of these ideas is simply and solely regulative. As regulative ideas, they give us a reasonable way of dealing with the constantly recurring questions raised by the metaphysics. His critical analysis of the scope of human reason led him to say that earlier rationalists had made the error of treating transcendental ideas as thoug h they were ideas about transcendental or actual beings. Kant emphasizes that there is a great difference between something given to my reason as an object absolutely or merely as an object in the idea. In the former case our concepts are employed to determine the object [transcendental]. He said that in the latter case there is in fact only a scheme for which no object, not even a hypothetical one, is directly given, and which only enables us to represent to ourselves other objects in an indirect manner, namely in their systematic unity, by their relation to this idea. He says that the concept of a highest intelligence is a mere idea [transcendental].[102] Similarly in theistic pan-psychic animism, God is an idea and a reality in subjective objective reality.

Kant argues that regulative ideas do not refer to any objective reality about which we can have knowledge; we must consider these ideas as being the product of our pure reason. As such we cannot bring to these ideas the forms of time and space or the category of cause and effect since these are

---

[100] Huemer, M., [ed] *Epistemology: Contemporary Readings.* London and New York Rutledge 2002, P. 132.

[101] Cahn, S.M., [ed], *Classics of Western Philosophy*, Indianapolis; Hacked Publishing Company, p. 310

[102] Audi, R., *loc. cit.*, P 77.

imposed by us only upon the sensible manifold. Science is possible because all people, having the same structure of mind, will always and everywhere order the events of sense experience in the same way: that is, we all bring to the given of sense experience the same organizing faculties of understanding. Hence for him, there can be no science of metaphysics because there is not the same kind of given when we consider the ideas of self, cosmos and God as when we consider "the shortest distance between two points."[103] What is given in metaphysics is the felt need to achieve a unity of the wide variety of events in experience at ever-higher levels and of discovering an ever wider explanation of the realm of phenomena.

This is the area where we disagree with him because theistic pan psychic mind goes beyond experience for which transcendental metaphysics or metaphysical science is possible. We can have scientific knowledge of phenomena but cannot have scientific knowledge of the noumenal realm, or the realm that transcends experience. Hence, our attempts to achieve a "science" of metaphysics, says Emmanuel Kant, are doomed to failure. Whenever we try to discuss the self, the cosmos, or God as though they were objects of experience the inability of the mind ever to do so successfully is indicated by what Kant calls the antinomies into which we fall. These four antinomies show us that when we discuss the nature of the world beyond experience, we can argue with equal force on opposite sides of various propositions namely that: (1) The world is limited in time and space or that it is unlimited; (2) Every composite substance in the world is made up of simple parts, or that no composite thing in the world is made up of simple parts since they nowhere exists in the world anything simple; (3) There is causality in accordance with freedom, or that there is no freedom since everything in the world takes place soley in accordance with the laws of nature; and (4) There exists an absolutely necessary being as a part of the world or as its cause or an absolutely necessary being nowhere exist.[104]

These antinomies reflect the disagreements generated by dogmatic metaphysics and disagreements that occur only because they are based upon "nonsense" that is upon attempt to describe a reality about which we can have no sense experience. Kant did, however, believe that these antinomies have positive value; namely, that they provide additional argument for saying

---

[103] Stumpt, S.E., *Philosophy History and problems*, New York McGraw-Hill Book Company 1994 P. 243

[104] Audi, R., *loc. cit.*, P. 772

that the world of space and time is phenomenal only and that in such a world freedom is a coherent idea. This follows because if the world were a thing in-itself, it would have to be either finite or infinite in extent and divisibility. But the antinomies according to Kant show that there can be no demonstrative proof that either alternative is true.[105] Insofar, then, as the world is phenomenal only, we are justified in affirming moral freedom and human responsibility.[106]

As regulative ideas kant says the concepts of the self, the world and God have a legitimate function for they help us to synthesize our experience, Also, to speak of a noumenal realm or the realm of the thing-in-itself is to respond to certain given experiences and tendencies of our thought. For this reason, we can think of a person in two different ways, as a phenomenon and as a noumenon, as a phenomenon, a person can be studied scientifically as a being in space and time and in the context of cause and effect. At the same time, our experience of mortal obligation suggests that people's noumenal nature, what they are like beyond our sense perception of them, is characterized by freedom. In this context the concept of freedom, as the idea of the self, of God, is a regulative idea. For Kant therefore there can never be any demonstrative proof either that people are free or that God exists because these concepts refer us beyond senses experience, where the categories of the mind have no data upon which to work.

Kant criticized all the traditional arguments for the existence of God used by past philosophers as invalid. He classifies them into there kinds namely, the onotologial argument, the cosmological argument, and the teleological argument. His argument against the onotological proof is that it is all a verbal exercise, for the essence of this proof is the assertion the since we have the idea of a most perfect being, it would be contradictory because the concept of a perfect being necessarily includes the predicate of existence. That is a being that does not exist can hardly be considered a perfect being. But Kant argues that this line of reasoning is "taken from judgments not from things and their existence."[107] Whereas the ontological proof begins with an idea of a perfect being the cosmological proof "takes its stand on experience," for its says that "I exist, therefore an absolutely necessary being

---

[105] *Loc. cit.*
[106] Audi, R., *loc. cit.*, P. 262
[107] Kaunitz, M.M., *A Popular History*

exist"[108] on the assumption that if anything exists an absolutely necessary being must also exist. The error of this argument, according to Kant, is that while it begins with experience, it soon moves beyond experience. Within the realm of sense experience it is legitimate to infer a cause for each event, but "the principle of causality has no meaning and no criterion for its application save only in the sensible world."[109] Here is the direct application of Kant's critical method, for he argues that we cannot employ *apriori* categories of the mind in trying to describe realities beyond sense experience.

The cosmological argument, therefore, lead us to a first cause of all things, for the most we can infer from our experience of things is a regulative idea of god. Whether there actually is such a being, a ground of all contingent things, Kant raises the same question posed by the ontological argument, namely whether we can successfully bridge the gap between our idea of a perfect being and demonstrative proof of its existence.Similarly, the teleological argument begins with considerable persuasiveness, for it says that,

> in the world we everywhere find clear signs of an order in accordance with a determinate purpose...The diverse things could not of themselves have cooperated by so great a combination of diverse means, to the fulfillment of determinate final purposes, had they not been chosen and designed for these purposes by an ordering rational principle in conformity with underlying ideas.[110]

To this argument Kant replies that it may very well be that our experience of order in the universe suggests an order, but order in the world does not demonstrate that the materials stuff of the world could not exist without an order. The most this argument from design can prove, says Kant, "is an architect of the world who is always very much hampered by the adaptability of the material in which he works, not a creator of the world to whose idea everything is subject."[111] To prove the existence of a creator leads us back to the cosmological argument with its idea of causality, but since we cannot use the category of causality beyond the things in experience, we are left simply with an idea of a first cause or creator, and this takes us back to

---

[108] Stumpt, *loc. cit.*, P 267.
[109] Kaunitxz, M.M., *loc. cit.*, P. 237
[110] Stumpf, S.E., *loc. cit.*, p. 286
[111] *Loc. cit.*

the ontological argument with its deficiencies. Kant's conclusion, therefore, is that we cannot use transcendental ideas or theoretical principles, which have no application beyond the field of sense experience to demonstrate the existence of God. It follows from Kant's critical remark about the 'proof', however, that we can neither demonstrate God's existence nor demonstrate that God does not exist. By pure reason alone, we can neither prove nor disprove God's existence. If, therefore, the existence of God cannot be effectively dealt with by the theoretical reason, which Kant has gone to such lengths to show its relevance only in the real sense experience, then some other aspect of reason must be considered as the source of the idea of God which in African philosophy is the metaphysical science of theistic panpsychism. Our disagreements with and subsequent conclusions on the possibility of metaphysics of science are; that God and spirits exist by virtue of this perfection discernable by post-reason or intuition, that empirical knowledge, deapherable by senses, exist and that analytical pure reason exist as well, the former and the later, all owning their origin and existence to the Almighty God. The realm of the ideal world or the cognitive or metaphysical science which is the theistic panpsychic animism of African philosophy is aptly delineated by the Christian Biblical teachings. According to 1 Corinthians 15:44, the spirit is "sown in natural body; it is raised in a spiritual body. This natural important and fundamental scientific proposition in the Bible has from the ancient of days in Africa, Asia and Europe, not only solved the problem of metaphysical science, but also provided answers associated with phenomena, nuomena space and outer space. This verse is the key to scienfic discoveries and will be the foundation of future scientific adventures it is what is called naturalized epistemology or what I call theistic panpsychic animism postulated as the framework for African contribution to the epistemology of outer space.

Naturalized space epistemology and Theistic panpsychic animistic universe

African or man's first contact with nature or the external world is the attempt to cognize the concept and objects of space: this is the method of Spinoza, Leibniz and Einstein. Cognitive science or more aptly naturalized epistemology is an area in which the African could contribute to the world of space exploration which already has the presence of United States, Britain, France, Germany, Russia, Northern Korea, Iran, China and India and so on. African may not have space science but it has beyond Kantian's notions of space and time the cognitive capacity of the space science and could develop this primary science as a naturalized epistemology with prediction and control. This cognitive science called epistemology is not unique to African philosophy, but special to it and hence can be a product for the global market. Quine's statement of naturalized epistemology is striking: „I am a physical object sitting in a physical world. Some of the forces of this physical world impinge on my surface. Light rays strike my retina, molecule bombard my eardrums and fingertips; I strike back emanating concentric airwaves…"[112] as idea of naturalized epistemology is narrow to the extent that it is the problem of how we learn to talk about or refer to objects (scientific and non scientific), the conditions that lead to reference and the possibility of scientific discourse. But the form which is amenable to African philosophy, and which is necessary in the external world of outer space is "how starting with experience in the form of immediately given impression or sense-data, we justify our claims to know objects such as tables, chairs or molecules."[113] That is to provide a foundation of certainty for sciences by standing outside of them.

Space epistemology as a naturalized epistemology is the logic of understanding the external world of our outer space. It is important to reflect on the claim that thus, methodology is one, an epistemology and two, a naturalized one. Epistemology is the concern and an exercise or enterprise whose objective is to investigate and acquire knowledge. Nature is the physical world comprising of man, water environment, and objects including the outer space. A naturalized epistemology is therefore a concern or an enterprise starting with or without the experience of space and all that is contained in it. Space epistemology is a naturalized epistemology because it is only and only through it that a good understanding of outer space can be achieved. A true grasp of the scientific realities in space and outer space must be preceded by this epistemology. Previous and several American, Britain and Russian satellites into the outer space were or ought to be guided by an epistemology, indeed, a naturalized one. It is the epistemology in the external world of outer space. This kind of epistemology has inclination to a spiritual connotation. It has to be acknowledged that the creeping in of the spiritual

---

[112] See Quine, W.V. The wages of paradox and other Essays (New York, Random House, 1966). P.215 and *Theories and Things* (Cambridge Mass Harvard University Press).

[113] Orebstin, Alex. "Epistemology naturalized - nature know the self" in Nigel Warblerton (ed) *Philosophy Basic Readings* (London, Routledge, 1999) p. 270.

element is natural too. It is in this sense that African philosophy's contribution to a space epistemology that is based on experience and subjective spiritual nature is theistic panpsychic animistic epistemology.

The logic of epistemology which is space naturalized epistemology could be logic of future successes in space explorations. It is by peculiar circumstances and methodology a specialized logic. The failures of British, America and Russian space shuttles in the past could be as a result of the absence of a sustainable logic of inquiry and inadequate epistemology of the outer space. The unsustainablility of the successful ones could be as a result of lack of logic of the external world of space. Then, what kind of logic and epistemology is necessary for the *prolegomena* for future metaphysics and epistemology of the outer space? Is it the same, beyond or different from, the informal and formal logic? The questions raised the applicability of the law of identity, non-contradiction and excluded middle; it will also question the amenability of the rules of replacement from modus ponens, modus tollens through material equivalence to exportation, predicate logic and logic of relations.

The Columba Shuttle provides inkling into the nature of outer space and its comparism with the earthly space. It is said that the effect of gravity is the same but we are not told the extent of the similarity and at which point the difference and similarity exist, breaks down, otherwise how can one explain a number of space causalities. The experience of Columbia shuttle also reveals that most physical feelings peculiar to our world of earthly space are not present in Mars. All this, among others suggest that the laws of thoughts, with its criticisms within the earthly context, may not all be applicable to the external world of outer space. What African philosophy will offer to the global space exploration is theistic pan psychism, which is the realm of nature and absolutes because space and time as well as theistic panspychic predicates subsist in the same absolute continuum and totality save the laws may be different. For African philosophy the constants and designators for the understanding of the external world of outer space are the panpsychic modalities of God, gods, spirits and forces.

Our lead investigative question following discussion on Kantian epistemology above is scientific discourse possible in the external world of out space and time? This requires the investigation into the properties of space and time and what African philosophy can offer as an alternative with the objective of conquering the galaxies and the planets. How can African philosophy go beyond the general theory of relativity to answer the question of an outer space scientific discourse? General theory of relativity presupposes that gravity is relatively distributed from one point to another in spaceio-temporal reality. Hence predictions in spacetime often are equally relatively made. For African philosophy the prediction about what happens around black holes, for instance, is a subject of theistic pan psychic analysis because the hole is not only a scientific puzzle but also a mystical infinity and reality. A successful theistic panpsychic understanding of the black hole will make for possible logical discourse about the external world of outer space in Mars, Jupiter, Venus, Moon, Sun, and so on.

The endless investigations into the relationship among the sun, the moon, the earth and other planets namely mercury, Venus, Mars, Jupiter, Saturn, Uranus and Neptune are veritable subject matters of theistic panpsychic naturalized epistemology. That the planets are all hanging independently without any demonstratable connecting rods in a mechanistic way is beyond the laws of thought but an issue in natural science of theistic panpsychic naturalized epistemology. The challenges of the natural science or naturalized epistemology or the theistic panpsychic naturalized epistemology is to discover the laws, possibly beyond the laws of thought, governing the external world of outer space or the planets. These laws are mystical and they could be invariable because God does not play a dice with His creations. There may be limits to scientific knowledge in the areas of the rotation of the planets faster than the earth around the sun, the violence associated with these movements and within the planetary bodies themselves as well as the accidents of gaming and collapsing stars and black holes. That in these external world of outer galaxies 'tidal forces are so strong that a moon's internal gravity can no longer hold its pinnacles together' is evidence of another scientific question beyond science itself; "particles are continuously leaving and being replaced-either escaping from the outer edges or being pulled inward from opposite side and destroyed through atmospheric friction."[114] Catastrophic destruction of meteorites and satellites and the systematic emergence of new ones with new ring systems in the form of giant planets namely, Jupiter, Saturn, Neptune and Uranus could not be accounted by their mechanical properties alone. They are more active and agile compared with other planets orbiting the sun; they have powerful magnetic field, strong atmospheric worlds and extremely violent weather

[114] Obatala J.K., "The Solar System 13" in Science Guardian, *The Guardian*. Thursday April 19, 2007. p 33.

systems with awesome lightening lashes; all these raise the question of logic of outer spaces which a more penetrating one would be the transcendental reality of Theistic panpsychic naturalized epistemology.

There are still some lingering epistemological questions about the gravitational measurement of the solar system; given rise to 'beyond Emc^2'. Einsteinism is the highest and latest explanation of the properties of space and time as well as the measurement of gravity in and around the solar system. "But predictions about what happens around black holes and other places where gravity is extremely strong remain largely untested. There are paths and systems of the outerspace and time that cannot be computed or measured by mechanical devices along,"[115] for instance, the nature and shape of gravity in the black holes orbiting one another and about to merge. It has been observed that "the question of general relativity can be easily written down but are notoriously hard to solve. Astrophysicists were also to simulate the head-on collision of two black holes three decades ago, the computing of the paths of orbiting black holes and their violent merger proved much harder."[116] One observe that in this era of space time enginering - computation, calculation and measurement are gradually disappearing giving way for intuitive calculation of the geometry and contours of theistic panpsychic animistic space-time absolutes. Some of the absolutes or symbols are called myths which in African philosophy are constants and in general relativity of Albert Einstein are relativities of space-time gravities.

The fact of relativity in both theistic panpsychic epistemology and general relativity presupposes the end of physical science and equation, but a two-dimensional analogy of space time. "Einstein theory of general relativity changed the idea of gravity from a simple force dragging apples from a tree to a puzzle of geometry. Imagine a rubber sheet pulled taut horizontally and then tossing a bowling ball and a tennis ball into it. The heavier bowling ball sinks deeper and the tennis ball will move towards the bowling ball because of a direct attraction between the two, but because the tannis ball rolls into the depression around the bowling ball"[117] the space -time universe that belong to the outspace or the solar system beyond the earth, there are curves,

---

[115] Ibid.,

[116] See "When Black holes collide, gravity quivers," New York Times Science Service in the *Punch Thursday*, May 11, 2006 p. 14.

[117] Ibid.

values, holes and mountains, existing ones and those coming into existence which are all planks established or created by the laws of God, embedded in the mystical spectrum of holy grail of immortality of theistic panpsychic animism but discoverable by the logic of intuition and naturalized epistemology. Black holes are transcendental infinities created by colliding stars just as objects in their relative densities created depressions and holes on surface of the earth. In the African theistic panpsychic universe, the ideas should be black hole and black holes because the later subsist by the limited perception and delusion of man but which in reality, descend, merge or sink into one unit infinite black hole which is properly theistic panpsychic apperception of unity of infinity. Also in African philosophy the idea of collapsing star is not a myth or fiction, because there is a one that occurs on daily bases in the African Theistic panpsychic animistic universe. Although these collapsing stars, said to be the creations of African native wizards, do not subsist or exist in the same space and substrum with the terrestrial sky and its stars. Yet heir epistemology and logic could be a veritable hypothesis for understanding the complexity of spacio temporal reality and the dead end of the predictability of General Relativity theory.

THEISTIC PANPSYCHIC ANIMISTIC UNIVERSE

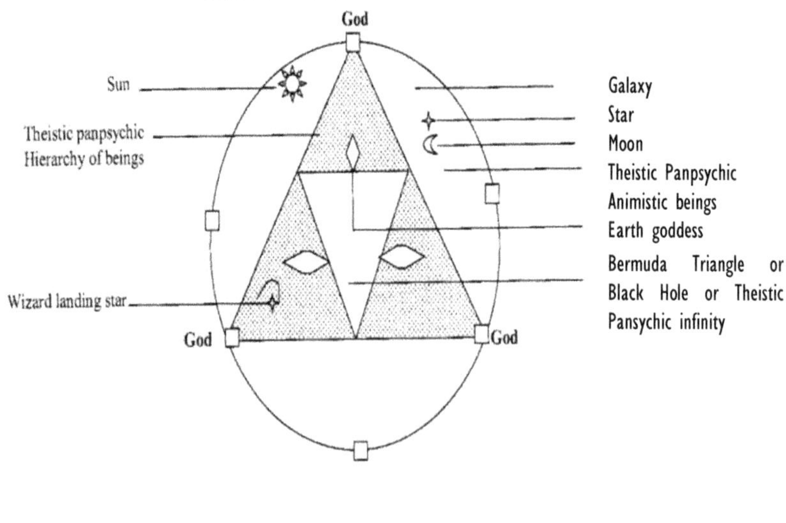

SYMBOL AND SYMBOLISM IN INFO-TECH EPISTEMOLOGY*

Symbols and Symblosmysticism

There is a difference between symbol and symbolism. Symbolism is esoteric, weird, mystical and supernatural. Symbol on the other hand could be grammatical, technical, logical or mystical. Also symbol could pass as a sign but not all signs are symbols. Man is prone to symbol formations. Men cannot do without symbols in his existence. Mans understanding of the world, himself and the environment is characterized and associated with symbol formation. The evolution of human mind was accompanied simultaneously with the evolution of symbols and concepts; "Concepts are mental particulars,"[118] so also symbols. The evolution of mind has to do with language formation just as man's scientific development starts from childhood, irrespective of his education. Western education is irrelevant here. The mastery of the cultural milieu and language is symbolization in itself. Even deaf and dumb people communicate with symbols. "Language makes every speaker, and even every deaf-mute who has some equivalent, for speech and its reception, a thinker; ideas of things, of moves to make, and if possible events fill his mind, and things, acts and happenings which realize or contradict his ideas fill his senses..."[119] Therefore, symbols were natural to man before formal language. Senses can only work when there are symbols. Even Kant recognizes them when he talks of categories of understanding. There are also sensibilities, that is, the intuition of space and time. These sensibilities function irrespective of whether the person is deaf or dumb. Hence symbolism could be called a second order system, a method, a medium.Symbols are unseparable from the evolution of man. Hence wine tapers and the local artisans understand and make use of symbols, despite being illiterate. The discovery of computer started with primitive signs and symbolisms: the computer language is characterized by formation and or use of symbols.

Symbol, in general sense, refers to that which expresses, represents, stands for, reveals, indicates or makes known another reality. For firth, symbols in general are signs with hydra-headed meanings. In other words

---

* Symbol and Symbolism in Info-Tech Epistemology was first published in *Nnamdi Azikiwe Journal of Philosophy, Vol. 2, No. 1, 2009. Nigeria*

[118] Sephen Laurence and Eric Margolis, "Concepts and cognitive science" in *Concepts, Core readings* (eds.) Eric Marsolis and Stephen Laurence (The MIT Press, England 1968) P. 9

[119] Langer, Susanne K., *Mind: An essay on human Feeling*, Vol. II (London, the John Hopkins University Press, 1972) p. 317

they are signs with complex referents which are often associated with man's emotions and sentiments.[120] He notes that symbols as instrumental tools in any cultural set-up are characterized by their expressive, communicative, cognitive and regulative qualities.[121] It is believed to have a psychical function of revealing the deeper aspects of reality which cannot be attained through any other means to man. Symbols are subjective realities whose objectivity is metaphysical while that of science is physical. Hence the objectivity of symbols could be defined in terms of inter subjective objectivity. This inter-subjectiveobjectivity implies that we as individuals in a society or culture agree on certain things based on our mode of living and religious experiences; that object of agreement or belief becomes for us an objective reality. Onwubiko distinguished three types of symbols namely, direct symbols, which are symbols whose material image express what they mean ideologically. Another is indirect symbols, which represent symbols whose material object signify a different thing which is not immediately observable in the material. Finally, there are non-material symbols, which are expressed in gesticulations and linguistic symbols which are forms of expression in which the actual meaning of the signs and words are known through an in-depth reflection. This is examplified in propositions, insensiblings proverbs. There is the possibility of confusing the symbol with the symbolized. The question of symbol is ultimately about the revelation or representation of reality. Thus symbol is a medium of representation according to certain determined norms or characteristics.[122] Furthermore, symbolism plays a vital role in the search or revelation of truth. Aylward Shorter sees a universal criteria of truth in symbolism when he writes that "...if there were no universal criteria of truth, people would be incapable of expressing their ideas and beliefs in languages and systems of symbols, and it would be impossible to have any scientific knowledge about such languages and symbol system."[123] Symbolism is the source or origin of most scientific knowledge.

Ukaegbu points out that „the distinction between scientific and symbolic thought is only analytical and does not imply that one is superior

---

[120] Firth, R., *Symbols: Public and Private* (London, George Allen and Unwin. 1973) P. 75

[121] Ibid., pp. 77-90

[122] Onwubiko, O.A., *African Thought, Religion and Culture* (Enugu, Snaap, Press Ltd., 1991) pp. 35

[123] Ayhward Shorter quoted by Ukaegbu, Igbo identity and personality vis-a-vis Igbo cultural symbols (Salamanca, 1991) p. 2.

to the other...[124] The simple fact as it is known today is that symbolic thought feeds scientific thought, even though symbolism forms its own science of symbols. Symbols pervade the African life and give meaning to their communal existence. Symbols make for unity in various aspects of their belief and existence. Old age and grey hair often symbolize a fulfilled life and may earn one the right to courtesy and politeness.

Again proverbs, gestures and even facial marks are symbols that may convey direct or indirect messages to people. The sign and the gesture require the association of certain conscious ideas in order to fully express or comprehend what is meant by them. To this extent, the symbol object has an esoteric-veiling-and at the same time an esoteric revealing function. The discovery of its meaning presupposed an understanding of a culture, because as a rule, it is based on the convention of a group that agrees on its meaning. Symbols can also in many ways be individually and subjectively construed.

There are many different ways of knowing reality, but symbolism has it as a primary objective to reveal the real; in other words to reveal the truth-the reality. Therefore symbol is nothing more than authentic truth. For Ukaegbu, the question of symbol revolves around order that is ontological. This ontological cosmic order opens an endless horizon of philosophical enquiry. It is this element of order in symbol that represents one of the main factors that direct and fashion all symbolic operations under the influence of symbolic logic. According to him; numbers and mathematics are known to represent some of the prehistoric symbols. For instance, the calculation of time and consequently the calendar gives us the different paradigms or cultural models that try to approximate the existing order in the phenomenon of natures.[125] Bonachritus Umeogu submitted that "the Igbo African thinks in symbols. He thinks with symbols. He thinks of symbol. He thinks through symbols. The system of thought of Igbo African is symbolismic.[126] The thesis is an attempt to reduce the framework or theory of further research in information technology to African *symbolismysticism* epistemology. *Symbolismysticism* or *symbolismystic* science is hereby adduced to be the epistemology of digital consciousness or information technology. *Symbolismystic* science is defined as digital, modularstic and

[124] Ukaegbu, Ibid., p. 36

[125] Ibid.

[126] Umeogu Bonachristus, *African symbolismic philosophy: Tractatus Symbolismico-Philosopheicus Africans* (Cifogne, Awka, 2003) p. 5

conceptualistic consciousness which, from Bantu or Igbo African metaphysics constitute the epistemology of information technology. In African Igbo, Yoruba, Akan or Bantu truth tabanacle, the neural structures of the brain are reducible to theistic panpsychic foundationalism. Theistic panpsychism as the metaphysical superstructure of the Black African philosophy is characterized by symbolism, *symbolismysticism*, monism and monadology all of which individually and severally presuppose digital consciousness; the digital human mind or consciousness is the digital world-write-large. It is the prototype or archtype proposition or word of digital machine or computer in the world of information technology. *Symbolismysticism* is the theistic panpsychic and the universal domain of digital consciousness where information is primitively stored *sympolismystically* or *symboliscientifically* in the theistic panpsychic consciousness from where it is evolutionally and subsequently released to the digital world or information technological world.

The Logic of Symbols and Symbolism

Wittgenstein in a logical and epistemological manner elucidated the concepts of sign, symbol and meaning in his *Tractatus*; a sign is what can be perceived of a symbol. A sign is the perceptible aspect of a symbol. It is a mark on a piece of paper, or a sound. A symbol will be a meaningful sign, a sign considered together with a meaning. Occurrences of a symbol will be those occurrences of its sign in which the sign bears a certain meaning. A symbol is a sign together with its meaning or sense.[127] For instance, in the proposition, 'Green is green' - where the first word is the name of a person and the last an adjective - these words do not merely have different meanings: they are different symbols.[128] Difference of symbol, Wittgenstein implies, is strictly stronger than difference of meaning. One and the same symbol may have different meanings on different occasions.

A symbol does not involve a meaning as a matter of its identity. What it does so involve, however, is a mode of signification. "So one and the same sign (written or spoken, etc.) can be common to two different symbols-in which case they will signify in different ways."[129] Difference of symbol with identity of sign implies difference of mode of signification, and difference of

[127] Johnston Colin, "Symbols in Wittgenstein's Tractatus" in *European Journal of Philosophy* vol 15, No. 3, Dec. 2007 p. 367

[128] Wittgenstein, *Tractatus Logico-Philosophicus* 3. 323

[129] *Tractatus Logico-Philosophicus* 3.32

mode of signification implies difference of symbol. In the sentence 'Green is green' the two instances of the sign 'green' are instances of different symbols, and this is entailed by the fact that the first is the name of a person and the second is an adjective.[130] Now something entailed here weaker than difference of meaning is difference of syntactic type. The thought is that a mode of signification of a sign will be, for Wittgenstein, a syntactic use. A sign signifying in a certain way will be a sign in use as a syntactic element of a certain kind (as an adjective, perhaps). Of course syntax here will mean logical syntax rather than surface syntax, and the proposal will accordingly be that a mode of signification is a logico-syntactic employment.

Further support both for the identification of a mode of signification with a syntactic use, and also for the proposal that a symbol is a sign together with a mode of signification, may be gained first by noting that a key symbol type for Wittgenstein is the proposition: A proposition is itself an expression and the signifying of a proposition is a depicting: A proposition is a picture of reality.[131] In addition: A propositional sign with its mode of depiction is the proposition and:

> If...then infinitely many propositions of different content follow logically from that first one. And this of itself that proposition itself is a matter of fact infinitely complex. That is, not the propositional sign by itself, but it together with its syntactical application.[132]

A symbol, for example, a proposition, is a sign together with a mode of signification. Or again, it is a sign together with a syntactical application. A mode of signification, the proposal will thus run, is a syntactic employment. A symbol is a syntactic element. A proposition, 'is a picture of reality.'[133] A proposition is essentially connected with the situation it represents, and this connection is precisely that it is its logical picture.[134] The essential connection between a proposition and its sense lies in the fact that the one is a logical picture of the other. If a fact is to be a picture, it must have something in common with what it depicts. There must be something

---

130 Tractatus Logico-Philosophicus 3.323
131 Tractatus Logico-Philosophicus 4.01
132 Wittgenstein, *Note Books*, 1914-1966 G.H. Vom Wright and G. Eni Annscombe (eds) Oxford Blackwell, 1998. p. 64
133 Tractatus Logico-Philosophicus 4.0
134 Tractatus Logico-Philosophicus 4.03

identical in a picture and what it depicts, to enable the one to be a picture of the other at all. What any picture, of whatever form, must have in common with reality, in order to be able to depict it-correctly or incorrectly-in any way at all, is logical form, i.e. the form of reality.[135]

That a proposition is a logical picture of a situation entails that the proposition and the situation share a logic form. It is a matter internal to a situation that it has the logical form it does. Equally, we should note, a symbol bears its logical form internally. Wittgenstein is quite clear that a sign does not by itself determine a form.[136] A sign does not determine a logical form unless it is taken together with its logico-syntactic employment. Only together with their syntactic use do [name signs] signalize one particular logical form.[137] It is a necessary condition for the determination of a form that the sign be considered together with its syntactic employment.

Therefore, names may and do stand for the most various forms, and it is only the syntactical application that signalizes the form that is to be presented. Pictorial form is the possibility that things are related to one another in the same way as the elements of the picture. That is how a picture is attached to reality; it reaches up to it [*es reicht bis zu ihr*].[138] A picture shares a form with the reality it represents; that is how the two are internally attached. Thus Wittgenstein comments on logical Form: a proposition reaches up to reality, and by this I meant that the forms of the entities are contained in the form of the proposition which is about those entities.[139] A proposition contains the form, but not the content, of its sense. A proposition and its sense stand in the internal relation of formal identity; external to a proposition, however, is the content of its sense. Given that a dualism of form and content is that of nature and particularly, we can express this by saying that a proposition determines the inner nature but not the particularity of its sense. It determines the type but not the token. A proposition contains the inner nature of the situation, that is, its sense, and thereby the possibility of representing it (being of the same form as a situation is, the only condition on the proposition itself for it to represent

---

[135] *Tractatus Logico-Philosophicus* 2 -1

[136] *Note books 1914-1966* G.H. Vom Wright and G. Eni Annscombe (eds) Oxford Blackwell, 1998. p. 53

[137] Tractatus Logico-Philosophicus 2.51-2, 1511.

[138] *Philosophical Occasions*, J.C. Wagge and A. Nordmann (eds) "Hackett, Indianapolis, 1993". p. 34

[139] Colin Johnston, *op. cit.*, pp. 373-374

that situation), but it does not contain that particular situation which is its sense.[140]

Sense Representation and Identity, here, need some clarification. Working with the Russellian categories of particular, property, dual relation etc., one might naturally say that 'Socrates is identical' predicates identity of Socrates and that this is nonsense because identity is a relation and not a property. Frege says that any legitimately constructed proposition must have a sense. And I say that any possible proposition is legitimately constructed, and, if it has no sense that can only be because we have failed to give a meaning to some of its constituents.[141] 'Socrates is identical' represents nonsense. The thought was that 'Socrates is identical' is nonsense because it predicates identity of Socrates and identity is a relation and not a property. 'Socrates' means Socrates, 'identical' means identity, and the proposition is of the subject-predicate form. Wittgenstein, will find here insensitivity to the sign-symbol distinction. Once it is note that it is symbols and not signs which are the (primary) bearers of semantic significance we will find ourselves with no reason to suppose that the symbol 'identical' appearing in 'Socrates is identical' means identity. If 'Socrates is identical 'is to be a subject-predicate proposition, then its component symbol 'identical' will have to be an adjectival symbol.[142] (Mr. Green's name shares a sign with a colour word but this does nothing to suggest that the two symbols share also a meaning)

Thus the reason why 'Socrates is identical' says nothing is that we have given no meaning to the word 'identical' as adjective. For when it appears as a sign for identity, it symbolizes in an entirely different way-the signifying relation is a different one: the two symbols have only the sign in common, and that is an accident.[143]

When 'identical' appears as a sign for identity its mode of signification is quite different from that found in 'Socrates is identical'. The two signs thus belong to quite different symbols, and when this is seen we lose all reason for supposing that they have the same meaning. Wittgenstein holds that a symbol and its meaning must share a form, and from this it follows that the 'identical' of 'Socrates is identical' could not mean identity. The former is an

---

[140] *Tractatus Logico-Philosophicus* 8.4733
[141] Colin Johnston, *op. cit.*, p. 380
[142] *Tractatus Logico-Philosophicus* 5.4733
[143] Colin Johnston, *op. cit.*, p. 380

adjective and the latter a relation. Generally, Wittgenstein's insistence on identity of form between a symbol and any semantic value it can have rules out, given the impossibility of ill-formed propositions, the representation of a logical nonsense. A proposition (propositional symbol) may be nonsense if it lacks a sense (fails to represent a situation)-and this will be so just in case it has a meaningless part-but it may not be nonsense in that it has a logical impossible sense. The proposition (propositional symbol), 'Socrates is identical', does not represent nonsense on account of what 'identical' means (that is, on account of its meaning a relation): rather it lacks a sense because no meaning has been given to its component adjectival symbol 'identical'.[144] The relations among signs, symbols, propositions and reality can therefore be summarized as follows:

> A sign is the perceptive aspect of a symbol.
> A symbol is a meaningful sign.
> Difference of symbol is stronger than difference of meaning. Difference of symbol with identity of sign implies difference of mode of significance, and difference of mode at signification implies difference of symbol. Signification is a logico-syntactic employment.
>
> A proposition is an expression symbol,
> The signifying of a proposition is a depicting.
> A proposition is the picture of reality.
>
> A symbol, a proposition is a sign together with mode.
> of signification or syntactical application.
> A mode of application is a syntactic employment.
> A symbol is a syntactic employment.
>
> A proposition is essentially connected with the situation it represents.
> The essential connection between a proposition and it's sense lies in the fact that the one is a logical picture of the other.
> Therefore, that a position is a logical form, i.e. the form of reality, of a situation entails that the proposition and the situation share a logic form.
>
> A symbol bears its logical form internally

[144] Langer Sussanne K., *op. cit.*

A sign does not by itself determine a form A sign determines a logical form only when it is taken together with its logico-syntactic employment.

A picture shares a form with the reality it represents
A proposition contains the form
A proposition and its sense stands in the internal relation of formal identity
External to a proposition is the content of its sense
A proposition contains the inner nature of the situation that is its sense and hence the possibility of representing it, but it does not contain that particular situation which is its sense.

Symbols and not signs are primary bearers of semantic significance.
Symbol and its meaning must share a form.
A proposition (propositional symbol) is non-sense if it lacks a sense.

In African metaphysics whether in Bantu or Igbo or Yoruba or Akan or Zulu cultures, words, propositions and sentences are theistic panpsychic and animistic and have the existential and commanding force of the divine authority. They represent symbols and tokens of understanding and reason in the exploration of the intentional, mental or empirical objects of the universe in form of reified or of objectified existents. They are windows to understanding and cognizing the external and the metaphysical world. "Words designating things carve out and fixate our objects, quite apart form the acts in which they figure, giving them a defined status they probably do not have for animals, for which they seem to be build into acts. So they are parts of acts and may not keep their identity from one situation to another.[145] Propositional symbols in African languages are primary bearers of culturally semantic meanings; they are pictures of reality with which they share a logical form. It has been argued forcefully, and I do agree indeed that the influence of language on human life goes much deeper than communication because it is intrinsic to thinking, imagining, even our ways of perceiving. In African epistemology, conception is not only generated from innate ideas but also abstracted from experience. The tokens for these conceptions are words, propositions and sentences, which in African philosophy or ancient Egyptian metaphysics are metaphysical. "Verbs are very interesting elements in our essentially static conceptual frame of entities

[145] Ibid., p. 320.

and properties, because they have the further function of referring the propositional complexes to the actual world of events, and therewith creating the entirely new dimension of truth and falsehood. Truth and its negative, falsehood, are not logical concepts, but basically metaphysical."[146] Truth and falsehood are properties of propositions in African metaphysics and epistemology, although false or true propositions have ontological existence either as good or evil; falsehood could be good or evil and truth could be good or evil. Propositions, falsehood, truths are metaphysical existents reflecting in empirical entities. That is why African epistemology is all together an idealist, rational and empirical inquiry.

Synthetic *A priori* and Symbolismysticism

Rationalism and Empiricism created a great problem for epistemologists. For rationalists, knowledge of fundamental features of the world is acquired through reason alone, for Descartes, basic principles of physics are derivable from geometric principles. For Spinoza and Leibniz, details of the world would be deducible from an ideal mind. Rationalism generally would indeed give a foundation for knowledge, but could not give an accurate picture of how knowledge about the world of nature can be acquired. For empiricism, experience is the sole grounding of the knowledge of the world. Therefore, our knowledge of natural facts are inductive, hence the casual laws are inferred from experience; we observe one event succeeding a prior one as the effect. Kant inherited many problems from rationalist and empiricist traditions. How can there be the possibility of having the knowledge of the sort obtainable in the sciences? Again, how to distinguish the three different kinds of objects of knowledge namely: (a) that based on tautologies; (b) empirical observation; and (c) general principles of nature, law and causation. His concern was how he can integrate the three forms of knowledge because Hume did not see the possibility for such knowledge, he ended up in skepticism. Immanuel Kant's Critique of Pure Reason resulted, in part, from the fact that he took David Hume's skeptical conclusions about such basic principles as causes and effects seriously, and the implication of such skepticism is Kant's grounding in rationalism.[147] Hume's position stems from extending the deductions made from the rising science of his

---

[146] Coupleston F., *A History of Philosophy* vol. 6, *The Enlightenment, Voltaire to Kant* (London Condium; 2005) p. 218.

[147] Scruton, R., *A Short History of Western Philosophy from Descartes to Wittgenstein*,2nd ed., 2002; p. 140

day, especially the physics of Isaac Newton. As stated above, science was making itself a universal discipline whose premises were certain and methods disputable only by an adoption of the stance of philosophical scepticism.[148] The new position of science and its finding made metaphysics a discipline of no consequence. The repute of metaphysics as a domain of knowledge became greatly questioned. The very position of metaphysics was thrown into doubt, and this very doubt was only exacerbated by Hume's radical skepticism- a skepticism which, according to Kant, aroused him from his dogmatic (Leibnizian) slumber.[149] For Hume, all knowledge concerned either relation of ideas or matters of fact. This is, more or less, Kant's distinction between analytic and synthetic truths. Hume held further that knowledge of the relations of ideas could be attained by intuition and demonstration; what, in Kant's terminology, means that it could be attained *a priori.* Hume however claimed that all knowledge of matters of fact comes from experience, what Kant calls synthetic aposteriority of knowledge. But then, how do we arrive at knowledge on the basis of experience? Hume suggests two ways; one of them is observation. If we observe a thing, surely we can know of its existence. But critics argue that very few of a man's beliefs about the world are beliefs about things directly observed. The enormous bulk of what man thinks of as knowledge requires what Hume calls his second method of acquiring knowledge which is experimental inference. From observation, man makes inferences about what must cause or explain them. But experimental inference always has to do with cause and effect. For example, from observation of B one may infer A. But of course to arrive at this conclusion one need more than mere observation of B; one need also the knowledge of the casual laws relevant to the production of B. Most of our synthetic knowledge comes from experimental inference, and experimental inference requires knowledge of casual laws. The dogmatic theory that woke Kant up was associated with Leibniz. At one time or another, Kant addressed all of Leibniz's main doctrines, including his defence of living forces against the Cartesians, his attack on absolute space and time against the Newtonians, his immaterial atomism or monadology, his theodicy, and his various principle and laws like the identity of indiscernible, continuity, noncontradiction and sufficient reason. His quarrel with the doctrine of

---

148 Quine W.V.O. "Two Gogmas of Empiricism" in (eds) Eric Margolis and Stephen Laurence), *op. cit.*

149 Ibid., pp. 140-141.

rationalism is that it posits knowledge of the kind it has no foundation to talk about or to possibly establish. His task then becomes the bridging of the gap between rationalism and empiricism by building upon what he thought was significant in both and rejecting what could not be defended.

Modern empiricism, by the over whelming influence of Kant's distinction between analytic and synthetic truth, Hume' relations of ideas and matters of fact and Leibniz distinction between truth of reason and truths of facts has been conditioned by what V.O. Quine called a dogma of empiricism. The Other dogma is of the belief that each meaningful statement is equivalent to some logical construct upon terms which refer to immediate experience.

These he called two Dogmas of empiricism. Although Quine seems to be in disagreement with Kant here it is only tangible and intelligible in degree, not in substance, and indeed the same applies to his relationship with African philosophy. In African philosophy, Kantian transcendentalism and Quinean epistemology, relations of ideas or truths of reason and matters of fact have a link in the symbolismystical form, which though tenous is not epistemologically negligible. In African philosophy, the relationship is characterized by symbols and symbolism in active and epistemological interactions. Kant reduced relation of ideas and matters to the common ground of synthetic *apriori* in which he postulated knowledge based in experience and innate possibilities. Quine's rejection of the dogmas of empiricism is based on a ground similar to the above with regard to African theistic panpsychic smbolismysticism and Kantian synthetic *apriori* or rather more pointedly to what Quine calls naturalized epistemology or what I call theistic panpsychic naturalized epistemology of the Bantu and Igbo people of Africa. All these posits are characterized by a collapse of the boundary between speculative or metaphysic and natural science and a shift towards pragmatism. Quine, like the Bantu, the Igbo or the Akan, is a pragmatist and an empiricist who identifies truth with the coherence atomistic and total field of experience. For him, to total of knowledge is man-made fabric which impinges on experience only along the edges while total science is like a field of force whose boundary conditions are experience a conflict with experience at the periphery occasions readjustments in the interior of the filed. Truth values have to be redistributed over field. Truth values have to be redistributed over some of our statement. Re-evaluation of some statements entails e-revolution of others, because of their logical interconnections."[150] Quine, therefore, can be interpreted to discountenance fragmented regimented pieces of experience in favour of total experience I coherence and pragmatic form. This is of course, consistent with his naturalized epistemology and very reminiscent but not purely linguistic form, of African theistic panpsychic naturalized epistemology both of which is characterized by coherence, pragmatism and *symbolismysticism.*

The bridging of the gap between empiricism and rationalism before Kant was the old corner stone of African philosophy; in other words *synthetic apriori* antedate Immanuel Kant. Kant's synthetic *apriori* is another or newer version of what I call *symbol-symbolism* in African philosophy. The 'symbol' is the 'synthetic' while the 'symbolism', is the *apriori* which can only be assessed by the substance of pure reason in the Bantu or Igbo peculiar process which I call *symbolismysticism.* Transcendental ideas in Kant's transcendental dialectics are symbolisms in *symbolismysticism. Symbolismysticism* as a theistic panpsychic transcendentality is a bridge between the phenomena and *nuomena. Symbolismysticism* is the metaphysical or symbolic interpretation of reality. Therefore, contrary to Kant's transcendental analytic, knowledge is not limited to experience only. Reason in theistic panpsychic *symbolismysticism* produces *apriori* concepts and ideas which demand only metaphysical and transcendental deductions. Bantu and Kant postulated the role of transcendental reason in streamlining and regulating understanding. While David Hume discusses cause and effect only at impressionable physical level, the African Bantu or Igbo traces the origin of cause and effect to the *symbolismystical* transcendentality and by theistic panpsychic reason. And Kant similarly postulates reason as a regulative instrument between the experience and the categories of mind which are transcendental, where *synthetic apriori* knowledge relies on the legislative authority of reason as its cause. In Kant and African Bantu or Igbo philosophy, therefore, categories and ideas are *symbolismystical* or transcendental concepts which in African philosophy is aided by theistic panpsychic deductive and inductive reason to explain cause and effect relations in arts and science, communications and neuroscience or cognitive epistemology.

---

[150] Copleston F., *op. cit.*, p. 278

Kantian Categories or Symbols?

In Kant, categories (symbols) are embedded in judgment forms while ideas are embedded in the forms of inference. Understanding is the power of making objective, perceptual judgment by the application of categories Understanding is, therefore, the faculty of immediate inference. On the contrary, reason is the power of making mediate or syllogistic inference whereby it does not concern itself with intuitions as understanding does in the process of making immediate judgments. Reason is concerned with concepts (symbols) and judgments and has no immediate relation to objects and intuitions.[151] Understanding brings about the unity of experience by means of intuitions and application of its concepts on those intuitions, but reason seeks the unity of judgment through arranging them in syllogistic order, that is, it tries to find the unconditional ground to the conditional knowledge of understanding so that the later be brought to its completion. In Kant the origin of categories (symbols) was sought in the four logical forms of judgments of the understandings (Quantity, Quality, Relation and Modality) while the origin of ideas is found in the three forms of syllogistism, categorical, hypothetical and disjunctive forms. Accordingly the concepts of reason founded on them contains: (1) the idea of the complete subject. (2) The idea of complete series of conditions (3) the determination of all concepts in the idea of a complete complex of that which is possible. The first is the idea of the absolute and unconditioned unity of thinking subject, the second is the idea of the absolute unity of series of conditions of appearance and the third is the idea of the absolute unity of the condition of all objects of thought in general.[152] The first idea is psychological and gives rise to paralogisms, the second is cosmological and gives rise to autonomy of reason and the third is theological and gives rise to idea of reason. Ideas have transcendental use and value. For Plato ideas are archetypes of things themselves, not in the manner of categories.Plato's ideas originate from the reason and since human reason is no longer in its original state it tries to recall by a process of reminiscence the old ideas which have become obscured. It is in Plato's ideas that Kant finds support for his transcendental ideas. But for Kant, Plato's Theory of ideas is impracticable because "it is judged in accordance with precisely those empirical rules, the invalidity of

---

[151] Smith N.K., *A commentary to Kant Critiques of Pure Reason* (New York., The humanities Press, 1980) p. 426.

[152] Mishra Sabbajeet "Nature and source of transcendental illusion," *Indian Philosophical Quarterly*, Special Number 200 years of Kant, January-October, 2004, vol. 31, Nos. 14 p. 31

which regard as principles it has itself demonstrated."[153] Kant says idea is a necessary concept (symbol) of reason to which no corresponding object can be given in sense experience, hence the pure concept of reason are transcendental ideas (symbolismystical concepts). In Kant, ideas are not arbitrarily invented; they result from the very nature of reason itself and stand in necessary relation to the whole employment of understanding. Since they overstep the units of all possible experience, no object adequate to the transcendental idea can ever be formed in experience. Ideas as transcendental concepts of reason are of great service to the understanding as a canon for its extended and consistent employment. But in Bantu or Igbo or Akan or Yoruba metaphysics, ideas or *symbolismystical* concepts stand on necessary relation to both the employment of understanding and theistic pantheistic reason. The ideas of pure reason can ever be dialectical themselves. This is because for Kant, they arise from the very nature of our reason. Reason as the highest tribunal of all the rights and claims of speculation should not itself be the source of deception and illusion. Hence, where there is misemployment of the ideas of reason they give rise to deceptive illusion. Good use or misuse of the ideas consist in their immanent and transcendental use respectively and when they are taken to have constitutive employment or conveyed to be supplying certain real objects, they become pseudo-rational and dialectical concepts. The values of ideas are pure. They guide the understanding towards greater knowledge and they make secure the field of the application of practical reason. The demand for the completion of the knowledge obtained through understanding pave the way for genuine metaphysics. The transcendental ideas can neither be evaded nor can be realized in experience, yet they point out the bounds of the pure reason and at the same time point out the way to determine them. As the presuppositions of reason, they take us to the realm of metaphysics. Transcendental ideas, therefore, are self-conscious regulative efforts of reason to find unity to the possible experience gained by understanding. But they are unable to present that unity as an object. Reason, according to Kant, is banned from making such an effort as it would lead to transcendental illusion. The values of the ideas consist in the fact that they enlarge the area of our knowledge without actually giving any knowledge.[154] Immanuel Kant's faculty of understanding and reason is meant to understand Mind in

---

[153] Ibid., p. 32.
[154] Kant, *Critique of Pure Reason* B. 375, A 319.

its complexity; thinking, intellect, natural intelligence or cognitive psychology in the history of Western philosophy.

Philosophers like Socrates, Plato, St. Augustine, St. Thomas Aquinas, John Locke, George Berkeley, Rene Descartes, Wittgenstein, and Bertrand Russel, etc., have contributed immensely to the understanding of ideas and legitimate preoccupation of reason in understanding objects of experience and innate ideas. Whether in empirical or rationalist tradition, ideas and knowledge are expressed propositional symbols. Kant's transcendental ideas and categories are *symbolismystical* concepts, properties and archetypes. But emphasis has shifted from the study of natural intelligence to the study of artificial intelligence or cybernetics starting with mind design, how it is built, how it works and how it can be transferred to machines. This has resulted to todays, Turing machine, today be computer and information technologies. Suffice it to say that computer and information technology is the height of the evolution of symbols of reason in the rationalistic and empirical interpretation of the world of matter and the supra-natural. Symbols have esoteric formations and they would continue to intervene mysteriously but innovatively in future computers and information technology which will rely heavily on the development of human mind. Yet some scientist and philosophers do not believe intelligence depends on anything immaterial or supernatural such as vital spirit or an immortal soul.

They believe that mind is nothing but matter in motion.

Cybernetics, Cognitive Science and Symbolism

Accordingly, A.M. Turing, the pioneering computer scientist, suggested that "intelligence is a matter of behaviour or behavioural capacity; whether a system has a mind, or how intelligent it is, is determined by what it can and cannot do."[39] Hence, combining the rationalist psychology and Turing's idea in what they call New Synthesis Nativism (NSN) mind gives a computational theory according to which, thoughts, have their causal roles in virtue of their logical form supervening on the syntactic form of the corresponding mental representation and mental processes as computations are reliably truth preserving in indefinitely many cases.[155] This view kept creating ripples leading to the idea that the mind is modular in nature as introduced by J. Fodor in 1983. He says that the mind is made up of modules and non-modular systems, which are characterized by the distinct roles marked for

[155] Mishra, *op. cit.*, p. 35

each of them. "While modules as input systems perform the task of transforming the information to which they are privy into a format comprehensible to the central system, central systems are responsible for undertaking large scale searches necessary for determining the relevance of current computations and responsible for fixation of belief."[156] The most salient feature of the central systems as computer machines is their cognitive penetrability. Computation machines "are essentially machines for recording numbers, operating with number and giving the result in numerical form"[157] and it is the rationality and predictability involved here that is being compared to the human mind. It is therefore, a project into the possibility of assigning a neural mechanism to John Locke's notions of ideas, David Hume's concept of impressions and Immanuel Kant's categories of understanding. For Locke the association of ideas occurs according to three principles: the principle of contiguity, the principle of similarity and the principle of cause and effect. Locke and Hume reduced the third to nothing more than constant concomitance and so is subsumed under the first, that of contiguity. For Kant the principles of contiguity and cause and effect are reducible to what he calls synthetic *a priori*. This is accepted by most materialist and cognitive scientists. However, the cognitive scientists have to prove that the modules, symbols or tokens operational on machines are not of reason and ideas and secondly that propositions of reason and ideas are not of the transcendent and first originated from matter. More often than not they do contradict themselves by confessing beliefs in the philosophies of Lebniz, Spinoza, etc., and invariably in panpsychic animistic philosophy or theistic panpsychic animism as the philosophical foundation of their works. Some are sandwiched between rationalism and materialism, a somewhat being aloof and some have camouflaged under a pseudo intentionality.

Brentano thought that "mental phenomena were one kind of entity, and material or physical phenomena were a completely different kind"[158] and that the mental state (belief, desire and so on) has the possibility of being related to another. Daniel C. Dennett accepts Brentano's definition of the mental but proposes a materialist view of intentionality that is, thinking intelligence is a matter of how a system behaves, but unlike Turing, he also

---

[156] Haugeland, John. "What is Mind Design?" in Haugeland John (ed) Mind Design II, Philosophy, Psychology, Artificial Intelligence (England, the MIT Press, A Bradfod Book, 1997) p. 3.

[157] Singh R.M., "Mind, Modularity and Evolution" in India philosophical quarterly, vol. XXXII, No. 1-2, Jan. Apml 2005.p. 110.

[158] Ibid., p. 107

has given an account of what it is about behaviour that makes it intelligent or endows the behaviour of a system with intentional or mental state. The idea consists of: (i) behaviour should be understood not in isolation but in context and as part of a consistent pattern of behaviour (that is often called holism); (ii) for some systems, a consistent pattern of behaviour in context can be construed as rational (such construing is often called interpretation).[159] Rationality for Dennett means acting so as best to satisfy ones overall goal given what you know and can tell about your situation. Generally, whether human or machine it is a consistent pattern of rational behaviour manifesting the same cognitive states and capacities repeatedly. Because of this, Dennett says, "rationality is the mother of intention."[160] This is the condition under which a system is said to take intentional state, i.e. manifesting beliefs, desires and goals. The point that must be emphasized here is that the intentionality of man is original *symbolismystical* system while that of artificial intelligence systems is derivative. One important epistemological deductively valid statement to fall out from this is that symbols and symbolisms or categories in the intentional state of man are original while that of machines and systems are derived from the former. But a formal system or machine is like a game in which tokens (originating from symbols) are manipulated. Similarly formal logic or a logical system is a token manipulation game, all having their origin from the mysterious man's mind or *symbolismystical* universe. The idea of a formal system emerged first in mathematics, and was inspired by arithmetic and algebra. When people solve arithmetic or algebraic problems, they manipulate tokens according to definite rules, sort of like a game. Numerals, for instance, represent numbers (either of specified items or in the abstract), while arithmetic signs represent operations on or relationships among those numbers. Tokens that mean something in this way are often called symbols. "Chess pieces, checkers, and go stones, by contrast, represent nothing, they are not symbols at all, but made formal tokens."[161] Symbol manipulation, however, is natural while that of the tokens or formal systems like chess and checkers is a second order intelligent network.

---

[159] Wiener Mobert, Cybernetics: or control and Communication in the Animal and machine (Massachusetts, the MIT Press 1965) p. 116

[160] Haugeland, John, *op. cit.*, p. 5.

[161] Ibid., p. 5

It can be argued that some connectionist networks in the brain, machines, computers and so on can only implement symbol manipulation because the primitive original prototype is "internal symbol manipulation."[162] A system or machine lacks feelings emotions, ego, imagination, moods, consciousness and invariably understanding, simply because it is artificial and fabricated from the prototypes in the primitive seat of consciousness and mind of man. However, the evolution of cybernetics and cognitive science has resulted to inducing understanding into formal systems on the condition that the prototype symbols from the mind or consciousness are applied correctly, adequately and in terms of their spacio-temporal possibility and verifiability. This has with limited success, challenged the African theistic pansychic animistic conception of the self or subject as the epicentre of knowledge, symbolismysticism, cognition, experience and action.

However it is important to prove, as this thesis is elected to achieve, the relation between the computational mind (information technology) and the phenomenological mind (consciousness) against the postulates of the cybernetic phase of cognitive science. Cognitive argument is that intelligent behaviour presupposes the ability to represent the world as being certain ways. It argues that intelligence and intentionality (semantics) are physically and mechanically possible. This reinforces the hypothesis that computers provide a mechanical model of thought or, in other words, that thought consist of physical, symbolic computations. Therefore cognitive science "becomes the study of such cognitive, physical symbol systems."[163] Similarly the cybernetic cognitive science originates from the idea of a logical calculus of ideas immanent in nervous activity "which aimed to achieving two things. "First, the proposal that logic is the proper discipline with which to understand the brain and mental activity, and second, the claim that the brain is a device that embodies loqueal principles in its component elements or neurons…"[164] This simply means that the brain acts as a prototype machine to other machines. But the cognitivists claim that the symbolic level of the brain is physically realizable, but it is not reducible to the physical level. They argue that because of this non reducibility it is quite possible that what corresponds to some symbolic expression at physical level is a different

---

[162] Ibid., p. 6
[163] Ibid., John, *op. cit.,* p. 16.
[164] Ibid., p. 25

and global, highly distributed pattern of brain activity. One source of confusion in the cognitive science or cybernetics is the perchance to void the separation of the brain and the mind as is the case in Bantu metaphysics or theistic panpsychic existentialism. The other source of confusion is the erroneous conception of the reducibility of the symbols expression of the mind to physical level. Yet in the theistic panpsychic existentialism, the brain is a physical container that houses the mind, the seat of consciousness, which is a universe of its own. And secondly in the *symbolismystical* thought or science, as case may be, every physical symbolic representation is reducible to the theistic panpsychic mind or consciousness. It is therefore intuitively obvious that symbols in the brain or in the conscious mind can be realized in numerous physical philosophical forms; with the former is the archetype or prototype while the later is the type. The former as is the original type that epistemologically substantiates the existence of the later, which could be multiplied in numerous but coordinated ways.

Cognitive Paradigms Compared

Cognition as an epistemology predates the cybernetic and scientific phase. As a philosophy, it is an all-round inquiry into the mental, objectives and spiritual experience of man, in relation to his environment, politics, economics and history. It predates "information processing as symbolic computation-rule based manipulation of symbols…through any device that can support and manipulate discrete functional elements-the symbols', the symbols appropriately represent some aspect of the real world…"[165] The assumption and the implication of cognitive research programme for an understanding of human experience are as follows: "(1) cognitivism postulates mental or cognitive processes of which we are not only unaware but of which we cannot be aware; (2) cognitvism is thereby led to embrace the idea that the self or cognizing subject is fundamentally fragmented or nonunified."[166] It also stipulates processes that are mental but cannot be brought to consciousness at all. Sigmond Freud supported this idea by denying any essential connection between the mind and consciousness. Dennett concluded that all cognitive theories are at "sub-personal level"[167] and that cognition is fundamentally a symbolic computation because none of us has any awareness of computing in a internal symbolic medium when

[165] Francisco J. Varela *et al.*, *The Embodied Mind* (England, the MIT press, 1993) p.41
[166] Ibid., p. 38
[167] Ibid., p. 42

we think. These argments are thread bare and completely dislocated from human nature and the history of the theories of overself and consciousness. The argument of the nonunified nature of the subject or the self, the separation of the personal from the impersonal or sub-personal and the question of the mental without consciousness at all suffer from a serious fallacy of separating the progenitor from the progeny, of severing the relationship between a child and his or her mother, of denying the consequent. We can understand the problem better from the perspective of the argument of form and matter. Platonism and African theistic panpsychic animism would postulate the originality, globality and universality of form while Aristotle would emphasize matter perhaps without denying its relations with form. But what the cognitive scientist is doing is declaring their independence after transplanting the picture of the mind consciousness and reinventing it in the physical space. But what one of the greatest scientists of our time, Philip Emegwali is doing does not seem to accord fully with cognitivism. His postulations on Super computer, Telepathic mail and Bionic brain predicated on a pantheistic-Super being paradoxically has an epistemological and metaphysical background on the subject, self, overself and theistic panpsychic animistic consciousness. In the Kantian sense of transcendental ideas and concepts; we agree with Philip Emegwalu that "anybody of knowledge has its "kernel of knowledge".[168] This is the irreducible essence from which that body of knowledge emanates in geometry. The theorems in geometry were constructed from a few rules of logic and some axioms. The axioms of geometry are what we called 'self evident truths'. They are ideas or presuppositions of reason. "The axioms of geometry are to geometers what the constitution is to lawyers. The self-evident truths in the law books are the statements written in the United States kernel of knowledge from which all laws were derived."[169] He says, that the computer and the Internet are similarly the kernel technologies behind the information technology field. By that he means that if all the computers in the world and the Internet were to disappear today, the IT field will for all practical purposes also disappear.

According to Philip Emeagwalu, information technology's conceptual foundation rests on the concepts of computation and communication. In other words, computation and communication are to IT what zeros and

---

[168] Ibid., p. 48
[169] Ibid.

ones are to computers. Therefore, information technology's kernel of knowledge is derived from two concepts: computing and communicating. But we argue that the conceptual foundation of computing and communication rests on concepts, symbols of reason or logic and by logical extension the pillar of information technology are tokens and symbols. Hence, the supercomputer as the driving force behind the computer, the supercomputer of today and the computer of tomorrow will be embedded in the categories of understanding and the symbolimystical ideas of pure reason. He says that "The engine that drives a supercomputer is the tightly-coupled thousands of processors which we have harnessed to compute and communicate simultaneously."[170] In these processors are highly complex networks of micro-field comprising first atoms and then tokens and symbols that are overtly given as concepts of understanding. He says again that, the engine that drives the Internet is the loosely-coupled millions of computers that we have harnessed to compute and communicate asynchronously. "Therefore, both the supercomputer and the Internet, in essence, comprise of interconnected computing and for transmitting and receiving data. And so on. Therefore, both the supercomputer and the Internet germinated from the same conceptual ideal, namely, the knowledge that thousands of processing nodes can compute and communicate, simultaneously."[171] But Philip Emeagwalu would be wrong on some theoretical fronts in the light of our postulation of tokens and symbols, metaphysical as they were, as the irreducible essence. He says: "the irreducible essence of a supercomputer is computation and communication, but the supercomputer places a greater emphasis on computation. The irreducible essence of the Internet is computation and communication, also but the internets place a greater emphasis on communication."[172] The use of irreducible essences by Emeagwalu however, is thread-bare and misleading.

Supercomputer and Internet cannot be the irreducible essence of computation and communication just as computation and communication cannot be the irreducible essence of information technology. Hence, all these alleged 'irreducible' are reducible and the only irreducible in science and technology are tokens, symbols, numbers and axioms. In other words, the

---

[170] Emeagwalu, Philip, "My Search for the Holy Grail of Immortality," keynote lecture, Black Data Processing Association, Augusta, Georgia, April 26, 2003.
[171] Ibid.
[172] Ibid.

irreducible essence of the supercomputer, the Internet and the information technology fields are the same. Softwares such as communication protocols, email, the web and graphic browsers as well as hardwares such as window operating system and PC evolved from atomic and molecular symbols, axioms and postulates. Therefore, the driving force behind the Internet was the atomic symbols and not the supercomputer.

We believe that the studies on scientific import of symbolism and symbolismysticism will remain the driving force behind the next generation of Internet or superbrain. One of the main missions and objectives of the cognitive scientist is to construct and promote an impersonal selfless mind and ignore the mysterious entity called personal identity. They were prone to achieve the notion and subsistence of selfless mind out of the separation of consciousness and intentionality from the other forms of artificial intelligent. Indeed the atheistic and nonpanpsychic approach of the cognitive scientist is as a result of its ancestry in the history of philosophy. It arose from the idea that experience or what the phenomenologists would call the life-world could be analysed into a more fundamental set of constituents. The aim of cognitivists scientist were not achieved as this project was deemed to be purely, abstract and theoretical. The project of the cybernetics and cognitivist received further impetus from the analysis and the analytic of the rationalist tradition in the West as exemplified by Leibniz, Frege Russell and the early Wittgenstein whose concern is with "analysing complex aggregates of societies-whether these be things in the world, linguistic or logical descriptions, mental representations or direct experience into their simple and ultimate constituents."[173] Therefore in cognitivism and computer, analysis as an abstract, theoretical exercise became descriptive and pragmatic. In this scientific tradition, the great tradition of the interaction of the mind and body at the pineal gland is set tumbling. Instead of the mind (soul) influencing the body, it is rather the body or the physical that does so. This yielded the argument, "the symbol-system hypothesis implies that the symbolic behaviour of man arises because he has the characteristics of a physical symbol system. Hence, the results of efforts to mould human behaviour with symbol systems become an important part of the cadence for the hypothesis, and research in artificial intelligence goes on in close collaboration with research in information-processing psychology."[174] The

---

[173] Ibid.
[174] Ibid.

argument here is an attempt to delineate the origin of symbolic human behaviour in the physical symbol system, a kind of epiphenomenalist approach to the mind and body problem. On the contrary, acknowledging the symbols in human mind or self as irreducible essence, research in information-processing psychology and technology involves the conduct of observations and experiments on human behavior in tasks requiring intelligence and the programming of symbol systems or *symbolismystical* existents to model the observed human behaviour. These propositions led us back to the evidence that the subjective, the self or the theistic panpsychic unity of apperception is the founding father or the guiding light of information processing technology in the empirical and global senses.

There is another argument that levels of cognition should not be thought of by analogy to the levels of computer system but with the acknowledgement that mental structures are like higher-level descriptions of a physical system only. This is because, just as "Newtonian concepts provide approximately valid descriptions of physical phenomenon that are more described with quantum concepts, so the symbolic concepts of folk psychology provide, approximately valid descriptions of cognitive phenomena that are more accurately described with sub-symbolic concepts."[175] Paul Smolensky, however, is of the view that the subsymbolic connectionist system of neural structures like areas, pathways, columns, neurons, membranes, nuclei, synapses, transmitters predicts and explains the actual cognitive behaviour of mental structures like goals, inference, perception, actions.[176] We could regard this argument as the theoretical paradigm and plank for the cognitivist scientist in puncturing the theistic animistic paradigm of science; this is and other paradigms are represented thus:

---

[175] Francisco J., Varela, *op. cit.*, 117-118

[176] Allen Newell and Herbet A. Simon, "Computer Science as Empirical Inquiry: Symbols and Search" In John Haugeland, *op. cit.*, p. 94

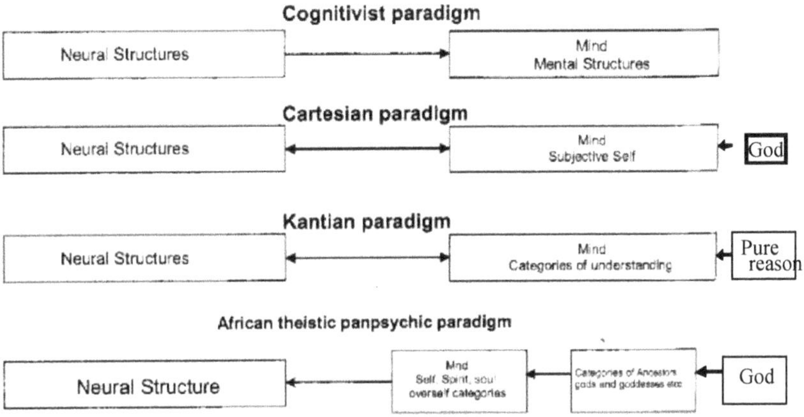

The above are sketchy illustration of the cognitive science and Cartesian, Kantian and African theistic panpsychic paradigms on the material and mental relations. The cognitivists do not make any pretention in their avowed belief that anything about man is physical or physical manifestation. That is why they have described human goals, belief, concepts schemata, knowledge, inferences, perceptions, actions as mental structures instead of mental concepts, and hence reduced mental structures to the neural structures. This is informed by the epiphenomenal framework of inquiry which they have accepted and consequently biased their method. On the other, in the Cartesian philosophy these goals, beliefs, knowledge etc are concepts of the subjective self; in Kantian epistemology, they are concepts of understanding, while in African theistic panpsychic animistic metaphysics they are concepts of the self or the soul. Therefore in African symbolismystical science they can be appropriately described as mental concepts or more appropriately concept of self or understanding without any physical connotations.

In Cartesian dualism, the neural structures (body) interact with the subjective self (mind) which is said to be subject and inferior to God as the most superior and powerful governor. The interaction is asymmetrical. Yet for Descartes, the mental state or the subjective nature of mind is not reducible to the brain nerveus: that is that the mind is not identical with the brain. The mind is a non physical substance. In Kantian transcendental idealism just like in Catesian dualism, there is the interaction of the neural structure (body) and the mind and that is why the arrows point both ways but assigning superiority to the mind. Some scholars, following Descartes supported the hypothesis that mental states such as perceptions, thoughts feelings and sensations are states of a different substance. According to this hypothesis, "no reduction of psychological theory to neuroscientific theory is forthcoming because the former is a theory about states and processes of mindsubstance, whereas the latter is a theory about the states and processes of a material substance, the brain."[177] This means that each substance (the mind and the brain) is thought to have its own laws and its range of properties. The argument of Catersianism or Theistic panpsychism is that one should not be led astray by the mathematized ideologies. According to Giovanmi Battista Vico, "mathematics is created in the self-alienation of the human spirit. The spirit cannot discover itself in mathematics, the human spirit lives in human institution."[178] To find things that cannot be mathematized then, we must look away from the physical world. Therefore, "if you are more of a human being, you will be aware that there are such things as emotions beliefs, attitudes, dreams, intentions, jealousy, envy, yearning, regret, longing, anger, compassion, and many others. These things, the inner world of human life, can never be mathematized."[179] There is an explanatory gap between the mental and the physical. The conceivability argument says: "it seems conceivable that there could be a creature physical like us (or functionally like us) and yet for which there is nothing it is like to be this creature; for which sensory states are very different from what they are like for us. If we really understood what it is about our physically or functional structure that is responsible for our sensory states being like what they are like (or being like anything at all), then it would no longer be conceivable that such a creature could exists."[180] The neutral structures in the brain are names that stand for various forms. They are: (1) forms in the Plato's sense; and (2), pictorial forms that are attached to transcendental *symbolismystic* scientific reality. They are physical symbols but there are existential or pictorial symbols which they share logical forms with which we

---

[177] Paul Smolensky, "Connectionist modelling: Neural computation and mental connections" in John Haugeland 238, *op. cit.*
[178] Ibid., p. 237
[179] Churchland Smith Patricia, Neuro Philosophy: Toward a unified science of the mind Brain (England, A Bradford Book, The MIT Press (1998). P. 318
[180] Davis J. Philip and Harsh Reuben, Descartes Dream: The world according to mathematics (U.S.A: Harvester Press, 1986)

contend represent reality. As concepts and propositions the neutral structures and their connectivist mechanisms or functional relations contain the logical forms of reality but not the content or sense which subsists in the *symbolismystic* reality. The dualism of form and content is reminiscent of Plato's world of forms, Cartesian doubt, and Kantian transcendental idealism and Africa theistic panpsychism.

Propositions of cognitive science or information technology determine the inner natiure but the particularly of the senses of the concepts as well as the type but not token. What determine the inner nature but not the particularities of the senses of the concepts are the symbols and symbolism in the *symbolismystic* transcendentality. It is with this connectivist network of propositions, words symbols that we say that a proposition represent reality. Representation here is logical and meaningful strictly in the sense of logico-syntactic employment and *symbolismystic* signification in a less determined but more of stochastized world of theistic panpsychic transcendetality which is a real, objective and fundamental aspect of the world."[181] The stochastization of the world crowd our digital consciousness, modular tenacity, *symbolismystical* expressions and equally the computer of today's information technology and cognitive science. Its major planks are probability, modularity and symbolism. Stochastization is part of "our thinking and behaviour that it can be said to be one of the characteristics features of modern life."[182] For instance "quantum physics is probabilistic, theory of experimental measurements is probabilistics", Stochastization, symbolism, *symbolismysticism* and modularity are all planks of African theistic panpsychic animism. In Kantian transcendental idealism, the categories of understanding namely, quantity, quality, relation, modality, interact with and enlighten the neural structures, which play the objective sensory organs, without which the external objects confronting the later would be intelligible. Also the relationship between the neutral structures and the categories of understanding is asymmetrical. But the concept of pure reason constitutes the highest magisterial authority and is the end of reason's enterprise, beyond which is transcendental illusion. In the sub-symbolic paradigm of the cognitivist, the neural structures are endowed with the

---

[181] Ibid., p. 13.

[182] Levine Joseph, "Conceivability, identity and the explanatory gap," in Hameroff *et al.* (eds.). Towards a sciences of consciousness III, the Third Tucson discussion and debates (A Badford Book, The MIT Press, Cambridge, Massachusetts, London, England, 1999 Davis J. Philip and Harsh Reuben Ibid. p. 18.

possibility of globality while the mental structure is local. On the other hand in the symbolic description of cognition in Cartesian dualism and Kantian transcendental idealism, the subjective self or the categories of understanding respectively, is the universe-writelarge, a micro-world, the innate or primitive globality, the original source of information processing psychology, and global consciousness without which the global attributes ascribed to the neutral structures by the cognitivists or epiphenomenalists would not exist.

Symbolismystic theistic panpsychic information technology[183]

The African theistic panpsychic soul or self, though lacks the sophistication and simplicity of modern information processing technology, remains the archetypal blue-print for all other paradigms of symbolic description of cognitivism in their complex interconnectionist network, as consciousness function as panpsychic animistic information processing psychology and technology; it is where symbols and symbolism primitively do the function of Kantian categories of understanding, and Cartesian subjective self in information processing. In the African theistic panpsychic animistic paradigm, a higher level of information processing psychology is accomplished by the theistic unity of the symbolic descriptions and representations of the ancestral and spiritual influences. It is in this sense that Bonachristus Umeogu conceives African *symbolismic* philosophy to be a "system or circuit of philosophy that moves from the logic and language of symbols which are either material or non material, to the consciousness, thought and understanding of symbolisms of such symbols, and moves on to the knowledge, truth, and meaning of the symbolismic expressions of such symbolisms ...a representative system of theories and practices, governing thought and conduct in relation to the meaning investigation of the principles and laws that regulate culture and existence."[184] Yet the powerful influence of God remains the most symbolic in connectionist networks of the subjective, spiritual and the neural objective symbolisms. In African philosophy, unlike in Kantian transcendental idealism, metaphysical knowledge is not only possible but also a reality and it is in this sense that the concept of universal Almighty God exist as the father concept of not only global information network but also the father concept of the universal

---

[183] Ibid. 19

[184] Umeogu B., *op. cit.*, p. 6-7

information network examplified in African theistic panpsychic animistic information network.

The theistic panpsychic animistic mind is globality write-large, micro universal mind of God or the divine spark of the cosmic reason, the reason of God which in connectionist network of yet unaccounted symbols and concepts generated the neural structures and patterns from where the computers are formed. This theistic panpsychic human mind or soul is neither rangimented nor nonunified but remains coordinated before the pure reason or the reason of God. Information processing technology in Cartesian dualism, Kantian transcendental idealism or African theist panpsychic animism is the view that consciousness is not a natural phenomenon and therefore cannot be understood in naturalistic terms but in the terms of theistic and panpsychic symbolism. Some adherents of this view think that "consciousness can be made intelligible if it is understood as a power of a nonphysical substance or as composed of nonphysical properties."[185] This thesis accepts conscious essentialism in cognition and the skeptics have no ground because incompetence is not knowledge or an argument. Consciousness is a world of its own with invisible mansions, moods, musings and mysteries. To prove it is difficult but not impossible. To prove it might require an agreement between mysticism and science. If according to Karl Marx consciousness is matter in motion,[186] then consciousness may contain atoms, neutrons, electrons, quanta etc. But this has an obvious difficulty in sustaining the existence of spirits, ancestors, Holy Spirits, and God. However, consciousness is the ultimate reality. "The universe is a creation of consciousness. The world did not come into existence suddenly as a finished product but it was created to acquire its present shape gradually by a process of evolution. Creation took the form of evolution because all creation, whether human or divine, takes this form."[187] However, it is safe to argue that consciousness remains a superior and independent domain of cognition that inform and create the mechanical universe and its machines including the information processing technology.

Consciousness as an interconnected network of symbolisms constitute a theistic pantheistic super structure of a super being, immanent and

---

[185] Flanagan Owen, *Consciousness Reconsidered* (England, the MIT Press, Cambridge, 1998) p. I.

[186] Sea Marx Karl on Economic Manuscript and Marx and Engels, 'Note' On Religion (Mosco Publishers 1981

[187] Ashrof Muhammed SH, Ideology of the Future (Pakistan, Ashraf Press 1970) p. 15

transcendental, from where artificial intelligence and computers originated and will inform the super computer and telepathic mail of tomorrow. This is in accordance with creation or evolution of theistic panpsychic nature. This is because, "the urge of human consciousness is not only to reach its own perfection but also to bring the whole of humanity to a perfection because the urge of human consciousness is the same as the urge of divine consciouness."[188] Philip Emeagwalu says, "We will gain a clearer understanding of the Internet if we observe it from another planet."[189] This is however a mechanical and physical perspectives. A clearer understanding of the Internet of today and tomorrow will be from immanent and transcendental authority of pure *symbolismystical* reason. He says, "Attempting to understand the Internet while standing on the earth reminds me of the parable of the nine blind men and an elephant. Each blind man based his descriptions of the elephant on a generalization of his sensory perceptions. The first blind man touched the elephant knee cried that the elephant is like a tree. The second blind man touched the tail argued that it is like a rope. And so on."[190] Well this parable only shows that discerning reality is difficult, grasping it is problematic and that the possibility of its understanding is a function of pure reason. The most popular software on the internets is email and the World Wide Web. As a result, most people cannot explain the difference between the webs with the Net. Like the blind men, people use the Web and then generalize and assume that the Web and the Net are the similar. Because the fibre-optic networks underneath the Internet is physically 10,000 miles wide and is metaphorically speaking is like an elephant, it is difficult to find two people who will agree on the best definition of the Internet.

To those of us standing on the earth, the Internet is tool for sending email and surfing the World Wide Web. But to an alien from out to space, the Internet will be seen as millions of interconnected computing and communication nodes. The alien will see the Internet as a spherical object as large as the entire earth that is used for transmitting and receiving data. I believe that it is the alien, who is observing the Internet from outer space that will see the true picture I will ask you to visualize yourself as that alien

---

[188] Ibid., p. 10
[189] Emeagwalu, *op. cit.*
[190] Ibid.

observing the Internet from the moon. I will also ask you to also travel with me, 100 years into the future.[191]

When the Internet becomes a zillion more powerful, faster and more intelligent: something weird will then happen. What will happen is that the computer as we know it today, will become obsolete instead we will be computing without computers. The computer will, in effect disappear into the future generation Internet, called "Internet X" or SuperBrain. by Emeagwalu What will also happen is that the Internet, as we know it today will become obsolete. Even the email, will become obsolete. Instead, we will be communicating by t-mail or telepathic mail. It makes sense to predict that the Internet will disappear into the "'Internet X' or SuperBrain. Since Superbrain is closer to a computer than to the Internet, it will make sense to predict that the Internet will disappear into the universal computer which, itself will literally be as large as the earth."[192] However this world of computer is a form of symbolic representation of consciousness that is yet to be determined. The growing trend in the scientific world is the evolution of symbols at different stages of scientific development leading to bionic brain implant, Superbrain, T mail or telepathic mail. Emeagwalu believed that: "We are determined to redesign ourselves. Our compelling urge to redesign ourselves is deepseated as we have to embark on a self-propelled evolution in which we are both the creator and the created."[193] This evolutionary scientific paradigm is wittingly or unwittingly supported by a pantheistic view of the universe which theistically retains God consciousness but which he calls Superbrain minus God. Is this possible? He says,

> the theory of evolution taught us that we evolved from lower order primates. But SuperBrain will help us understand that the human specie collectively existed as one SuperBeing. We will understand that we are not human beings that exist separately from other beings. Instead, we may come to believe that we are small and separate beings that exist within a Super Being...The big idea is not that from the theory of evolution, we may infer that the Super Being has been undergoing self-directed evolution since life first appeared on planet earth. It is a selfdirected evolution along the direction of greater complexity: a self-directed evolution that resulted in higher collective

[191] Ibid.
[192] Ibid.
[193] Ibid.

> intelligence. Super being is a coherent and self-organizing network of all living biological entities, which possessed a unique intelligence that is above and beyond the sum of intelligences of the separate living entities.[194]

Deductively, he concluded pantheistically that the animals and plants are not distinct beings. And that the species co-exist, interact and learn from each other. Gaia hypothesis also pantheistically argues that the earth is a living planet. From the moon, we see a zillion species that are isolated entities that swim within the earth's inert atmosphere, oceans or subsurface soil. "All living things are inextricably connected and work together as a team to ensure its survival as a Unified Being. I am not merely directly connected to every person, animal and plant. We are all one being. A Super Being."[195] What Emeagwalu is talking here is a universal consciousness symbolized by his Superbeing as an information processing agency, whether this is information processing consciousness or psychology or technology is another thing. He says:

> I began by studying the interconnectedness between millions of computers configured around the earth. I learned that interconnected computers do emulate on supercomputer. I then interfered that we could use that knowledge as a metaphor for living entities, which we also know, are interconnected. Therefore, I have interfered that interconnected animals and plants do emulate one Super being. Along the way, I learned a lesson that wasdeeper and one that transcended computing. It was epiphany. It changed the way I looked at myself, humanity and the Supreme Being or what we call God. I said a Super Being. Not a Supreme Being. I am not talking of the God that transcends space, time and all things physical. I am not talking about the theological God described in the Bible or the Koran. In fact, I did not talk about the existence of an ultra Supreme Being who is omniscient and omnipotent Super Being exists in a biological sense while the Supreme Being exists in the theological realm. Therefore, the acceptance of my theory will be based on reason, not faith.[196]

---

[194] Ibid.
[195] Ibid.
[196] Ibid.

From the above, Philip Emeagwalu thesis led him to what he does not want to believe. His thesis presupposes (which implied theism or God) pantheism, but as cognitivist scientist, he does not want to call it pantheism for fear of an obvious contradiction. As a pantheist who believes in the Superbeing as a content and selforganizing network of all living biological entities, he paradoxically denied the existence of an all powerful God but ascribed a directing intelligence to pure reason. Yet paradoxically he talks of cognitivist science with the consciousness paradigm of pantheism. However, Philip Emeagwalu pantheistic cognitivist scientific thesis, if explored further could lead to unraveling the mystery in African theistic pantheistic animistic consciousness and how it can contribute to the bionic brain computer, supercomputer and telepathic mail. This direction of research would also benefit from Newtonian physics, Boyles animism and Albert Einstein theistic panpsychism and animism.

We have tried to argue that the epistemological basis of information technology and science is largely the African theistic panpsychic naturalized epistemology, Kantian *synthetic a priori* and Quinean naturalized epistemology. It is a particular and unique theistic panpsychic consciousness which synthetic panpsychic and pantheistic digital universal consciousness which n Africa philosophy culminated in one, single ultimate principle, the God-concept. This realm of conscious is inhabited by a complex network, interconnected symbols in modular and monadistic interactions in a pantheistic or panpsychic interactions in a pantheistic or panpsychic universes where information is complete gained but not lost. That is why Godconcept is the prime mover in interconnected network of information axis and galaxies; that is equally why all the mental neurons in the brain are ducible to the galaxies of human mind and the large galaxies of the u niverse in the theistic panpsychic or panthesistic sense. Quine escaped from strick empiricism in his rejection of the dogmas of empiricism into African theistic panpsychic totality or the Sarterian or Jasperian encompassing totally otherwise known as universal consciousness of the Godconcept, the prototype of digital consciousness and modular *symbolismystal* cognitive science. This is nothng short of

Cartesian 'I think therefore I am', Spinoza monism, Leibinz monadology, Kantian transcendental unity of apperception of African theistic panpsychic animism all of which collectively constitute the centre of universal information assimilator, transmitter and disseminator rendered either as psychineses, telepathy, etc. The transcendental or theistic panpsychic centre of information consciousness is, therefore, the irreducible essence of information technology. All other corporeal and mundane information networks are separate forces that exist within the transcendental or theistic centre of information gravity otherwise, called unity of consciousness. Accordingly in the future researches into the information technology and the allied cognitive sciences, telepathy, psychinesis super-computer, Internet or super-brain are reducible to the universal transcendental consciousness, digitalized or otherwise, called theistic panpsychic cognitive science.

BIBLIOGRAPHY

Aasdair, Macintyre." Is understanding Religion compatible with Believing?," in *Rationality,* ed. Barryan R. Wilson, Oxford, Britain, Basil Blackwell, 1997.

Abdu-Aguye, I. "Venereal Diseases" in Ed. Aguwa, C. N., *Therapeutic Basis of Clinical Pharmacy in the Tropics*, London, Macmillan, 1986

Abiodun, Oladele, Balogun, "The Belief in God (*Oludimare*) and Divinities in Traditional Yoruba Thought," in *Essence Interdisciplinary International journal of Philosophy, No 2, 2005.*

Abiola, Irene, "The Tragic Conflict in Achebe's Novels," *Black Orphans*, IT, Ibadan, 1965.

Abiola, Irene. *The Crisis of Cultural Memory in Chinua Achebe's Things Fall Apart*, New York; Anchor Books, 1994.

Achebe, Chinua, *Things Fall Apart* (Heinemann, London, 1958 Ade, Adegbola E. A., *Traditional Religion in West Africa,* Ibadan Day Star Press 1983.

Adeboye, Oyesanya, "*IFA,* The Do It yourself. For the Beginners" in *Orunmila Magazine, Issue No. 2 June 1986.*

Adedayo, Festus, "The Dilemma of a snake" in *Guardian newspaper Ltd, online article, Tuesday, February 1 2005,* *http://adilinet/news/source/2005/feb/146html*http://adilinet/news/source/2005/feb/146html

Adele, Bangbose."The Place of Deities in African Political Systems" in *Essence Interdisciplinary International Journal of Philosophy, No2, 2005,*

Afanasyev, U. G. *Marxist Philosophy*, Moscow, Progress Publishers 1953.

Afigbo, Adiele. *Ropes of Sand, Studies in Igbo History and Culture*, Nsukka Nigeria University of Nigeria Press, 1987.

Agera, Cassian R., "Some Reflections on Indian Syllogism" in *Indian Philosophical Quarterly, Vol. XVI, No. 4, Oct. 1989,* 205..

Aghamelu, F.C., Culture and Freedom," in *Essence Interdisciplinary International Journal of Philosophy, No2, 2005,*

Aghamelu, Heken U., "Traditionalism and the woman Question in Nigeria." in *Essence Interdisciplinary International Journal of Philosophy, No 2, 2005,*

Ajayi, S.A. *West, African Traditional Religion*, Ado-Ekiti, Omolayo Standard Press, 1981. 103.

Aderibigbe, I., *Religion, Study and Practice*, Lagos, Almon School Press Ltd. 1997.

Ajikola, J.O., *Owe Yoruba*, Ibadan University Press Ltd. 1974.

Akere, Funso, *Linguistic Assimilation in Socio-Historical Dimension in Urban and Sub-urban Lagos,* 1985.

Akinlade, Kola, *Owe ati Humo*, Ibadan, Abiprint Publishing Company Ltd, 1982.

Alasdair, MacIntyre, 'Myth'" in *Encyclopaedia of Philosophy, Vol. 5 & 6,* New York, Macmillan Pub. Co. 1967.

Albert, Mosley, "The Metaphysics of Magic: Practical," *in Indian Philosophical Implications", Second Order, African Journal of Philosophy,* Vol. VII 1 & 2 and July 1978

Albert, W. J., "Art and Otology" in *Indian Philosophical Quarterly* Vol. XXII, No. 2, April, 1995

Allen Newell and Herbet A., Simon, " Computer Science as Empirical Inquiry: Symbols and Search in Haugeland John (ed) *Mind Design II, Philosophy, Psychology, Artificial Intelligence*, England, the MIT Press, A Bradfod Book, 1997.

Altelkar. "Quantum gravity: Some Philosophical Reflection" in *Indian Philosophical Quarterly,* Volume XVIII No 2. 1991

Alterkar. "Quantum Gravity: Some Philosophical Reflection " in *Indian Philosophical Quarterly,* Volume XVIII, No. 2, 1991.

Amo, Anton, William., "*Treatise On The Art of Philosophising Soberly and Accurately",* ed. Professor T. Nzodinma Nwala, Special Publication of William Amo Centre for African Philosophy, Department of Philosophy, University of Nigeria ,Nsukka, 1990.

Ananda, Reddy. V., 'The Process of Physical Transformation," in *Indian Philosophical Quarterly* Vol. XVIII No.2, April 1991,

Anders, Wedberg. *A History of Philosophy, vol. 3*, Britain Oxford, Clarendon Press 1984,

Anigboi, Francis. "Igbo Deities and metaphysical Ethics" in *Essence Interdisciplinary International Journal of Philosophy, No2, 2005,*

Anyanwu, K. C., "The Problem of Method in African Philosophy," in Momoh C. S. (ed*) The Substance of Philosophy,* Achi, Nigeria, African Philosophy Projects" Publications, 1989.

Anyanwu, K. C., "Presupposition of African Socialism" *The Nigerian Journal of Philosophy,* Journal of the Department of Philosophy, University of Lagos, Nigeria. *Vol. No. 1 & 2. 1983.*

Anyanwu, K.C., "Scientific Attitude and African Humanistic Values" *The Arts and Civilization of Black and African peoples Vol. II, Black Civilization and Philosophy,* Lagos, Centre for Black and African Arts and Civilization 1986

Anyanwu, K .C., "Mario Formulation of causal law" in *The Nigerian Journal of Philosophy, Department of Philosophy University of Lagos, Nigeria vol. 5, Nos I and 2 1985.*

Anyanwu, K. C., Presuppositions of African Socialism" in *The Nigerian Journal of Philosophy,* University of Lagos Vol. 3, No. 1 & 2, 1983

Anyanwu, K.C. "Philosophical Significance of Myth and Symbol in Dogie World-view" *in* C.S.Momoh, *The Substance of Philosophy*, Auchi, Nigeria, African Philosophy Projects" Publications, 1989.

Appiah, Kwame, Anthony, *Introduction to Things Fall Apart*. New York" Knoof, 1992,

Appiah, K. A., *In My Father's House*, New York and Oxford: Oxford University Press, 1992.

Arinze, F. A. *Sacrifice in Ibo Land*, Ibadan, Ibadan University press, 1978.

Arthur, Koester, *The Roots of Coincidence: an Excursion into Parapsychology*, New York, 1973.

Ashrof Muhammed SH, *Ideology of the Future*, Pakistan, Ashraf Press 1970.

Augustine, *St. Confessions*, England, Penguin Books Ltd. 1970.

Aurobindo, Sri, *On Himself*, Birth Centenary Library, Sri Aurobindo Ashram Trust, 97 46

Auther, Pap. "Does Science have metaphysical Presuppositions" in Herbert Feigle and May Brodbeck, *Readings in the Philosophy of Science*, New York, Appleton, Century Crafts Inc. 1953.

Ayantayo, J.K., "Social Signifinance of Traditional Religious Rituals"in *Essence Interdisciplinary International journal of Philosophy, No2, 2005,*

Ayhward Shorter quoted by Ukaegbu, *Igbo identity and personality vis-à-vis Igbo cultural symbols*, Salamanca, 1991

Azikiwe, Nnamdi. "Africa in Renascence" *Reading in African Political Thought* Gideon-Cyrus et al, London, Heinemann, 1975. Bail, D. R., *Introduction to Philosophy,* New Delhi, sterling Publishers Private Ltd., 1997.

Baldwin, Tom. "The Inaugural Address:, Kantian Modality" *Joint Session of the Aristotelian Society and The Mind Association, University of*

Glasgow, July 5-7 2002"- in The Supplementary Volume LXXVI 2002, The Aristotelian Society.

Bannerman – Richer, Gabriel, *The Practice of Witchcraft in Ghana,* California, Gabriel Publishing Company, 1982.

Barry, Hallen,"Phenomenology and the Exposition of African Traditional Thought" in Sophie Oluwole (ed) *Readings in African Philosophy: An Anthology,*Lagos, Nigerian Meastech Publications, 1989.

Baruch, Spinoza, *The ethics of Spinoza*, edited by Dagobert D. Runes, Citadel Press, London, 1957,

Beck, L. W., *Kant: Critique of Practical Reason,* Indianapolis: Boobs-Merrill Educational Publishing Company, 1996.

Beier. ed.:"Introduction of African Literature: An Anthology of Critical Writing" from Blach *Orpheus* London: Longman, 1967.

Benjamin, B., Wolman, 'Kant Immanuel" In *International Encyclopedia of the social sciences*

Bannerman-Richer, Gabriel. *The Practice of Witchcraft in Ghana.* California, Gabari Publishing Company, 1982.

Berkeley, George, Justus, Hartnack. (ed) New York, Humanities Preside Inc. 1973.

Bernstain, Richard .J., *Habermas and Modernity, MIT* Press, Cambridge, Massachusetts

Bernstein, Richard .J., (ed) "Introduction" in *Habermas and Modernity* Cambridge, Massachusetts, the MIT Press.

Bertrand, Russel. "On Scientific method," *Mysticism and Logic*, 1914.

Bertrand, Russell. *The Problem of philosophy*, New York: Oxford University Press 1980

Bridgrian, P. W., "The Logic of Modern Physics" in Herbert Feigle and Ma Broadbeck (eds). *Readings in the philosophy of Science,* New York, Appleton, Century Crafts Inc. 1953.

Bodunrin. P., *"The Question of African Philosophy" Philosophy Vol. 56, 1981.*

Broad, C. D., *Kant: An Introduction*, New York: Cambridge University Press, 1978.

Brown, Radcliff. *Structure and function in primitive society,* London, Cohen and West, 1952

Bruce, Aune. *Rationalism, Empiricism and Pragmatism: An Introduction*, New York, Random House, 1920.

Bruthl, Levy, *Postumus Notebook,* New York, A. M. Press 1978.

Bynum, Edward, *The African Unconscious, ,* New York Teachers College Press 1999.

Bernth, Lindfors, and C.L., Innes. (Eds.) *Critical Perspectives on Chinua Achebe,* Washington, D.C., Three Continents Press. 1978.

Calm, S M., (ed), *Classics of Western Philosophy*, U. S. A.: Hacket Publishing Company, Inc. 1990.
Chambers 20th Dictionary, ed B. M. Kirik Patrick, Britain, Wand R. Charibar Ltd.
Chijioke, J. O., "The Role of Shrine /Deities in the Dispensation of Justice in a Traditional African Society" in *Essence Interdisciplinary International journal of Philosophy, No2, 2005,*
Chisholm, R.M., "Law statements And Counterfactual Inference" in Ernest Sosa
Christian, L .J., *Philosophy: An Introduction to the Art of Wondering*, Calif: Rinehart Press,
Churchland Smith Patricia *Neuro Philosophy*: *Toward a unified science of the mind Brain,* England, A Bradford Book, The MIT Press, 1998.
Collier, Eugenia. "The African Presence in Black American Literary Criticism" in *The Arts and Civilization of Black and African People, Vol. Three, Black Civilization and Literature*. Copi, Irving M., *Symbolic Logic 5th edition, New York*, Macmillan Pub. Co. Inc., 1979.
Coupleston F., *A History of Philosophy vol. 6, The Englithenment. Valtaire to Kant,* London, Condium; 2005
Coupleston, F.*A History of Philosophy; Vol. 6, Modern Philosophy; part 11 Kant,* New York, Image Books, 1964.
Critchley, Simon. "Philosophies As Poetry" in Havi Carel and David Gamez, *What is Philosophy*, London, Continuum, 2004
Crowder, Michael. *The Story of Nigeria*, London, Faber, 1962.
Crowder, .J., (ed) , *Oxford Advanced Learner Dictionary*, Oxford University Press New York. 1995
David, G., and P., Gwynne. "Proning the Universe" in *Newsweek, the International News Magazine, March 12, 1979,*
David, Gelman, "Field Theory: Glimpse of Unity" in Newsweek, March 12,
David, Gelman and P., *Gwynne, "Probing the Universe* "In Newsweek, the International News Magazine, March 12, 1979.
David, Hume, quoted by Bruce Aune, *Rationalism, Empiricism and Pragmatism, An Introduction,* New York, Random House 1970
David, Thompson, ed *Political* Ideas ,Britain, Penguine Books 1966.
Davis J., Philip and Harsh Reuben, *Descartes Dream: The world according to Mathematics, U.S.A*: Harvester Press, 1986.
Debrekerinert, *Witchcraft in Ghana,* Brown Knight and Truscott Ltd., 1961.
Descartes, R. *Principles of First Philosophy*. Trans by Anscombe, E., Geach, P. T. London: Thomas Nelson & Sons Ltd. 1968.
Deshande, Shard, "Causation, Explanation, and Understanding", in *Indian Philosophical Quarterly Vol. XXII, No. 4, Oct: 1995*

Dioka, Walter."The Evolution of Nigerian International Boundary 1961-1989" eds. A. Adefuye, B. Agiri, and J. Oshuntokun in *The History of the People of Lagos State* (Lagos, Lantern Books 1987)
Diyanm, Robert, *Critical perspectives; Approaches to the Analysis and Interpretation of Literature*, New York, McGraw Hill, Inc. 1995.
Dostoevsy to Satre (New York, A memdian Book, Now American Library, 1956) 128.
Ducasse, C. J., "On the Nature and the absorbability of the Causal
Relation" in Causation And conditionals Ernest Sosa (ed) (Oxford Readings in philosophy, Oxford University Press 1980.
Dukor, M., "African Polymonotheism And Existentialist Humanistic Culture" in *Philosophy and Social ActionVol.5 No.1, 2nd June 1989.*
Dukor, M. "African Concept of Man" in *Orunmila*, No.6, June 1990.
Dukor, M., "God And Godlings in African Ontology" in *India Philosophical Quarterly Vol, Xvii No.1, January 1991.*

Dukor, M., "African Cosmology And Ontology" in *India Philosophical Quarterly, Vol. Xvi, No. 4, October, University Of Pooma; 1993.*
Dukor, M., "Idealism, Coherence And God; A Critical Inquiry" in *Haggadah LASU Journal Of Christian And Philosophical, LASU Vol. 1993.*
Dukor, M., "Rationality of An African Science" in *Journal of Oriental And African Studies, Athens Greece, Volume 7, 1995.*
Dukor, M., "Epistemology As The Foundation of Scientific Reasoning" in *Essence International Journal Of Philosophy Vol. 1, No. 1, 1996.*
Dukor, M., "Perception, Intuition and Knowledge of the External World: Scienticizing African Philosophy" in *Indian Philosophical Quarterly Xxvii No. 4, October 2000.*
Dukor, M., "Theistic Humanism; African Philosophical Tradition" in *Journal of India Council of Philosophical Research, Volume Xviii No.3*
Dukor, M., "Afro-Theodicy: Freedom And Determinism": in *Journal For The Scientific Study Of Religion.* Vol. 2, No.1, February, 2002.
Dukor, M., "Emotion, Reason and Scientific Inquiry: Conceptual Relativism in Western And African Philosophies" in *Jadavper Journal Of Philosophy Vol. 12, Nos. 1 And 2, 2000.*
Dukor, M., "Kant Epistemology and African Faculty of Knowing" in *Philosophy and Progress, University of Darkha, Bangladesh June - December 2002.*
Dukor M., "Philosophy and Scientific Paradigms", the concept of space and time in African philosophy and quantum Gravity" in *Philosophy and Praxis Vol. 1, 2005, Journal of Nigerian Philosophical Association,*

Dukor .M.,"African Philosophy and the Pathology of Traditionalism", Editorial, in *Essence, Inter-disciplinary – International Journal of Philosophy No: 2, 2005.*

Dukor .M., "African Philosophy in World Scientific - Heritage" in *Essence, Interdisciplinary – International Journal of Philosophy No: 2, 2005.*

Dukor, M., "The Great Debate: Deconstruction, Recognition and Cognition of African Philosophy" in *Philosophia, Philosophical Quarterly of Irsael, Vol. 33, Nos. 1-4, (2005).*

Dukor M., "The Doctrine of Humanism Revisited" in *The Nigeria Journal of philosophy* vol 1, 2006.

Dukor M., Theistic Pansychic Animism of African Medicine" in *Essence Interdisciplinary -International Journal of Philosophy,* No 3. 2006.

Dukor M., "Propositions of African Cultural Values" *Arts and Humanities Quarterly, vol. 2 January-Nov. 2007r.*

Dukor M., "God, Man and Nature in Spinoza" Fitche"s and Leibniz" in *Nnamdi Azikiwe University Journal of Arts* and Humanities, Vol IX Sept 2007.

Dukor, Maduabuchi. *Symbolic and Philosophical Logic*, Lagos, Essence Library, 2004.

Dukor, M., (ed) "How not to Empower Women" in Dukor, M. *Philosophy and Politics: Discourse on Values, Politics and Power in Africa*, Lagos, Malthouse Press Ltd. 2002.

Dukor, M., "Echoes of Horishima" Poetry: *The Guardian, Saturday,*

Dukor, M., "Father"s Death" in *Guest Poet:* The *Post Express on Sunday,*

Dukor, M., Ph.D Thesis, *The Concept of African Freedom,* University of Nigeria, Nsuka 1993.

Dukor, M., "Justice and the Principles of Necessity" in *Philosophy and Politics* ed. Dukor Maduabuchi, Nigeria, Malthhouse PressLtd, 2003.

Dukor, M., "Corruption and Social Action in Nigeria" in *Philosophy and Social Action Vol. 16, No.3* July – Septembe,. 1990

Dukor, Maduabuchi. "Guest Poet" in *Poetry, The Post Express On Sunday, August 4, 2002.*

Dummett, M. *Frege; Philosophy of Language,* London, Duckworth.1973.

Olorunleke, Ojo. "Aproaches to Literary Criticism in the 20th

Century" in Ojo Olorunleke, *Material ist Essays in Literature,* Ibadan, Olu-Akin Pub. 2004.

Kwame, Gyekye, *Beyond Culture: Perceiving a Common Humanity*, Ghana Academy of Arts and Sciences Accra, 2000

Egudu, R.A. "Africanity in Modern African Literature" in *The Arts and Civilisation of Black and African Peoples; Vol. 3, Black organization and Culture,*

Echekwube, A. O. "The Basic Principles of African Philosophy" in *Essence: Interdisciplinary, International Journal of Philosophy No2 . 2005.*
Edward, W. Blyden. "Ethiopia stretching out her hands unto God; or Africa"s service to the world" in *Readding inAfrica Political Thought* eds. Gideon Cyrus n Mutiso and S.W. Rohio, London, Heinnman 1975.
Egonwa, Osa D, *African Art* , Edo, Nigeria; Edo State house of Assembly Printing Press ,1994.
Egudu, Romanus, *"Achebe and the Igbo Narrative Tradition". Research in African Literatures. Vol 12, No 1, Spring, 1981.*
Einstein, Albert, *"In Time person of the Century, Dec. 31, 1999, Vol. 154, No. 27*
Einstein, Albert. *"The Fundamentals of Theoretical Physics"* in F. Feigl and M. Brodbeck (eds) *Reading in the Philosophy of science*, New York. Appleton-century-Crofts. Nc., 1953.
Einstein, Albert, "The laws of Science and the laws of Ethics" in F. Feigl and Brodbeck (eds) *Reading in the Philosophy of Science,* New York. Appleton –century-Crofts. Nc., 1953.
Einstein, Albert." Geometry and Experience" in F. Feigl and M. Brodbeck (eds*) Reading in the Philosophy of science*, New York. Appleton-century-Crofts. Nc,. 1953.
Einstein, Albert, *Relativity: The Special and the General Theory*.(Trans) R. W. Lawson, New York, bonanza Books.
Ejiza, C. I. "Continuity and Discontinuity for Igbo Traditional Religion," in Metuh ed. *The God"s in Retreat*, Enugu, fourth dimension, 1986.
Ekiyor, Henry, "The Philosophy of Traditionationalism; A Brief case Study of Corruption in Nigeria" in *Essence Interdisciplinary International journal of Philosophy, No2, 2005,*
Ekwueme, Laz. *Teasers; Poems, Proverbs and Puns,* Lagos, Lenaus Advertising and Publishing Ltd., 1993
Elizabeth, Young – Bruehl. Freedom and Karl Jaspers Philosophy, London, Yube University Press 1981..
Elizabeth, Young Bruehi. *Freedom and Kari Jasper Philosophy, London Yube University Press 1981*
Elwes, R. H. M., *Benedict De Spinoza Ethics, Including the Improvement of Understanding,* Promotheus books, U.S.A. 1989.
Emeagwalu, Philip, "My Search for the Holy Grail of Immortality", keynote lecture, Black Data Processing Association, Augusta, Georgia, April 26, 2003.

Emmanuel, Obiechina, *Culture, Society and the West African Novel.* Cambridge: Cambridge University Press, 1975.
English, Paker. and Kibujjo, M. Kalumba, (eds) *AfricanPhilosophy: A Classical Approach,* New Jersey, Prentice Hall, 1996.
Erivwo, S. U., "A Consideration of the Charismatic Movement among the Urhobo and Isoko Speakers: 1929 to date" *in Orita, Ibadan Journal of Religious Studies Vol. XV/1 June 1983*
Ernest, Cassirer. *Substance and function and Einstein's Theory of Relativity,* Dover Publication Inc. 1953
Evans-Printehard. *Witchcraft, Oracle and Magic Among the Azande,* Clarendon Press, 1976.
Eucke, Rudolf. *The fundamental Concept of Modern philosophic Thought,* New York: D. Appleton and Company, 1980
Ezeabasili. *African Science, Myth or Reality,* New York, Vantage Press, 1977.
Martin F. David & Leo A. Jacobus. *The Humanities Through The Arts,* 3rd ed., ,USA, McGraw – Hill, 1983
Fietcher, Joseph. "Elective Death" in Paula Rothenberg Struhl and Karsten
Finch, C. S. lll. *The State of Deep Beginning, the Genesis of African science and Technology,* U.S.A., Knenti, Inc. 1998.
Firth, R. *Symbols: Public and Private,* London, George Allen and Unwin. 1973
Fortes, M and G., Dieterlen. *African Systems of Thought: Studies Presented and Discussed at The Third International African Seminar in Salisbury Dec. 1968,* London, Oxford Press 1972.
Francisco J. Varela *et al. The Embodied Mind,* England, the MIT press, 1993
Freud, Sigmund. *Beyond The Pleasure Principle (Trans) Jame* Strache New York, W.W. Norton and Company Inc. 1961
Gaarder, J Sophies, *Word,* Ibadan: Spectrum Books Limited, 1997.
Gail, M., Presby et al. *(Eds) Thought and Practice in African Philosophy,* Nairobi Kenya, Konrad Adenauer Foundation, Nairobi, 2002.
Gbadebo, Moses, Debo. "Gods and in Traditional African Religion and Philosophy" in *Essence Interdisciplinary International* Ethics *Journal of Philosophy,* No2, 2005,
Gekaisy, Diana and Peter, Geschiere."Containing Witchcraft: Conflicting Science In Post- Colonial African" *African Studies Review* Vol. 41, No. 3 December 1998.
Geoffrey, Parrinder. *African Three Religious,* London, Sheldon Press, 1969.
George, G.M., James, *The Stolen Legacy,* New York, Philosophical Library, 1980.

Geshiere, Peter. and Francis, Nyamnjoh. "Witchcraft as an Issue In The "Politics of Belongings: Democratization And Urban Migrants Involvement with Home Village" *African Studies Review, 1998.*

Gikandi, Simon, „Reading Chinua Achebe; Language and Ideology" in *fiction; An Antholoty of Critical Writing*, Black Orpheus 1991

Gluckman. *Custom and Conflict in Africa,* Oxford Max and Blackwell Based 1970.

Goodman, Nelson. *Fact, Fiction and Forecast*, U. S., Harvard University Press, 1983,

Gottleb, Frege: *Logical Investigations*, Britain, Basil Blackwell, 1977,

Gray, Glenn, J." The Problem of Dearth in modern Philosophy" in Paula R. Struhl and K.J. Sruhl (eds) *Philosophy Now*, Random House, New York, 1980

Gretel, Adorn, Adornom, and Rolf Tiedemann. "Art, society, Aesthetics" in Aesthetics *Theory*, ed. Trans. C. Lenhardt, London: Routledge and Kegan Paul, 1984.

Grills, and Livingston, "African Concept of Consciousness, Contributions from Kenetic Concepts" in *African Concept of Consciousness project, Project Think Tank Meeting, Roundtable 11, Accra, Ghana, July 1999.*

Grills, C T, and A. Livingston, "Akan Conceptualization of Consciousness, Executive Summary" presented for African Concept of Consciousness Project, Roundtable 11 Accra, Ghana Oct. 1999,

Grills, C. T. "African Psychology and concepts of Consciousness" in *African Concept of Consciousness project, Project Think Tank Meeting, Roundtable 11, Accra, Ghana, July 1999.*

Grills, C. T *and Livingston A.*, Akan conceptualization of Consciousness, *Project, Roundtable11, and Accra, Ghana.*

Grills, C. T. "African psychology and Concepts of Consciousness" in *African Concept of Consciousness project, project Think Tank Meeting, Roundtable* 11, Accra, Ghana, July, 1999,

Gustavus, Hindman, Miller. *The Dictionary of Dreams*, Preface Britain, Blaketon -Hall Ltd, 1983.

Gyekye, Kwame, "Political Corruption: A Philosophical Analysis of aMoral Problem" in Dukor M. (ed) *Philosophy and Politics: Discourse on Values, Politics and Power in Africa,* Lagos, Malthouse Press Ltd. 2002.

Gyekye, Kwame, "The Akan concept of Person" in *International Philosophical Quarterly,* vol xiii No.3, 1978

Gyekye, Kwame, *An Essay on African Philosophical Thought: The Akans Conceptual Scheme* Revised Edition, U.S.A., Philadelphia, Temple University Press 1995.

Gyekye, Kwame, *The Akan Concept of Person" in International Philosophical Quarterly,* Vol. Xiii, No. 3, 1978.

Gyekye, Kwame, *Tradition and Modernity: Philosophical Reflections on the African Experience,* New York, Oxford University Press 1997.

Habermas, and the *unfinished project of modernity: critical essays on the philosophical Discourse of modernity "introduction" (eds)* Maurizio P and Seyla B,,U.S.A. Mitprers 1997

Hafstadter, A.*Principle of Philosophy: A Simplified summary and Instant Reference.*

Hale, Bob, "Knowledge of Possibility and of Necessity" (Presidential Address) in *Proceedings of The Aristotelian Society, Vol. III, Part 1,* 3003.

Hallen, Barry, "Phenomenology and the Exposition of African Traditional Thought" in Oluwole Sophie B. In Sophie Oluwole (ed) *Readings in African Philosophy: An Anthology* Lagos, Nigeria, Meastech Publications. (1989).

Hamlyn, D.W. *The Theory of Knowledge,* Macmillan Press London, 1971

Hamlin, Greg, *Revelation: A mystery Revealed* Fab Anieh Nigerian Limited Jos, Nigeria.2001

Haring, Bernard, *Medical Ethic,* Indiana, USA. Fides publishers Inc. 1912

Harris, M. *The Rise of Anthropological Theory,* New York, Thomas Y. Crowell, 1968.

Harris, M., *The Rise of Anthropological Theory,* New York, Thomas V. Crowell, 1968

Haugeland, John, "What is Mind Design?" in Haugeland John (Ed) *Mind Design II, Philosophy, Psychology, Artificial Intelligence*, England, the MIT Press, A Bradfod Book, 1997

Hegel. *Die Philosophic der Gerschichte,* Stuttgart, Reclaim Verlag, 1961,

Hart. H.L.A., "Separation of Law and Morale" *The Philosophy of Law.* Dworkin, R.M. ed. Oxford, Oxford University Press 1977..

Hegel, George, *Philosophy of History,* Trans. J. Shree, New York, Dover, 1956

Nwoga, "The African Imagination" Research in African Literature" *Vol. 12 No 1 Spring, 1981,*

Helaine, K. Minkus, 'Causal theory in Akwapim Akan Philosophy" in *African Philosophy, An Introduction,* Richard Right ed. University Press of America 1977

Henigo, D., *Oral Histomography*, London, Longman 1982.

Herbert, Herring. 'Cartesian and Kantian Revolutions in Philosophy" I*n Indian Philosophical Quarterly, Special Number, Rene Descartes,* Vol. No XXIII, Nos 1-2. Jan-April 1996.

Herrick, Jim, *Humanism,* in *"Introduction"*, Ibadan, Gadfly publishers 2006.
Hesten and Wanjohi. *Anointing and Healing in Africa,* Kenya, G"aba, Spearhead no. 71, 1982.
Hodgson, David, *The Mind Matters,* U.S.A.: Oxford Press, New York, 199.
Honderich, Ted, *The Oxford Companion to Philosophy*, Oxford University Press, USA, 1995,
Horton, Robin, "African Thought and Western Science", in*Rationality,* ed. Barryan R. Wilson, Oxford, Britain, Basil Blackwell, 1997.
Hountondji, Paullin, *African philosophy; Myth or Reality,* (Trans) Henri Evans with Jonathan Ree, Introduction by Abiola Irele, Bloomington, Indian University Press, 1983.
Hountondji, Paulin, "African Philosophy, Myth or Reality" in Sophie Oluwole (ed), *Readings in African Philosophy, An Anthology,* Lagos, Nigeria, Masstech publications, 1989.
Houston, Smith, *The Religion of Men,* New York, Perennial Library, 1958.
Howard, Jonathan, *Darwin*, Oxford, Oxford University Press 1982
Idowu, E. B., *African Traditional Religion, A Definition,* GreatBritain, SCK Press 1975.
Ikeobi, G. "The Healing Ministry and Igbo Christianity" in *Religion and African*Culture, A Nigerian perspective (ed) Elochukwu E. Uzukwu, Enugu, Snaap, 1988.
Ilogu, E., *Christianity and Igbo Culture*, Leiden; Brill 1974
Irene, F., Abiola 2000. *The Crisis of Cultural Memory in Chinua Achebe"s Things Fall Apart.* New York; Anchor Books, 1994
Iroegbu, Panteleon. "The Ocultic and the metaphysical: where they Differ" in *Essence Interdisciplinary International Journal of Philosophy, No2,* 2005,
Isaac, Kwesi, Otabil. Notes on African Traditional Religion, Book 2 (5th ed.) .Ghana Asempa Publishers, Accra.
Isaac. O. Delano, *Owe Lesin Oro Yoruba Proverbs*, Ibadan, and Oxford University Press 1972.
Isaaior, James, Tar. "Those Days" and "These Days"NeoTraditionalism, Postmodernism and Culture of misgovernance in Africa" in *Essence Interdisciplinary International journal of Philosophy, No2, 2005,*
Iwuoha, Chiemeka, "A forum on Culture and Development" *in Champion Vol. 10, No. 50, Tuesday, March 11 1997,*
Jacobs, A.B. *A textbook on African Traditional Religion*, Ibadan, Aromolaran Press Ltd. 1997.
Jagat pal, D., Lewise on Causeation" in *Indian Philosophical Quarterly Vol. XXVI No. 4, Oct. 1999.*

Jamal, Anwet. "Problem of Induction" in *Indian Philosophical Quarterly* Vol. 22, No. 3 July, 1995.
James, B., Wilbur; *Spinoza"s Metaphysics* Van, Corcum, Assen, Netherlands January 20, 2002.
Jarvie, I.C., "Explaning the Cargo Cult" in *Rationality* ed. Bryan R. Wilson, Oxford, Basil Blackwell 1977.
Jaspers, K. *Introduction a'la philosophy*, Libraire Plon, Paris, 1974.
Jaspers, Karl, *Reason and Existenz: "Introduction "By William Earle,* New York, The Noonday Press 1955.
Jay, Van, Hook, "The Universalist Thesis Revisited: What Direction for African philosophy in the New York Millennium" in Gail M. Presbey *et al., Thought and Practice in African Philosoph,y* Nairobi, Kenya, Konyrad Adenauer Foundation, Nairobi, 2002.
Jeyifo, Biodun "Okonkwo and His mother – Things fall Apart and issues of Gender in the constitution of African post colonial
Discourse" *Callalloo Vol. 16 No 4. on "Post Colonial Discourse" A Special Issue ,Autumn 1993.*
Joad, C. E. M., *An Introduction to contemporary knowledge* , London, EJ Arnold and Sons Ltd.
John, Hick. *Evil and the God of Love*, London, the Macmillan Press Ltd. 1985.
Johnston Colin, "Symbols in Wittgenstein"s Tractatus" in *European Journal of Philosophy vol 15, No. 3, Dec. 2007*
Kant, Immanuel, *Prolegomena to Any Future Metaphyisics* .New York, The Liberia Arts Press, 1950.
Kari, Jaspers. *Research and Existen,* New York, The Noonday Press, 1955.
Kartiyeya, C. Pate! "Wittgenstein on Emotion" in *Indian Philosophical Quarterly* Vol. XVII, No. 4, Oct. 1990,
Kelkar Ashok, "Language as Empowerment" *Indian Philosophical Quarterly, vol. XXII* No. I,1995, *Journal of the Department of Philosophy, University of Poona.*
Keita, L., "Progress in Science: A critique of Kuhn's incompatibility Thesis" of scientific change" in *Nigerian Journal of philosophy, Department of Philosophy University of Lagos vol, 4, no., 1 and 2.*
Khanna, Raj. *Philosophy and some contemporary issues.* , Chandigorh, India, Arun Publishing House, 2002.
Kirk, G.S., *Myth: its Meaning and Functions in Ancient and other Cultures,* London, Cambridge University Press, 1970.
Kola, Omotosho, Kola. "Season of migration to the South," A review in *The African Guardian, August 15, 1994,*

Kuhn, Thomas, S. The Copenican *Revolution*, London: Harvard University Press, Cambridge, 1976.

Kwame, Anthony, Appiah. *Introduction to Things Fall Apart,* New York" Knoff, 1992,

Kwame, Gyekye. Essay African Philosophical Thought, The Akan Conceptual Scheme.

Kwasi Agueman, "Marriage: The most important social value of all Human Relations" in Dukor M (ed) *Philosophy and Political Discovers on Values, Politics and Power in Africa*(Lagos, Malthouse Press 2002).

Lacey, A. R., *Dictionary of Philosophy*, London, Rutledge and Kegan Paul, 1976.

Landau, Siddey I. *International Directory of Medicine and Biology*, New York, John Willey and sons. Inc 1986.

Langer, Susanne K., *Mind: An essay on human Feeling*, Vol. II, London, the John Hopkins University Press, 1972.

Laximinarayan, Lenka. "An Understanding of Contemporary Foundationalism", *Indian Philosophical Quarterly, Vol. XXI, No. 4,* October, 1994,

Laxminarayan, Lanka, „*Indeterminancy: An Exposition" in Indian Philosophical*

Laz, Ekwueme. *Junior Teasers for Schools, Poems, Proverbs and Puns* , Oko, Nigeria, Le Naus Advertising and Publishing Ltd. 1995.

Lemon. "Sentences, Statements and Proposition" in *Readings in the Philosophy of Language,* J.F. Rosenberg and C. Trans (ed) New Jersey, Prentice Hall, Inc. 1971

Lepold, Sedar, Senghor. "What is Negritude?" in *Reading in African Political Thought*, Gideon-Cyrus et al London, Heinemann, 1975

Lesile, Stevenson," FreudPsychoanlysis" In *Seven Theories of Human Nature,* New York. Oxford University Press, 1973.

Levine Joseph, "Conceivability, identity and the explanatory gap" in Hameroff, et. al. (eds.). *Towards a sciences of consciousness III, the third Tucson discussion and debate* (A Badford Book, The MIT Press,Cambridge, Massachustts, London, England, 1999)

Levy- Bruhl. *Luciem, les fontions mentales dan les societes inferieures:* Paris, F. Alcan, 1912

Magesa, L. *African Religion, The Moral Tradition of Abundant Life*, Nairobi, Kenya, Pauline publications, Africa, 1998

Makinde, Akin. M., "Philosophy in African" in Momoh C. S. (ed) *The Stbstance of Philosophy,* Auchi, Nigeria, African Philosophy Projects" Publications, 1989.

Malinowski, Bronislaw, *Crime and causation in savage society*, Peterson, N.J. Litter field, Adams 1959.

Marimba, Ani, i *An African-centred Critique of European Cultural Thought and Behaviour* ,New Jersey, African World Press, 1994,

Marimba, Ani, *in An african-centred Critique of European Cultural Thought and Behavour,* New Jersey, African World Press, 1994.

Marx and Engels, Notes *on Religion, Moscow*, Progress Publisher, 1981

Max Planck, Scientific Autobiography and other papers, tr.Frank Gaynor, New York: Philosophical library, 194.

Mazumdar, D Rinita, "Dream effects, Reference and Naturalised epistemology" in *Indian Philosophical Quarterly, Vol.XIIX, No.2*

Mbamara, C. I. C., *Modern Natural Health Counselor on Common Diseases, Prevention and Their Natural Remedies, Osuchukwu* and Sons Printing Press Ojo, Lagos, 2002.

Mbamara, C.I.C., "Creation of Deity in African clinical And social setting" in *Essence Interdisciplinary International journal of Philosophy, No2, 2005,*

Mbiti, J.S., *African Religions and Philosophy*, London, Heinemann Pub. 1996.

Mbiti, J.S. 1969 *African Religions and Philosophy*, Heinemann Educational Books Ltd. Ibadan.

Meenalm, M. Katarnikar, "Critical note on Professor L. Banjour, The structure of empirical knowledge" in *Indian Philosophical Quarterly, Students Supplements Vol.XX, No.4, October, 1993.*

Metuh, E. I., *God and Man in African Traditional Religion*, London, Geoffery Chapman, 1981.

Metuh, Ikenga. *African Religions in Western Conceptual Schemes: The Problem of Interpretations,* Pastoral Institute, Bodija, Ibadan. 1985.

Mishra Sabbajeet "Nature and source of transcendental illusion" *Indian Philosophical Quarterly, Special Number 200 years of Kant, January-October, 2004, vol. 31, Nos. 1-4* p

Woodword, Keneth L., "Physics and Mysticism?" in *Newsweek August 13, 1979*

Momoh, C. S., "The Logic Question in African Philosophy" ed. Momoh C. S., *The substance of African Philosophy*, Auchi, African Philosophy Projects" Publication 1989

Momoh, C. S., *The Substance of African philosophy, Auchi NigERIa, Philosophy Projects" Publications, 1989.*

Morse, Warner. *Study Guide for Logic and Philosophy,* 2nd edition, California, Wadsworth Pub. Company, 1971,

Mudimbe, V. Y., Appiah Kwame*A. and Jean O'Barr (eds) Africa and the Disciplines: The Contributions of Research in Africa to the social Sciences and Humanities, London, the University* of Chicago press, 1993.

Mudinbe, V. Y., Appiah K. A., *"Impact of African Studies on Philosophy". In Mudimbe V. Y. and Appiah K. A. and Jean O'Barr (eds.) African and the Disciplines; The Contributions of Reasearch in Africa to the Social Sciences and humanitiess, U.S.A., The University of Chicago Press, 1993.*

Naatey, A. A., "The African Archetypal Psychology (AAP) and Contemporary African Concepts of Conciouness", *in .African Concept of Consciousness Project, Roundtable 11, November 1999, Accra, Ghana.*

Nigosian, S.A., *World Religions*, London, G Clark Publishing Co. Ltd, 1974

Nkeonye, Otokpor, "Pragmatism and Traditionalism in the concept of God in African Culture: A reply to Dr. C. Nze" *in Uche Journal of Philosophy the Dept. of Philosophy, University of Nigeria*

Nkrumah, Kwame, *Consciencism: Philosophy and Ideology of Decolonization*, Monthly Review Press, U.S.1964

Nkwo, Nnabuchi, "*Ofo: Igbo Symbol of Authority:* in *Ogirisi – Igbo Annual Lecture, Department of Philosophy, Nnamdi Azikiwe University, Awka,* 2002.

Nomans, Geoge, "Bringing men Back in Ryan Alan, The *Philosophy of social explanation*, Oxford 1973

Nora, Pierre. *Great Introduction, Between Democracy and History*, 1989

Nwala, T. Uzodinma, *A Modern Introduction to Philosophy and Logic, Nsukka*, Nigeria, Niger Books and Publishing Co. Ltd., 1997,.

Nwala, T. U., The concept of Traditional African Philosophy", in *Essence Interdisciplinary International journal of Philosophy, No2, 2005,*

Nwala, T. U., (ed) (1989), *"Anton William Amo's Treatise on the Art of Philosophising Soberly and Accurately" Special Publication of William Amo centre for African Philosophy Department of Philosophy, University of Nigeria Nsukka.*

Nwoga, Donatus, "The African Imagination". *Research in African Literature.*

Nyerere, Julius.*Ujamaa, London, Oxford Press, 1968*

Nze, C. B., "Logic in African Charm and Medicine" in *The Nigerian Journal of Philosophy.*

Ocansey, James, "The African Egyptains Concept of God, of Satan and Man", *in African Personality Vol. 4,No. 1, January/February 2000.*

Oruka, Odera, Henry, (1989), "Principles of African Philosophy" in Oluwole Sophie. B. In Sophie Oluwole (ed) *Readings in African Philosophy: An Anthology*, Mastech Publications.Lagos, Nigeria,

Odera, Oruka, "The Fundamental Principles of the Question of African Philosophy", *Second Order, Vol.4, No. 1, 1975.*

Odera, Oruka. *Sage Philosophy, Indigenous Thinkers and Modern Debate on African Philosophy*, Kenya, Nairobi, African Centre for Technology Studies 1991.

Odujinrin, J.S.A. *Modern Lessons in Yoruba*, London Waterloo, Press Ltd,1984.

Oehieng, Ochiambo F., *African philosophy An Introduction,* Nairobi, Consolata Institute Press, 1995.

Ogden, C.K and I.A., Richards. *The Meaning of Meanings, London,* Routledge and Kegan Paul Ltd., 1972.

Oguah, B. E., "African and Western Philosophy: A Comparative Study" in *African Philosophy, An Introduction,* Richard A. Wright,(ed).

Ogugua, P.I "Understand Deities in Igbo – African world: A Religio-Philosophical perspective" in *Essence Interdisciplinary International journal of Philosophy, No2, 2005,*

Ohia, C. P., *Definite Casual Operations of Witchcraft and Magiccraft in Africa,* Owerri Springfield publishers Ltd 2005.

Okafor, F. U., *Igbo Philosophy of Law,* Enugu, Nigeria, Fourth Dimension Publishing Co. Ltd., 1992.

Okolo, C. B., "African Philosophy and Reconstruction", in *Journal of African Studies, Vol. 13, No. 1, 1985*, California, U.S.A.

Okolo, C.B., *Problems of African Philosophy and Other Essays*, Enugu Nigeria, Cecta Nig. Ltd., 1990.

Okolo, C.B., "Negritude: A Philosophy of Social Action" in *International Philosophical Quarterly,* New York, 1984.

Okolo, C.B., "Problem of Self in African Philosophy", in *International Philosophical Quarterly, New York, December 1992.*

Okolo, C.B., "African Philosophy, A Process Interpretation," Africana, *Marbugensia, 2 1983.*

Okolo, **C**.B., *African Philosophy, A Short Introduction, Revised Edition,* Enugu, Cecta, Rug LTD, 1993.

Okolo, C.B., "Self as a Problem in African Philosophy" in *International Philosophical Quarterly Vol. XXXII, No. 4 issue No. 128* (December 1992

Okonkwo, Paschal, "Traditionalism And Christianity Compromise or dialogue" in *Essence Interdisciplinary International journal of Philosophy, No2, 2005,*

Okporobaro, F.B.O., and Umovon, J. A., *Nigerian Proverbs: Meaning and Relevance Today*, Lagos, Nigerian Magazine 1994.

Oladele, Taiwo, *An Introduction to West African Literatures*, Hong Kong, Thomas Nelson Ltd, 1967

Oladipo, Segun, *The Third Way in African Philosophy. Essays in Honour of Kwasi Wiredu*, Ibadan, Nigeria, Hope Publications. 2002.

Olela, Henry, "The African Foundation of Greek Philosophy" In *African Philosophy, An introduction ed.* Richard A. Wright University Press of America, 1984

Oluwole, Sophie. B., *Philosophy and oral Tradition, Lagos*, Nigeria, African Research Konsultanc, ARK, 1991.

Oluwole, Sophie B., (1999), *Philosophy and Oral Tradition*. Lagos, African Research Konsultancy, ARK.

Oluwole, Sophie B., (ed), *Readings in African Philosophy: An Anthology*, Lagos, Masstech Publications. 1989

Oluwole, Sophie B., " Africanness of A Philosophy", in Oluwole Sophie B., in Sophie Oluwole (ed) *Readings In African Philosophy: An Anthology*, Lagos, Nigeria, Meastech Publications. 1989

Omotosho, Kola, „Season of Migration to the South, A review" in the *African Guardian, August 15, 1994.*

Onwuejeogwu, M. A., *An Igbo civilization: NRI Kingdom and Hegemony*, London,

Onwubiko, O.A., *African thought, Religion and culture*, Enugu, Snaap, Press Ltd., 1991

Onyenwuenyi, Innocent, *The African Origin of Greek Philosophy: An Exercisen in Afrocentrim,* Nigeria, University of Nigeria Press 1994

Onyewuenyi, I.,"*African Belief in Rciocarnation:* A Philosophical Reappraisal "Enugu, Nigeria. Snaap Press 1998.

Orenstein, Alex, "Epistemology naturalised – nature know thyself" in *Philosophyand Basic, Reading* (ed) Nigel Warburton, London, Routledge, 1999

Oruka, Odera, Henry, (1996) "Introduction, In defence of the Sagacity Approach to African Philosophy" in Parker English and Kalumba, Vubujjo (eds) *African Philosophy. A Classical Approach,* New Jessy, Prentice Hall.

Oruka, Odera, Henry,"Principles of African Philosophy" in Sophie Oluwole, (ed*) Readings in African Philosophy: An Anthology Lagos, Nigeria, Meastech Publications, 1989.*

Oruka, Odera, Henry, "Introduction, In Defence of the Sagacity Approach to African Philosophy" inParker English and Kalumba Kibujjo (eds)

African Philosophy: A Classical Approach, New Jessey, Prentics Hall, 1996.
Osuagwu, Chidi, 'Dynamics of Truth within Igbo Cosmology'" in Okere T. I.. *Religion in a World of Change: African Ancestral Religion, Islam and Christianity.*
Otubanjo, D. A. O.,"Determining The Impossible" in *The Nilgerian Journal of Philosophy of the Dept. of Philosophy University of Lagos - Nigeria* 1969 vol. 1, No. 2
Owen, Flanagan, *Consciousness Reconsidered*, England, the MIT Press, Cambridge, 1998
Owolabi, Kolawole, "Orientation in African philosophy. A critical survey" *in Indian philosophical Quarterly, vol .XXVI, No. 1, January 1999.*
Owomoyela, Berth L.O., *Yoruba proverbs*, Ohio, Owomoyela Press, 1973
Ozeman, Theodore, *Problems of the History of philosophy*, Moscow, Progress Publishers.
Panneerselvim. Derrida and the Philosophy of Deconstruction" *Discussion, Indian Philosophy Quarterly, Vol. 19, No. 3, July 1992 – January 1991*
Parrinder, Geoffrey. *Africans Three Religions*, London, Sheldon Press, 1969.
Parrinder, Geoffrey. *West African Religion*. Epworth Press: London, Epworth Press, 987.
Paul Smolensky, "*Connectionist modeling*: Neural computation and mental connections" in John Haugeland John (ed) *Mind Design II, Philosophy, Psychology, Artificial Intelligence* ,England, the MIT Press, A Bradfod Book, 1997.
Paulose, Mar, Gregorias. "On Postmodernism" in *Journal of Indian Council of Philosophical Research Vol. XIV, No. 3 May – August 1997,*
Peter, Gwynne, 'Cosmology: Boom or Bust?" in *Newsweek,* March 12, 1979.
Peter, Ogola, Onyang."A continuing Study on Sage Philosophy: Emphasis on Jaramogi Oginga Odinga in the New Millenium," in Gall M. Presgy *et al., Thought and Practice in African Philosophy* Nairobi, Kenya, Konyrad Adenauer foundation, Nairobi, 2002.
Peter, Winch .I., "Understanding a primitive society" in *Rationality*, ed. Barryan R. Wilson, Oxford, Britain, Basil Blackwell, 1997.
Philip, Frank., "Philosophical International and misinterpretation of the theory of Relativity" in Herbert Feigle and May Brodbeck (eds) *Radings in the Philosophy of science,* New York, Appleton-century-crafts.NC, 1953
-Philosophy Now; An Introductory Reader, New York, Random House, 1972.
-Philosophy in Paula Rothenberg Struhl and Karsten J. Struhl (ed)

Placed, Tempels, Bantu Philosophy (Introduction) in (eds) Parker English and K. Bujjo M. Kalum ba, *African Philosophy: A Classical Approach,* New Jersey, Prentice Hall 1996.

Planck, M., *Scientific Autobiography and other papers, tr. Frank Gaynor,* New York, Philosophical library. 1949.

Plato, (Trans).Tredennick H. "Apology" in *The last days of Socrates*, New York, Penguin classics 1982).

Plato, the Symposium ed. Betty Paidice, Penguin Books 1911.

Punaman, W.G., „"What is structuralism?" in Ryan Alan (Editor)

The philosophy of social explanation "Oxford, regions 1973 Quine, W V., *Word and object*, Cambridge Mass, M.I.T. Press, 1960.

Quine W.V.O., "Two Dogmas of Empiricism" in Concepts, Core Readings (eds) Eric Margolis and Stephen Laurence English ,A. Braford, The Mit Press, 1999

Quine, W V., *Ontological Relativity and other Essays*, NewYork, Columbia University Press, 1969

Quine, W. V., and Ullian. The Web of Belief, New York, Random House, 1970

Reichenbach, Hans, The Rise of Scientific Philosophy, University of California Press, 1962.

Raphael, D. D., *Problems of Political Philosophy, London*, Macmillan Press 1992.

Reichenbach, Hans, *The Rise of Scientific Philosophy* .University of California Press, 1962.

Rene, Descartes, 'Meditation 1, Meditations on the First Philosophy" in *Ten Great Wadis of Philosophy,* ed. Robert Paul Wolf, New York: Mentor Book, 1969,

Plato, Republic of Plato, Francis MacDonald Conford (Trans), London, Oxford University Press, 1979

Richard, Bernstein, *Beyond Objectivism and Relativism: Science, Hermeneutics And Praxis*, Philadelphia, University of Pennsylvania Press.1983

Richard, H., Hopkin. Avrum Stroll, *Philosophy made simple*, London, W. H. Allen made simple books, 1979.

Rinita, Majumda. "Dream Objects Reference and Naturalized Epistemology," in *Indian Philosophical Quarterly Vol. 19, No. 2, April 1992*

Robert, Audi. *The Cambridge Dictionary of Philosophy;* Second edition, Cambridge University Press. London, 2001.

Robert, Paul, Wolf. "Kant", *Ten Great Works of Philosophy,* New York: New American Library, 1969.

Rodney, Walter. *How Europe Undeveloped Africa*, Washington D.C., Howard University Press 1982.

Roper, Nancy, *Pocket Medical Dictionary*, Livingston ltd. 1969

Ross, Elizabeth, "On the fear of Death" in Paula RS and KJS

Roy, P K., "Logical structure of cybernetic and Magical phenomenon in African Traditional Thought" in *Uche, Journal of the Department of Philosophy University of Nigeria Nsukka* volume 8 1984, p. 6

Ruch, E.A. *The Ways of Knowing and Thinking*, Roma, National University of Lesotho, 1977.

Ruch, E. A. () "Is there an African Philosophy," in Sophie Oluwole (ed) *Readings in African Philosophy: An Anthology* Lagos, Nigeria, Meastech Publications. 1989

Ruch, E.A., and Anyanwu, K. C.,*African Philosophy,* Rome, Catholic Book Agency, 1984.

Russell, Bertrand, *The Problem of Philosophy*, New York: Oxford University Press 1980.

Russell, Bertrand, *History of Western Philosophy*, London, George Allen and Unwin, 1979,

Saam, Trivedi, "An outline of some problems in the philosophy of music composition" in *Indian Philosophical Quarterly* Vol. XIX, No. 3, July 1992,

Sajahan, Miah, "Russell"s Resolution of Realism-Empiricism dilemma" in*Indian Philosophical Quarterly* Vol. XXIV No.4 Oct. 1997

Sanda, A. O., "The Scientific or Magical Ways of Knowing, Implication for the Study of African Traditional Healers" in Second Order. *An African Journal of Philosophy,* Vol. VII, Nos. 1 and 2, January and July 1978.

Saurabh, Sanatani, *(2001)* "Metaphysics of Unobservable" in *Journal of Indian Council of Philosophical Research vol. Xviii No. 3, July – Sept, 2001*

Scheffler, Isreal, *Science and Subjectivity,* U.S.A., Bobbs Mervill Educational Publishing 1967.

Scruton, R., A *Short History of Western Philosophy from Descartes to Wittgenstein 2nd ed. 2002*

Senghor, Leopold, Sedar, *Negritude et Humanism,* Paris, 1964.

Simpton, J. A., (ed) *The Oxford English Dictionar, Vol. vii,*Oxford University Press, 1989

Singh R.M., "Mind, Modularity and Evolution" in *India philosophical Quarterly, vol. XXXII, No. 1-2, Jan. Apml 2005.*

Singh, R.P., "Micheal Foucault:A Critique of Immanuel Kant" *Indian Philosophy Quarterly, Vol 14, 3, July 1992*

. Smith N.K., *A commentary to Kant Critiques of Pure Reason*, New York., The humanities Press, 1980
Smoker, Barbara. *Humanism*, Ibadan, Gadfly publishers 2006.
Sodipo, J .O., *Notes on the concept of cause and chance in Yoruba Traditional Thought*,
Sogolo, Godwin,*Foundation of African Philosophy: A Definitive Analysis of Conceptual Issues in African Thought*, Nigerian, Ibadan University Press 1993
Sogolo, Godwin, *Foundations of African Philosophy* (University of Ibadan Press, Nigeria 1997.
Solagbade, Popoola. S., "Editorial, Quest For Knowledge" in *Orunmila Magazine, Issue No. 2 June 1986,*
Solomon, R. C. *Continental Philosophy Since 1950*, New York, Oxford University Press, 1988.
Spinioza, *Ethics*, New York, Hafner Press, 1949.
Sunil Baran Mondal "Development of Epistemology" *in Indian Philosophical Quarterly Vol. 18, No. 3, July 1991, Student Supplement.*
Sreekumar, N. A language and the Evolution of the self" *Indian Philosophical Quarterly, vol. XXIX, No 2 and 3.2002*
Stalnaker, R.C., "A Theory of conditional" in Ernest Sosa Stephen Laurence and Eric Margolis, "Concepts and cognitive science" in *Concepts, Core Readings (eds.)* Eric Marsolis and Stephen Laurence ,The MIT Press, England 1968
Steva, Vago. *Social change, USA, Prentice Hall, Inc 1996.*
Stumpf, S.E., *Philosophy of History and Problems*, U.S.A. McGraw-Hill, Inc., 1994.
Swedenbog, Emanuel, *Heaven and Hell*, New York Swedenborg
Taban, Lo Liyong. „Dark Areas in African Studies: How to Lighten Them, A Diagnostic Palaver", in *Essence, International Journal of Philosophy Vol. 1, No 2. And 3, 2000.*
Tandra, Patnaik, "Purusarthas in Aesthetics" in *Indian Philosophical Quarterly* Vol. XXII, No. 1, Jan. 1955.
Robert, Audi, ed., *The Cambridge Dictionary of Philosophy*, Cambridge University Press, 1995.
Tunji, Vidal, "Music and Musical instruments as modes of Communications in West Africa" in *African Unity: the Cultural Foundations,*
Ugwu, C.O. & Ugwueye, L.E., *African Traditional Religion: A Prolegomenia*, 2003.
Ukaegbu, J. O. *Igbo Identity and Personality vis-à-vis Igbo Cultural Symbol,* Salamanca 1991.

Umeogu Bonachristus, African symblismic philosophy: Tractatus Symbolismico-Philosopheicus Africans, Cifogne, Awka, 2003

. Urmson, J.O., *The Concise Encyclopedia of Western Philosophy and Philosophers*, New ed., S.V. "Aesthetics"

Valdez, Moses, *The Novel and the Globalization of Culture* 1995

Venkatalaskshmi, M. „Epistemology of Mysticism,"in *Indian Philosophical Quarterly* /Vol. XXIII No.3 and 4 July and October 1996

Vincent, Theo, "Africanity in Modern African Literature" in *The Arts and Civilisation of Black and African People; Vol. 3*

Walsh, W.H., "Kant Emmanuel" in *Encylopaedia of philosophy, 1972, Vols. 3 and 4,*

Warner, Rex, *The Greek Philosophers*, London, Mentor Book 1958.

Webster"s Third New International Dictionary, Volume 3, Chicago, William Benton 1971.

Weldon, T.S., "Preface" in *Introduction to Kan's Critique of Pure Reason Oxford Clarendon Press 1945*

Wiener Mobert, *Cybernetics: or control and Communication in the Animal and Machine,* Massachusetts, the MIT Press, 1965

William, P. Alston., *Philosophy of Language*, New Delhi, Prentice-Hall of India, 1988.

William, Shakespeare; *The Complete Works of William Shakespeare*

Wilson, C., Leibniz *Metaphysics: A historical and Comparative Study,* Manchester: Manchester University Press, 1989.

Wiredu, Kwasi. "On Defining African Philosophy," in Momoh C.S. (ed*) The Substance of* Philosophy, Auchi, Nigeria, African Philosophy Projects" Publications, 1989.

Wiredu, Kwasi, *Conceptual Decolonization in African Philosophy, Essays,* Selected and Introduced by Olusegun Oladipo, Ibadan, Hope Publications, 1995.

Wiredu, Kwasi,*Cultural Universals and Particulars: An African Perspective, Bloomington,* Indiana University Press, 1996.

Wiredu, Lwasi, *Philosophy and African Culture,* Accra, Cambridge University Press, 1980.

Wittsgenstein, *Tractatus Logico-Philosophicus*

Wittgenstien, *Note books* 1914-1966 G.H. Vom Wright and G. Eni Annscombe (eds) Oxford, Blackwell, 1998

Wolman, B., Benjamin."Kant Immanuel" In *International Encyclopaedia of the Social Science.*

Wright, G.H.Von, " On the Logic And Epistemology of the Causal Relation" in Ernest Sosa.

Young, Bruehl, Elizabeth, *Freedom and Karl Jaspers Philosophy*, London, Yube University Press, 1981.

Walter, Kaufmann, Existentialism from Dostoevsky To Sartre, New York, Ameridian Library 1975.

Index

CPSIA information can be obtained
at www.ICGtesting.com
Printed in the USA
LVHW011826090721
692292LV00013B/913

9 789785 878912